Links
To Your
Canadian Past

Tome 2
Quebéc Province

Peter J. Gagné

Quintin Publications
Pawtucket, Rhode Island

Copyright © 1999 by Peter J. Gagné

ISBN: 1-58211-119-7

All rights reserved for all countries. No part of this publication may be reproduced, stored in a retrieval system or transmitted in any form by any means, electronic or mechanical, by photocopying, recording, or otherwise, without prior written permission of the author or other duly authorized person or collectives.

Printed in the United States of America

First Edition
First Printing, March 1999

Quintin Publications
28 Felsmere Ave
Pawtucket, Rhode Island 02861-2903
Telephone: 401-723-6797
Fax: 401-726-0327

Website: http://www.quintinpublications.com

Cover: *Map of Quebec*, H.B. Walker, Montreal, 1910 in the possession of the publisher.

Table of Contents

Publisher's Notes v
Author's Notes vii
Introduction xi
Internet/Computer Glossary xiii
National 1
    Genealogical, Historical and Cultural Societies 1
        Individual Societies 1
        Professional Organizations 5
    Archives 6
        Directories 6
        Archive Centers 6
        Professional Organizations 8
    Libraries and Research Centers 10
        Directories and Catalogues 10
        Libraries and Research Centers 11
        Canadian Studies Centers and Programs 12
    Birth, Marriage, Death, Census and Other Data Online 18
        Vital Statistics and Parish Records 18
        Census Information 18
        Passenger Lists/Immigration Data 19
        Land Records 21
        Adoption Information and Groups 22
        Legal and Other Data 24
    Museums/Historic Sites/Groups 24
        Directories 24
        Museums and Historic Sites 26
    Military, Native and Historic Groups 32
        Military and Mounted Police 32
        Native and Métis Groups 36
        Loyalists 37
        Orangeism and Oddfellows 38
    National and Regional History and Historic Photos 39
        Exploration and Settlement 39
        General/Social History 41
        Timelines and "This Week/Day in History" 43
        Confederation 44
        Military History 45
        Professional Groups/Commercial History 46
        Geographical History and Information 49
        Regional History 51
        Cultural Groups 51
        Canadian Women's History 54
        Canadian Culture, Traditions and Symbols 55
    Family Associations & Surnames 56
        Nationalities and Cultural Groups 58
        Individual Surnames and Family Associations 58
    Chat Rooms and Mailing Lists 59

Quebec **63**
    Genealogical, Historical and Cultural Societies 63
        Directories 63
        Individual Societies 63
        Web-based Directories, Societies and Resources............ 72
        Professional Organization and Federations 73
    Archives 76
        Directories 76
        Archive Centers 76
        Professional Organization 79
    Libraries and Research Centers 80
        Directories and Catalogues 80
        Libraries and Research Centers 81
        Quebec and French-Canadian Studies Programs 83
    Birth, Marriage, Death, Census and Other Data Online 86
        Vital Statistics and Parish Records 87
        Vital Statistics and Parish Records - Local 89
        Cemetery Data 90
        Census Information 92
        Passenger Lists/Immigration Data 95
        Land Records 97
        Adoption Information and Groups 98
        Legal and Other Data 99
    Museums and Historic Sites 101
        Directories 101
        Museums and Historic Sites 101
        Government and Professional Organizations 126
    Military, Native and Historic Groups 128
        Carignan-Salieres Regiment 128
        Les Filles du Roi/The King's Daughters 129
        First Nations and Native Groups 131
        Other Military and Historic Groups 133
    Provincial and Local History and Photos 136
        Timelines/Historical Overviews 137
        Exploration, Immigration and Settlement 139
        Origins of the French-Canadians 142
        Military History/Wars 144
        Professional Groups/Commercial History 146
        Religious History 148
        Geographical History and Information 151
        Local and Regional History Photos 154
        Prominent Figures 165
    Cultural Groups and Traditions in Québec 169
        Cultural Associations and Groups 169
        Québécois French and Francophony 171
        French-Canadian Traditions and Culture 173
        The Huguenots: History, Culture and Traditions 176
        Other Cultural Traditions and Groups 178

  Family Associations and Surnames 178
    The *Dit* Name and Other Name Problems 179
    Province-wide and Regional Surnames 179
    Individual Surnames and Family Associations 182
  Chat Rooms and Mailing Lists 207

Other Canadian Provinces 209
  French-Canadian Genealogical and Historical Societies 209
    Directory 209
    Alberta 209
    Manitoba 210
    Nova Scotia 210
    Ontario 210
    Saskatchewan 210
  Archives, Libraries and Research Centers 211
    Ontario 211
  Birth, Marriage, Death, Census and Other Data Online 211
    Newfoundland 211
    Nova Scotia 212
    Ontario 212
    Saskatchewan 212
  Museums and Historic Sites and Groups 212
    Directory 212
    Alberta 213
    Manitoba 213
    Newfoundland 214
    Nova Scotia 214
    Ontario 215
    Prince Edward Island 216
    Saskatchewan 216
  Regional, Provincial and Local History 216
    National 216
    The Canadian West 217
    British Columbia 217
    Manitoba 218
    New Brunswick 218
    Nova Scotia 219
    Ontario 219
    Prince Edward Island 219
    Saskatchewan 219
    Yukon Territories 221
  French-Canadian Culture and Cultural Groups 221
    Directories/Canada-wide 221
    Alberta 223
    British Columbia 223
    Manitoba 224
    New Brunswick 224
    Newfoundland 225

Northwest Territories/Nunavut	225
Ontario	226
Prince Edward Island	226
Saskatchewan	226
Yukon Territory	228
Surnames and Family Associations	228
Alberta	228
Manitoba	228
New Brunswick	229
Newfoundland	229
Nova Scotia	230
Ontario	231
Prince Edward Island	231
Saskatchewan	232
Chat Rooms and Mailing Lists	232
Nova Scotia	232

United States 232

Genealogical, Historical and Cultural Societies	232
Archives, Libraries and Research Centers	236
Birth, Marriage, Death, Census and Other Data Online	241
Vital Statistics and Parish Records - General	241
Vital Statistics and Parish Records - By State	242
Cemetery Information	245
Census Information and Similar Records	246
Immigration/Border Crossings/Naturalization	247
Legal and Other Data	249
Museums and Historic Sites and Groups	249
Directories	249
New England and New York	250
Central and Western United States	251
The South	256
Regional and Local History and Historic Photos	258
New England and New York	258
Central and Western United States	259
Military History	261
Surnames and Family Associations	262
Regional Surnames	262
Individual Surnames	264
Chat Rooms and Mailing Lists	264

Publisher's Notes

Thousands, if not millions, of new genealogical websites have appeared during the past several years. At times, it seems to resemble a "Gordian Knot" — too many sites, poorly organized, if organized at all, and no regulation. This present publication, *Links to Your Canadian Past – Quebec* is the second of the QUINTIN'S LINKS SERIES and, will hopefully attempt to remedy that situation. Hundreds of hours have gone into the compilation of each book insuring its accuracy and completeness. We have taken particular care in choosing highly qualified authors to research each volume and hope that it will make your genealogical journey one of great pleasure.

Special Note to Readers: Please inform the publisher immediately of any broken links or additional links that you feel have either been left out or were created after the publication of this book.

Please send all correspondence to:
>Quintin Publications, Inc.
>28 Felsmere Ave
>Pawtucket, RI 02861-2903

>or

>E-mail: QuebecLinks@quintinpublications.com

Author's Notes

Names – All names of places and individuals are transcribed *as found* on each Web site. This includes British, American and First Nations spellings of words found in Web site titles.

Abbreviations – Sometimes abbreviations of the names of organizations are included in the site name or description. The full name should appear elsewhere in the title or description. Abbreviations used for states and provinces are as follows:

AL	Alabama
IH	Idaho
LA	Louisiana
MI	Michigan
NB	New Brunswick
NH	New Hampshire
OH	Ohio
PEI	Prince Edward Island
VT	Vermont
BC	British Columbia
IL	Illinois
MB	Manitoba
MN	Minnesota
NE	Nebraska
NWT	Northwest Territories
ON	Ontario
RI	Rhode Island
WI	Wisconsin
CT	Connecticut
IN	Indiana
ME	Maine
MS	Mississippi
NF	Newfoundland
NY	New York
PA	Pennsylvania
SK	Saskatchewan
YK	Yukon Territory

Searching – The term "searchable" has been used in this book to indicate that a search engine is available for the site or database being described, meaning you type in a keyword and the engine returns a list of results. When this method is not available, you can search an individual Web page yourself with your browser. Just hit [CTRL]+[F] at the same time to call up the search box in either Netscape or Internet Explorer.

Mailing Lists – Where possible, I have included a link to a Web page with instructions on subscribing to the list. When this was not available, an e-mail address follows the name of the list. Some lists provide you two methods of subscribing: All means you receive all postings individually. **Digest** means you receive a daily or occasional "digest" of postings. Use the address for the option you want. Send an e-mail with *no subject* and just the given text as the body of the message. If **all** or **digest** are not options, include only the word subscribe or the given text in the body of the message.

Don't Understand French? – Many of the sites included in this book are "French only" (indicated after the site name or before the URL for sites with long names). This means that the text on the site is only presented in French.
To get a translation, use the AltaVista Translation site
 (http://babelfish.altavista.digital.com/cgi-bin/translate?).
You can enter the URL for the Web page you want translated or type in a given section of text, and after a brief pause the translator will return the translation.

Submit a Site – Have you come across a site that isn't included in this book? Do you have a site of your own that you'd like included?
Send an e-mail to
Quebeclinks@quintinpublications.com.
Be sure to include the province, category (and subcategory) and URL (Web address) for the site.

Introduction

This book is the result of hundreds of hours of online research. It is meant to serve as a guidebook for your online genealogy and history research in Québec and for French-Canadian resources in the other provinces of Canada and the United States.

This book is meant to **save you time and confusion** in your online research. By organizing the information geographically, then by resource type, I have attempted to provide you the shortest route to find what you are looking for on the Internet. The Web can often seem overwhelming, and it's easy to get lost or caught in it and feel more like the fly than the spider.

Sure, there are many "lists" out there on the Internet, but none of them provide the **organization, descriptions** and **scope** that you will find in this book. Many lists just point you to another list, then another and take you to a site three or four clicks from what you are actually looking for – and good luck finding your way back to where you started. Others claim to link you to a specific site, but merely point the way and force you to find it in the context of a larger Web site. Still others merely give you a list of names with no description, and you waste time chasing down links that don't help you at all or miss sites that could provide valuable information for your research.

I have **personally visited every site** listed in this book and written the accompanying description, so you know that when you type in the URL, you'll be taken exactly where you want to go. In the case of pages contained within frames where all of the frame choices are not relevant to the topic, I have linked to just the individual frame that is appropriate.

This book in on paper and not on the Internet for one main reason: it can't be deleted, erased or "crash." Keep it by your computer and use it to **decide where you want to go before you go online**. That way, you'll save time surfing, reduce connection time and make your online time more efficient. If you find sites that you want to visit again, bookmark them or add them to your browser's "favorites." But in case you lose them, accidentally delete them or your computer crashes, this book will still be there. And if you use the Internet at your public library or another location where you don't have your own set of favorite sites, take this book along.

Good luck in your research, and happy surfing!

-Peter J. Gagné

Internet/Computer Glossary
Terms in italics refer to other glossary entries.

Bookmarks: A collection of your favorite sites (on Netscape Navigator). Bookmarks are basically a collection of links to sites that you visit often or want to go back to, without having to re-type the entire *URL* over and over. *See also Favorites.*

Bps: Bits Per Second. This is a measure of how fast data is transferred through your modem. "K" stands for thousand, thus 56k means 56,000 bits per second transferred.

Browser: The computer program that you use to view Web pages, images and other documents and files on the *Internet*. The two most popular browsers are Microsoft Internet Explorer and Netscape Navigator. (Netscape Communicator is a "browser suite" that integrates an e-mail program, *html* editor and other features.)

Cache: A reserved area of your hard drive or memory where files are stored temporarily for quick retrieval. Many Web pages or image files are stored in your computer's cache so they can be accessed quicker than downloading them off the Web each time.

Cookie: A piece of information stored on your computer that is used to identify you to Web sites. Some sites use cookies as a means of keeping track of your identity and password, so you don't have to type in a username and password every time you visit. Other sites keep track of your preferences or customized user options for activities on the site. Some sites may use cookies to try to find out information about you without your knowledge. You can set your browser to accept or reject all cookies or warn you before accepting cookies.

Discussion List: Also known as "mailing lists." A discussion list is a list of people who decide to send and receive e-mail messages pertaining to a certain subject or topic. List members join the list by "subscribing," and then send messages to the group by "posting" a message to the list. Some lists offer the option of subscribing to every message posted to the list or to just a daily or occasional digest of postings. "Moderated" lists are run by an individual who screens posted messages.

Domain: In the *URL* `http://www.YourName.com`, "YourName" is the domain. The domain is the identifier for groups or individuals on the Web.

FAQ: Frequently Asked Questions. Many sites provide them to reduce the amount of actual questions that they get posed through e-mail.

Favorites: A collection of your favorite sites (on Microsoft Internet Explorer). Favorites are basically a collection of links to sites that you visit often or want to go back to, without having to re-type the entire *URL* over and over. *See also Bookmarks*.

FTP: File Transfer Protocol. This is a way of sending files from one computer to another, and is most often used to download files from the Web or send files from an individual's computer to a Web *server* to be posted on the *Internet*.

GIF: Graphic Interchange Format, pronounced "giff." A type of image file used in Web pages. GIF files are usually drawings or computer-generated images. Some GIF files are "animated" and appear to move or change shape.

Host: A company or group that provides storage space on their *servers* for Web sites.

HTML: HyperText Markup Language. This is the language used to write Web pages.

HTTP: HyperText Transfer Protocol. This is the set of rules that computers use to allow you to view HyperText documents, or Web pages.

Hyper Link: Part of a Web page or *HyperText* document that allows the user direct access to another Web page or document.

HyperText: A type of computer file that allows the integration of text, images and other multimedia elements into a single file, usually a Web page. HyperText also allows the linking of one file to others through hyper links.

Internet: Commonly confused or interchanged with the *World Wide Web*. The Internet is the combination of the Web, e-mail, *ftp* and other means of exchanging data.

Interstitals: Small *browser* windows that pop up and display advertisements or other information. Interstitals are most common in *online communities*, where the *host* provides free Web space in exchange for displaying advertisements.

ISP: Internet Service Provider. These are the people that you pay to get on the Web. They provide the connection between your computer and the *Internet*. Some of the bigger national ISPs are AT&T WorldNet, MSN, EarthLink and MindSpring.

Java: A programming language used in Web pages to run mini-programs or "applets" on Web pages. Some of the more common examples of the use of Java are news tickers, changing images, chat rooms and buttons that change color or reveal another image or information when the pointer passes over them.

JPEG/JPG: Pronounced "J-peg." An acronym for Joint Photographic Experts Group, an industry collective that agreed on the standard for this type of image file, most often a scanned photo.

Online Community: A group of Web sites bound together by common themes and interests. Online communities commonly provide free Web sites to individuals or groups in exchange for displaying advertisements on these sites or in *interstitals*. Some of the more popular online communities are GeoCities, Tripod and Xoom.

Online Service: An ISP that provides its members with pre-packaged content or "channels." These channels are on the online service's *servers*, and while online services provide access to the *Internet* at large, they are not the Internet itself, but are more like a closed community or "Disney World" version of the Internet. Some of the more popular online services are America Online, Compuserve and Prodigy.

Plug-ins: Small programs that extend the capabilities of your *browser* to view different types of image, music or other files.

Protocol: A set of rules that computers use to communicate with each other. See *FTP, http* and *TCP/IP*.

Search Engine: A Web site that searches the *Internet* to find the site or keyword you are looking for. Many search engines don't search the entire Web, but rather the sites that have registered with them or which they have indexed. Some of the more popular search engines are Yahoo!, Excite, AltaVista, Lycos and HotBot. A search engine that searches other search engines is known as a meta search engine. Examples of meta search engines are Dogpile and MetaFind.

Server: A computer that stores files that are used by several other computers, known as "clients." A Web server stores the *HTML* and other files that make up Web pages.

Spam: Unwanted, unsolicited bulk e-mail, usually offering some sort of promotion.

TCP/IP: Transmission Control Protocol/Internet Protocol. TCP handles how computers send and receive information between each other. IP breaks up the information being sent into "packets" and assigns each a sequence order. The packets are then sent along different channels to their final destination and put back together in sequence.

URL: Uniform Resource Locator. Commonly called a "Web address." This is the line you type in (which usually begins with `http://`) to get to the site you want.

World Wide Web: Commonly confused with the *Internet,* of which it is a part. The World Wide Web is a network of computers connected via phone lines, and is thus a "dial-up network." The Web is the part of the Internet that stores and displays *HTML* documents and other files on Web sites.

Links to Your Canadian Past
Québec

National

Genealogical, Historical and Cultural Societies

Individual Societies

Alliance for Canada's Audio-Visual Heritage [English & French]
http://www.rcc.ryerson.ca/Alliance/
Preserves and facilitates access to heritage materials that include film, video, television and radio productions and sound recordings. Also conducts training programs and aids research projects.

Asian Canadian
http://www.asian.ca/
Dedicated to tracing and sharing the legacy of Asians in the fields of the economy, culture and politics in Canada. Links to professional and media groups, educational and cultural centers.

Association for Canadian Jewish Studies
http://fcis.oise.utoronto.ca/~acjs/
Formerly the Canadian Jewish Historical Society, the ACJS encourages scholarly research in Canadian Jewish history, life and culture. The Web site features news and events, a discussion list and links to research organizations, as well as the *Canadian Jewish News* Internet edition.

Canada GenWeb Project [English & French]
http://www.geocities.com/Heartland/6625/cngenweb.html
A collection of links to genealogical information and data for the entire country. Links to individual provinces' GenWeb sites (catalogued below), with county-level divisions.

Links to Your Canadian Past
Québec

Canada's National History Society [English & French]
http://www.cyberspc.mb.ca/~otmw/cnhs/cnhs.html
Dedicated to popularizing Canadian history through an admissions discount program, historical booklet publications, a heritage award and *The Beaver* magazine, with an online index.

Canadian Association for Irish Studies
http://www.usask.ca/english/cais/index.html
Fostering and encouraging the study of Irish culture in Canada. CAIS publishes a semi-annual newsletter (available online) and the twice yearly *Journal of Canadian Irish Studies*.

Canadian Aviation Historical Society
http://www.cahs.com/
Supports and encourages the preservation of Canada's flying heritage through research and collection of historical material. Publishes a quarterly journal. Several provincial chapters.

Canadian Committee on Labour History
http://www.mun.ca/cclh/
Promoting and publishing scholarly research in the field of Canadian labour history and related areas. Books for purchase and an index to the latest newsletter *Labour/Le Travail* available.

Canadian Doukhobor Society
http://www.kootenay.net/~cds/
Information on membership, events, workshops, publications and an online newsletter.

Canadian Friends Historical Association
http://home.interhop.net/~aschrauwe/
Preserving and documenting the social, cultural and pioneer heritage of the Quakers who immigrated to Canada, from their early settlement through today.

Links to Your Canadian Past
Québec

Canadian Heritage / Patrimoine Canadien [English & French]
http://www.pch.gc.ca/
The official page of the Ministry of Canadian Heritage, with the sections: The Department, Multiculturalism, Sport, Canadian Studies and Youth, Canadian Symbols, Human Rights, Cultural Development, Arts and Heritage, Parks Canada and Official Languages.

Canadian Heritage Information Network (CHIN):
http://www.chin.gc.ca/e_main_menu.html
Réseau Canadien d'Information sur le Patrimoine (RCIP):
http://www.rcip.gc.ca/f_main_menu.html
A directory of Canadian museums, galleries and heritage information. Subscribe to special resources, enroll in a course, purchase publications, view virtual exhibits and more.

Canadian Historical Association / Société Historique du Canada [English & French]
http://www.yorku.ca/research/cha/
The CHA advocates the study and preservation of Canadian history by lobbying governments, holding conferences and publishing a journal, historical booklet series and the *CHA Bulletin*.

Canadian Jewish Historical Society
http://www.oise.on.ca/webstuff/otherprj/cjhs1.html
Sponsors an academic journal, a members-only newsletter and an online discussion group.

Canadian Oral History Association / Société Canadienne d'Histoire Orale [English & French]
http://www.ualberta.ca/~fmillar/coha.htm
COHA helps individuals plan and carry out oral history projects. Includes guides and advice.

Links to Your Canadian Past
Québec

Canadian Railroad Historical Association – St-Constant, QC
[English & French]
http://www.exporail.org/
Dedicated to the preservation and dissemination of information, artifacts and archival materials pertaining to the history of railways in Canada. The association operates a museum/archives (*see National / Museums and Historic Sites*) and publishes a bimonthly magazine and newsletter.

Canadian Society of Mayflower Descendants
http://www.mayflower.org/canada/canada.html
The society is open to any person able to document his or her lineage to a passenger on the *Mayflower*. Includes research tips and a list of *Mayflower* passengers who left descendants.

Genealogical Institute of the Maritimes
http://www.shelburne.nscc.ns.ca/nsgna/gim/index.html
This organization, focusing on Nova Scotia, Prince Edward Island, Newfoundland and New Brunswick, certifies and registers researchers as either Genealogical Record Searcher (Canada) or Certified Genealogist (Canada). Certification guides available.

Icelandic National League of North America
http://users.imag.net/~sry.rasgeirs/default.html
Seeks to promote the Icelandic language, literature and culture among those of Icelandic descent in Canada and the US.

International Internet Genealogical Society – online resource
[English, French, etc.]
http://www.iigs.org/index.htm.en
This online "society" seeks to link genealogists and genealogical information throughout the world and also provides a chat room, monthly newsletter, queries and free online courses.

Links to Your Canadian Past
Québec

Mennonite Historical Societies Directory
http://www.goshen.edu/mcarchives/directory1998.htm
A contact list for North American Mennonite, Amish and related historical committees, societies, conference historians and interpretation centers.

Organization for the History of Canada
http://www.acs.ucalgary.ca/~osnhc/
Dedicated to fostering an interest in the "Canadian national experience" in the broadest sense. OHC publishes *National History*, a quarterly journal devoted to scholarly research and general interest in history, culture, biography, politics, geography, society, and economy.

Pier 21 Society
http://pier21.ns.ca/
A group dedicated to preserving and documenting the history of immigration to Canada through the historic Pier 21 in Nova Scotia and other entry points. Online newsletter and stories.

Ukrainian Genealogical and Historical Society of Canada
http://www.feefhs.org/ca/frgughsc.html
Basic information on the society, contact information and a link to the Ukrainian Research List.

Professional Organization
Federation of Canadian Genealogical and Family History Societies
http://www.rcip.gc.ca/f_main_menu.html
An umbrella organization for societies nationwide. Co-ordinates the exchange of information between societies. Members share current issues, concerns and information on heritage projects.

Links to Your Canadian Past
Québec

Archives

Directories
Canadian Council of Archives Directory of Archival Repositories
http://www.cdncouncilarchives.ca/dir.html
This site provides a comprehensive directory of member institutions and their collections. Archive centers are listed by province as well as theme or type (military, religious, native organizations, etc.).

Canadian Archival Resources on the Internet
http://www.usask.ca/archives/menu.html
This site, maintained by the University of Saskatchewan archives, provides a Web directory of archive centers, listed alphabetically, by region or type.

Archive Centers
Canadian Institute for Historical Microreproductions
http://www.nlc-bnc.ca/cihm/cihm.htm
The CIHM locates early printed Canadian materials, puts them on microfilm and makes them available to libraries and institutions. Includes a list of libraries with a complete or partial collection of the Early Canadiana research project, plus a searchable database of the project, with the possibility to order materials located via the search.

Canadian Pacific Railway Archives
http://www.cpr.ca/www/insidecpr/aboutcpr/cparchives/incprarchives.html
This private archive offers fee-based research services on its materials relating to the history of Canadian Pacific, including the railway, ships, hotels, promotion of immigration and tourism, etc. Images of sample documents, artwork and artifacts are available online.

Links to Your Canadian Past
Québec

Canadian Quaker Archives at Pickering College – Newmarket, ON
http://home.interhop.net/~aschrauwe/Archives.html
Information on available resources at the archives for researching Quaker genealogy and history.

Canadian Women's Movement Archives – Ottawa, ON
[English & French]
http://www.uottawa.ca/library/cwma.html
Located at the University of Ottawa, this archive center preserves the documents and archival material of the various women's organizations that collectively make up the women's movement in Canada. This site describes the various holdings and available finding aids.

Charles Denny Métis Genealogical Collection
http://www.glenbow.org/archhtm/denney.htm
This Web site lists the families included in the Denney collection of Métis genealogies housed at the Glenbow Archives in Alberta, giving the call numbers of the microfilmed files. The families included have some connection to the Red River settlement.

George Back Collection from the National Archives [English & French]
http://www.schoolnet.ca/collections/back/
An online presentation of several paintings, maps, documents and artifacts from Back's Arctic expeditions pertaining to Alberta, Manitoba, the Northwest Territories, Ontario, Saskatchewan, the Yukon Territories and the sea.

Hudson's Bay Company Archives
http://www.gov.mb.ca/chc/archives/hbca/index.html
Information on the holdings of the HBCA, how and where to access records, a catalogue of microfilm holdings, and a list of

libraries and repositories. The site also includes a brief history of the Company and online aids to help locate and order available records.

Métis Genealogical Research Services – Glenbow Archives
http://www.glenbow.org/archhtm/metis.htm
Contains information on the Métis genealogy research service of the Glenbow Archives in Alberta, including fees, contact information and records searched.

National Archives of Canada [English & French]
http://www.archives.ca/
Includes a comprehensive guide to using the archives and a Genealogy Research section with information on census, birth, marriage, death, land and many other records in the archives' holdings. There is also a page on How to Get Started and information on how to make inquiries.

United Church of Canada/Victoria University Archives
http://vicu.utoronto.ca/archives/archives.htm
Describes the holdings of the United Church of Canada and its antecedent denominations, including the Presbyterian and Methodist Churches in Canada. Also includes information on genealogical research and resources at the archives.

Professional Organizations
Alliance of Libraries Archives and Records Management (ALARM) [English & French]
http://www.fis.utoronto.ca/groups/ALARM/
A forum for those working in the various fields of information management, ALARM provides a Marketplace/Directory listing of educational and training resources in the field, plus an Open Forum/Personal Interaction area, where professionals can communicate and interact.

Links to Your Canadian Past
Québec

Association of Canadian Archivists
http://www.archives.ca/aca/
A group providing government advocacy, leadership, communication and awareness of archival concerns and issues in the professional community. Publishes a newsletter and scholarly journal.

Association of Canadian Map Libraries and Archives [English & French]
http://nexus.sscl.uwo.ca/assoc/acml/acmla.html
A group of map librarians, cartographic archivists and other interested in preserving geographic information. Promotes professional standards, research and publications. The ACMLA also offers maps of Canadian cities for sale on its Web site, with thumbnail previews.

Canadian Council of Archives [English & French]
http://www.cdncouncilarchives.ca/
The national coordinating body for federal and provincial archives groups. Their bulletin is available online, as is a list of publications and information about the Canadian Archival Information Network initiative to put archival information online.

Records Management Institute
HTTP://www.dfait-maeci.gc.ca/rmi-igd/menu.htm
A professional organization dedicated to the needs of those in the field of managing recorded information. The RMI promotes sound standards and practices, encourages and facilitates the exchange of information, organizes and promotes conferences and training. This site provides information on all their activities, links to articles, a mailing list and newsgroup.

Links to Your Canadian Past
Québec

Libraries and Research Centers

Directories and Catalogues
Canadian Libraries and Library Catalogues [English & French]
http://www.nlc-bnc.ca/canlib/eindex.htm
A searchable listing of libraries throughout Canada by province, name or type. Some libraries just provide information, while others allow a search of their catalogue.

Canadian Library Index
http://www.lights.com/canlib/
A listing, by province, of the Web sites of libraries throughout Canada. Each listing contains a link to the library's Web site and/or their telnet or Web-based catalogue.

Family History Centers in Canada
- http://www.shelburne.nscc.ns.ca/nsgna/fhc/cdnfhc.htm
- http://www.genhomepage.com/FHC/Canada.html

Lists (the first by province) of the addresses and phone numbers of LDS Family History Centers.

HYTELNET Library Catalogues: Canada
http://moondog.usask.ca/hytelnet/ca0/ca000.html
A listing of the TELNET sites, login names and procedures to search online catalogues of public and university libraries throughout Canada.

resAnet [English & French]
http://www.amicus.nlc-bnc.ca/resanet/
The catalogue of the National Library of Canada. resAnet is a free subset of the fee-based Amicus catalogue, providing brief records of the library's collections.

Links to Your Canadian Past
Québec

Special Collections in Canadian Libraries [English & French]
http://library.usask.ca/spcol/index.html
An index to the contents of special collections of libraries throughout Canada. Browse through subjects such as History, Cartographic Materials and Sociology or search for a specific keyword.

WebCATS – Canada
http://library.usask.ca/hywebcat/countries/CA.html
A listing of links to Web-based catalogues of public and university libraries across Canada.

Libraries and Research Centers

Canadian City Directory Collection – National Library of Canada
- http://library.usask.ca/spcol/collections/040e.html
- http://www.nlc-bnc.ca/services/edirect.htm

A description of this specialized collection – over 7,000 volumes of directories from across the country at different levels, with access and holdings information.

Gabriel Dumont Institute of Native Studies and Applied Research – Regina, SK
http://schoolnet2.carleton.ca/english/ext/aboriginal/metis-de/dumont.html
Promoting the renewal and development of Métis culture through research and education.

National Library of Canada [English & French]
http://www.nlc-bnc.ca/ehome.htm
Information on the collections and services of the National Library, which include access to its electronic collections and a description of Services to Genealogists and Family Historians. These services include the fee-based catalogue Access AMICUS and a listing of reference sources for Canadian genealogy.

Links to Your Canadian Past
Québec

Royal Military College of Canada: Massey Library
http://library.usask.ca/spcol/institutions/32e.html
Describes the Canadian Military History Collection and the Reginald E. Watters Collection at the library, with contact information for the library.

Canadian Studies Centers and Programs
Acadia University: Canadian Studies Program (Wolfville, NS)
http://ace.acadiau.ca/arts/canstud.htm

Association of Canadian Studies [English & French]
http://www.er.uqam.ca/nobel/c1015/e_acs.htm
The only national association dedicated solely to the promotion of research, teaching and publications on Canada. The ACS sponsors conferences, publications, awards and study programs at the college and university level, as well as other educational levels.

Association for Canadian Studies in the United States
(Washington, DC)
http://canada-acsus.plattsburgh.edu/acsus/i_acsus.htm
The only organization in the U.S. devoted to encouraging and supporting the study of Canada's political system, economy, history, geography, literature and artistic and cultural heritage. The ACUS sponsors conferences, grants and awards as well as various publications in the field, including a newsletter, *Canadian Studies Update*, available online.

Association Françaises d'Études Canadiennes/French Association for Canadian Studies
http://www.archimedia.fr/AFEC/index.html
A multidisciplinary association promoting Canadian studies in France through scholarships, a scholarly journal, conferences and communication among France's Canadian studies centers.

Links to Your Canadian Past
Québec

Athabasca University: B.A. Major in Canadian Studies (Athabasca, AB)
http://www.athabascau.ca/html/programs/b_arts/maj_cdst.htm
A description of the program and listing of sample courses in literature, geography, history, native and ethnic studies, politics and government.

Canadian Studies in the United States (online resource)
- **Main**: http://canada-acsus.plattsburgh.edu/index.htm
- **List of Programs**: http://Canada-acsus.plattsburgh.edu/programs/orgprog.htm

A joint project of the Center for the Study of Canada at SUNY Plattsburgh and the Association for the Study of Canada in the U.S., this site is an online resource center for material pertaining to Canadian Studies. Sections include Business, Conferences, Government, Grants, Newspapers, Outreach, Positions, Programs and Video, as well as recent news items.

Capilano College Canadian Studies Specialty (North Vancouver, BC)
http://www.capcollege.bc.ca/programs/cana_studies/index.html
A listing of courses offered in the specialty and overview of requirements.

Carleton University: School of Canadian Studies (Ottawa, ON)
http://temagami.carleton.ca/fass/CanStud/index.html
Information on the undergraduate and graduate programs, academic staff, faculty research interests, awards and bursaries, recent publications and the school's history and mission.

Links to Your Canadian Past
Québec

Center for the Study of Canada – SUNY Plattsburgh (Plattsburgh, NY)
http://canada-acsus.plattsburgh.edu/cesca/cesca.htm
A presentation of the programs of study offered at this institution, including major and minor programs, internships, study abroad, scholarships and grants and other activities.

Centre d'Études Amérindiennes [French only] (Chicoutimi, QC)
http://www.uqac.uquebec.ca/cea/cea.htm
The programs under the auspices of the CEA include a Certificate of Teaching in Amerindian Communities, Certificate in Native Technolinguistics, Certificate of Multidisciplinary Studies, a Bachelors Degree in Preschool and Primary Education and a Short Caseworker Program.

Centre d'Études Canadiennes, Université de Rennes (Rennes, France) [French only]
http://www.uhb.fr/langues/cec/
A multidisciplinary program focusing on research and teaching of all aspects of Canadian studies. The center organizes conferences, academic exchanges and publications.

Dalhousie University Canadian Studies Programme (Halifax, NS)
http://WWW.Registrar.Dal.Ca/calendar/ugrad/cana/
An overview of the requirements, faculty and courses included in the programme.

Institute of Canadian Studies – University of Ottawa [English & French]
http://www.uottawa.ca/academic/arts/cdn/
Offers undergraduate and Ph.D. programs, workshops, lecture series and seminars.

Links to Your Canadian Past
Québec

International Council of Canadian Studies
http://WWW.ICCS-CIEC.CA/eng_home.html
A group of 20 national and multi-national Canadian Studies associations, dedicated to promoting and supporting research, education and publications in the field of Canadian Studies.

McGill Institute for the Study of Canada (Montréal, QC)
[English & French]
http://www.arts.mcgill.ca/programs/misc/
The institute offers interdisciplinary and experimental courses in Canadian studies, provides graduate fellowships and hosts visiting students and seminar speakers. It offers both major and minor concentration programs in Canadian Studies and a minor in Canadian Ethnic Studies.

Mount Allison University Programme of Canadian Studies
(Sackville, NB)
http://aci.mta.ca/depts/canadian_studies/
Both undergraduate programs and courses for non full-time students are offered, with a particular focus on Maritime history. Course and faculty listing available online.

Mount Saint Vincent University Canadian Studies Program
(Halifax, NS)
http://www.msvu.ca/calendar/cana.htm
An interdisciplinary Bachelor of Arts if offered with either a major or minor in Canadian Studies.

Saint François-Xavier University Canadian Studies Program
(Antigosh, NS)
http://xel.stfx.ca/academic/Canadian-Studies/
An overview of various aspects of the program, including faculty, courses and students.

Links to Your Canadian Past
Québec

Saint Mary's University Department of Atlantic Canada Studies (Halifax, NS)
http://www.stmarys.ca/academic/arts/atlantic.htm
Course descriptions, offerings and time table, as well as faculty information.

Simon Fraser University Centre for Canadian Studies (Burnaby, BC)
http://www.sfu.ca/cns/
General information on the program, as well as faculty, courses and student groups.

Trent University (Peterborough, ON)
- **Canadian Studies Program**:
  http://www.trentu.ca/admin/ro/calendar/dynamic/canstudies.html
- **Summer Explorations in Canadian Culture**:
  http://ivory.trentu.ca/www/canstudies/summer.htm

University of Alberta: Undergraduate Programs in Canadian Studies (Edmonton, AB)
http://www.ualberta.ca/~polisci/canstud/ugrad.htm
Offers courses in Canadian regions, culture, literature, nationalism and contemporary issues.

University of British Columbia: Canadian Studies Program (Vancouver, BC)
http://www.arts.ubc.ca/canada/cdnstud.htm
An overview of the program, with major, minor and specialized course lists.

University of Calgary: Canadian Studies (Calgary, AB)
http://www.ucalgary.ca/pubs/calendar/current/What/Fac/GN/BBMP/DOP/CNST.htm
Details of the requirements for the program and the courses offered in various disciplines.

Links to Your Canadian Past
Québec

University of Manitoba Canadian Studies Program (Winnipeg, MB)
http://www.umanitoba.ca/faculties/arts/deans_office/cdnsp.htm
An overview of the program, including courses in Canadian history, economics, politics, and social and cultural traditions.

University of Prince Edward Island Canadian Studies Program (Charlottetown, PEI)
http://www.upei.ca/~regoff/canst_1.html
Requirements for a major or minor in Canadian Studies, with list of courses and faculty.

University of Regina Canadian Plains Studies Program (Regina, SK)
http://www.uregina.ca/printsrv/artscan.html
An overview of this graduate program to study the unique aspects of Canadian Plains life.

University of Toronto (University College) Canadian Studies Program
http://www.library.utoronto.ca/www/uc/can.htm

University of Victoria: Diploma and Certificate Programs in Canadian Studies for International Students
http://www.uvcs.uvic.ca/artsci/cs/
Admissions and application info, curriculum and courses covered in the programs.

University of Waterloo Canadian Studies (Waterloo, ON)
http://www.adm.uwaterloo.ca:80/infoucal/9596/INTER/can_studies.html
Information on the three-year Canadian Studies major, general and honours option programs, Canadian Studies minor, non-major degree and courses offered in the programs.

Links to Your Canadian Past
Québec

Birth, Marriage, Death, Census and Other Data Online

Vital Statistics and Parish Records
Canadian and Other Vital Statistics Offices
http://www.gov.ab.ca/ma/reg/vs/sa.htm
Contact information and an overview of fees for provincial Vital Statistics offices.

Records of Births, Marriages and Deaths at the National Archives
http://www.archives.ca/www/svcs/english/BMDRecords.html
An overview of the records contained in the National Archives classified into church records, marriage indexes, civil registration (birth, marriage and death by province) and marriage bonds.

Census Information
Census of Canada: History
http://142.206.72.128/cgi-bin/folioisa.dll/Focus-e1.nfo/query=*/doc/{t2}/pageitems={body}/hit_headings/words=4?
An overview of the need for a census of Canada, past censuses and an historical timeline.

Census Records in Canada [English & French]
http://www.archives.ca/www/svcs/english/GenealogicalSources.html#Census Records
An overview from the National Archives on what records are available, what they contain and where to find them for use in your research.

Information Collected by Canadian Censuses
http://www.virtuel.qc.ca/simmons/CENSINFO.HTM
A list of the categories of information collected in the 1825, 1831, 1842, 1851, 1861, 1871, 1881, 1891 and 1901 censuses of Canada.

Links to Your Canadian Past
Québec

Métis Census Indexes
http://www.televar.com/~gmorin/census.htm
Census information from 1827 to 1917 that includes Métis settlers in present-day Manitoba and parts of the United States (North Dakota, Minnesota and Montana).

National Registration File of 1940
http://www.geocities.com/Heartland/9332/natreg.htm
Information on this census-like registration, which is not as restrictive as other records, including what information is provided for men and women and how to obtain copies of the records.

1901 Census of Canada Information
http://www.tbaytel.net/bmartin/census.htm
An explanation of the column headings for this census, with a listing of National Archives of Canada and LDS film numbers for each district and subdistrict, listed by province.

Passenger Lists/Immigration Data

Early Maritime Disasters and Accidents Involving Immigrants to Canada
http://www.cadvision.com/traces/imigrate/disastr1.html
Includes the names of those passengers saved and lost in the disasters.

Emigration from Iceland to North America
http://nyherji.is/~halfdan/westward/vestur.htm
Articles and information on many aspects of Icelandic immigration to the US and Canada, including Icelandic Names, Settlers, Photos and the "Evergrowing Tree" of surnames.

Links to Your Canadian Past
Québec

Immigrants to Canada in the 19th Century
http://www.ist.uwaterloo.ca/~marj/genealogy/thevoyage.html
A wealth of information on immigration for this time period. Ship information, passenger lists, immigrant handbooks, information on specific cultural and national groups, etc.

Immigration Records at the National Archives
http://www.archives.ca/www/svcs/english/ImmigrationRecords.html
Includes information on available records for passenger lists prior to 1865 and from 1865-1935, border entry records 1908-1935, post-1935 immigration records, immigration from China and Home Children.

inGeneas Passenger and Immigration List Database
http://www.inGeneas.com/ingeneas/index.html
A searchable database of passenger and immigration information from the 18th, 19th and early 20th centuries. Returns age of individual, year and type of record found. For a fee, inGeneas will research further information and provide a more detailed account of the record.

Irish Emigrants
http://www.genealogy.org/~ajmorris/ireland/ireemg.htm
A series of passenger lists for ships leaving Great Britain or Ireland in the late 1800's.

Miscellaneous Immigration Index (National Archives of Canada/inGeneas)
http://www.inGeneas.com/free/index.html
Fully-searchable index of various immigration records from the NAC. Clicking on a returned name provides a complete record and clicking on "source" returns full source information.

Links to Your Canadian Past
Québec

Naturalization (Citizenship) Records at the National Archives
http://www.archives.ca/www/svcs/english/GenealogicalSources.html#Citizenship Records
Describes what records are available and where to write for detailed information.

Pier 21: The Ships of Pier 21
http://pier21.ns.ca/ships.html
A list of ships that arrived at Pier 21 carrying War Brides, Troops, Evacuees, Immigrants, Refugees, Displaced Persons and other groups. Links to info on some ships.

Profiles: Immigration Research Series
http://cicnet.ci.gc.ca/english/pub/index.html#reference
A series of reports on (recent) immigrants from several countries, describing settlement patterns, family status, education, demographics, income and other details.

Young Immigrants to Canada
http://www.ist.uwaterloo.ca/~marj/genealogy/homeadd.html
A collection of information on juvenile immigrants to Canada. Includes information on Roman Catholic organizations and other denominations, societies and organizations, reformatories and schools, groups for women and non-British immigrants.

Land Records

Land Records – Genealogical Sources in Canada [English & French]
http://www.archives.ca/www/svcs/english/LandRecords.html
Describes the archival materials available through the National Archives, including:
- **Index to Upper Canada Records**:
  http://www.archives.ca/www/svcs/english/INDEXRG1_E.html#Upper Canada

Links to Your Canadian Past
Québec

- **Index to Lower Canada Records**:
  http://www.archives.ca/www/svcs/english/INDEXRG1_E.html#Lower Canada
  Also provides information on provincial land records holdings.

Métis Land Claims
http://www.archives.ca/www/svcs/english/LandRecords.html#Métis land claims
Brief information on the records in the National Archives pertaining to Métis land claims and how to locate this information in the archives or obtain copies.

Adoption Information and Groups
Adopt: Assistance, Information, Support
http://www.adopting.org/
Sections include Especially for Adoptees, Especially for Birth Parents, Free Search Registry, a Chat room, Support Forums and a great deal of other information.

Adoptee Searcher's Handbook
http://www.login.net/inverc/search.htm
An online resource, created especially for Canadians, on Web sites, registries, records, archives, libraries, government and provincial departments and other sources of adoption information.

Adoptees Internet Mailing List
http://www.webreflection.com/aiml/
A forum for the discussion of search and reunion issues. Includes a chat room.

Adoption Information for Canadians
http://www.toddlersonline.com/adopt/
Primarily for those currently seeking to adopt children, this site provides information on agencies, newsletters, support groups, a book list and message board.

Links to Your Canadian Past
Québec

CANADopt
http://nebula.on.ca/canadopt/
Adoption information for each province and Canada-wide, including a national registry.

Canadian Adoptee Information Center and Reunion Registry
http://www.geocities.com/Heartland/Plains/1742/
An online registry for adoptees and birth parents searching for each other. Includes lists of adoptees searching, birth parents searching and an online form for sending data.

Canadian Adoptees Registry, Inc.
http://www.bconnex.net/~rickm/
A free service detailing what records are available and how to obtain them, plus a national registry of adoptees/foster children or parents or those seeking to find them.

Forget Me Not Family Society
http://www.portal.ca/~adoption/
Includes a Canadian adoption FAQ and Resources, Online Support Lists and Newsletter.

Parent Finders of Canada
http://www.ltinc.net/reunion/
This site includes adoption news and issues from across Canada, an adoption reunion registry form, online group support lists and links to other online resources.

Seekers of the Lost
http://www.seeklost.com/
A free international adoption search registry, with over 42,000 people registered.

Links to Your Canadian Past
Québec

The Triad Society for Truth in Adoption in Canada
http://www.sfn.saskatoon.sk.ca/community/triad/index.html
Dedicated to reuniting families separated by adoption. Triad volunteers provide service, support groups, peer counseling and conferences and also maintain a national registry.

Legal and Other Data
Wills and Estate Records
http://www.archives.ca/www/svcs/english/WillsEstates.html
A list from the National Archives of provincial sources of probate records.

Museums/Historic Sites/Groups

Directories
Artefacts Canada [English & French]
http://www.chin.gc.ca/Artefacts/e_artefacts_canada.html
Formerly National Inventories, this is an online catalogue of information on millions of museum objects, natural history specimens and archaeological sites throughout Canada.

Guide to Canadian Museums and Galleries (Canadian Heritage Information Network)
http://www.chin.gc.ca/Museums/ [English & French]
A searchable guide to the museums of Canada by name, collection or location. Information on hours, services, collections and activities, with links to Web sites of member institutions.

Links to Your Canadian Past
Québec

Heritage Directory (Canadian Heritage Information Network) [English & French]
http://www.chin.gc.ca/Museums/CHER/e_hp_cher.html
A searchable directory of over 450 private organizations and government departments and agencies engaged in heritage activities and conservation. Contact information and scope and type of activities are included in the listings.

History Lands – Canada's Heritage Sites
http://www.interlog.com/~parks/historyhome.html
An overview of this series on History Television, with links to individual episode summaries on various heritage sites throughout Canada, from Alberta's Head-Smashed-In Buffalo Jump to Québec's Grosse Île Immigrant Station, Victoria's Chinatown, and many more.

Images of Parks Canada [English & French]
http://parkscanada.pch.gc.ca/schoolnet/pcimages/homepage/homepage.htm
View photos from national historical sites and parks throughout Canada.

Parks Canada [English & French]
http://www.parkscanada.pch.gc.ca/
The government authority over Canadian National Heritage parks and sites. Individual sites are indexed in the *Museums and Historic Sites* section of each province.

SchoolNet Digital Collections [English & French]
http://www.SchoolNet.ca/collections/E/index.htm
This site provides access to many online presentations in the areas of History, Geography, First Peoples, Social Studies, Women, Government, Fine Arts, Business and Labour.

Links to Your Canadian Past
Québec

Ship Information Database (Canadian Heritage) [English & French]
http://susan.chin.gc.ca:8013/basisdbdocs/title1e.html
Search or browse databases containing information on vessels, masters, owners, builders and voyages for ships of Canadian registry or that sailed in Canadian waters.

Museums and Historic Sites

African Canadian Heritage Tour – Amherstburg, Buxton, Chatham, Dresden & Sandwich, ON
[English & French]:
http://www.ciaccess.com/~jdnewby/heritage/african.htm
Five connected heritage sites depicting the communities settled and developed largely by former slaves who escaped to Canada via the Underground Railroad.

Agriculture Museum – Ottawa, ON [English & French]
http://www.nmstc.ca/ag/index.htm
Showcasing Canada's agricultural heritage through exhibits and the only working farm in a national capital. Visit animal barns for the sights, sounds and smells of Canadian agriculture.

Alexander Mackenzie Voyageur Route Home Page – several provinces
http://www.amvr.org/
Stretching more than 10,000 km from Québec City to British Columbia, this route marks the first documented crossing of continental North America by a European. Find online information about the route, the man and the Alexander Mackenzie Voyageur Route Association.

Links to Your Canadian Past
Québec

Canadian Canoe Museum – Peterborough, ON
http://www.canoemuseum.net/
Boasting the "largest collection of canoes and kayaks in the world," the museum features birchbark, dugout and modern canoes and artifacts of the canoeing lifestyle.

Canadian Center for Architecture – Montréal, QC [English & French]
http://cca.qc.ca/contents.html
The CCA is a museum and study center devoted to the art of architecture and the related domains of urban planning and landscape design. While its scope is international, the Center features many local and national exhibits, activities and programs and includes an extensive library.

Canadian Military Heritage Museum – Brantford, ON
http://www.bfree.on.ca/comdir/musgal/cmhm/
Exhibits and artifacts recounting Canada's involvement in military deployments from the Seven Year's War to the Boer War, World Wars I & II, Korea and UN peacekeeping missions.

Canadian Museum of Civilization – Hull, QC [English & French]
http://www.civilization.ca/cmc/cmceng/welcmeng.html
In addition to information on location, hours and events, you can also visit the Virtual Museum, browse some of the permanent and temporary exhibits on the history of Canada and find out about research activities at the museum.

Canadian Museum of Flight – Langley, BC
http://www.canadianflight.org/
This site provides information about the museum and its 23 planes on display, as well as the history of aviation in Canada, aviation artwork and a special section for kids.

Links to Your Canadian Past
Québec

Canadian Museum of Rail Travel – Cranbrook, BC
http://www.crowsnest.bc.ca/cmrt/index.html
Restored railway buildings (station, freight shed and water tower) and a large collection of restored railway cars and artifacts depicting the history of rail travel in Canada.

Canadian Postal Museum – Hull, QC [English & French]
http://www.civilization.ca/cpm.html
The only museum in Canada dedicated to preserving and interpreting the material heritage of postal communications as an integral part of modern society and communications.

Canadian Railway Museum and Archives – Delson/St-Constant, QC [English & French]
http://www.exporail.org/musee/musee_CRM.htm
Historic train cars, streetcars, railway equipment and structures help tell the history of rail transportation in Canada and how this history is intimately linked to the history of the country itself.

Canadian War Museum – Hull, QC [English & French]
http://www.civilization.ca/cwm/cwmeng/cwmeng.html
Dedicated to the remembrance of Canada's military history from colonial through modern times. Information about the museum's exhibits and collections and a virtual tour of the galleries.

Canadian Warplane Heritage Museum – Mount Hope, ON
http://www.warplane.com/
Take a virtual tour of the museum, with 35 aircraft from World War II to the Jet Age, and a library/archives with books, photos and artifacts on warplane history.

Links to Your Canadian Past
Québec

Currency Museum of the Bank of Canada – Ottawa, ON
- **Information**: http://www.bank-banque-canada.ca/english/museum.htm
- **Collections:** http://www.schoolnet.ca/collections/bank/english/index.htm

The Information page gives location and activities information on the museum, while the Collections page presents some of the items from the museum's exhibits, which tell the history of currency, giving special emphasis to the history of coins and paper money in Canada.

Hudson's Bay Company Digital Collections – online [English & French]
http://www.schoolnet.ca/collections/hbc/
Part of the Manitoba Museum of Man and Nature, the HBC Digital Collection is a virtual exhibit of the former collections of the fur trading company. Includes documents, clothing, tools and more from native and Métis cultures, the fur trade and explorations.

Japanese Canadian National Museum and Archives Society – Vancouver, BC [English & Japanese]
http://www.multinova.com/jcnmas/index.htm
Information on this society, created to present and interpret Japanese Canadian history and culture from the 1870's to the present. The site contains historic images, membership and society information and a timeline of Japanese-Canadian history.

Maritime Command Museum – Halifax, NS
http://www.marlant.hlfx.dnd.ca/museum/
Features exhibits, artifacts, photographs and historical documents from the Royal Canadian Navy, in the residence of the commander-in-chief of the British North American Station.

Links to Your Canadian Past
Québec

Museum of the Fur Trade – Chadron, NE (USA)
http://www.furtrade.org/
Dedicated to the history of the North American fur trade, including artifacts from British, French and American trappers and companies, as well as American Indian and Spanish traders from the colonial period to the 20th century.

Museum of the Mountain Man – Pinedale, WY (USA)
http://www.pinedaleonline.com/MMMuseum/
Exhibits and a research library presenting the history of the western fur trade, located in the hub of the historic Rocky Mountain Rendezvous system. Includes exhibits and living history demonstrations on the fur trade, exploration and early settlement of the West.

National Aviation Museum – Ottawa, ON [English & French]
http://www.nmstc.ca/nam/index.htm
Museum information, as well as hundreds of images and lots of information on aircraft, upcoming exhibits and the history of aviation in Canada.

National War Memorial – Ottawa, ON
http://www.vac-acc.gc.ca/Memorials/Nationalmem.htm
A tribute to Canada's war heroes, with online photos and text about the memorial.

North American Black Historical Museum and Cultural Centre – Amherstburg, ON
http://www.city.windsor.on.ca/cvb/Northamericanbl.htm
Contains a research library with genealogical and historical materials, as well as African-Canadian exhibits, audiovisual presentations, workshops and conferences.

Links to Your Canadian Past
Québec

Royal Canadian Air Force Memorial Museum – Astra, ON
http://aeroweb.brooklyn.cuny.edu/museums/ont/rcafmm.html
Unofficial information and photographs about the RCAF museum and exhibits.

RCMP Centennial Museum – Regina, SK [English & French]
http://www.trakkerinc.com/rcmp/rcmphome.htm
Historical material and artifacts recounting the colorful history of the RCMP, North-West Mounted Police and Canada's western pioneer heritage.

Veterans Affairs Canada: Memorials
http://www.vac-acc.gc.ca/Memorials/memorials.htm
Links to memorial sites abroad commemorating the service of Canadians in foreign wars.

"We Will Remember": War Monuments in Canada
http://www.stemnet.nf.ca/monuments/
An attempt to preserve the history of the hundreds of war monuments throughout Canada in digital form to be accessible on the Internet. Searchable by province.

Professional Organizations

Canadian Conservation Institute [English & French]
http://www.pch.gc.ca/cci-icc/index~1.htm
CCI's mandate is "To promote the proper care and preservation of Canada's moveable cultural property, and to advance the practice, science, and technology of conservation." To this end, they carry out and assist in research, training, funding and advocacy for conservation.

Canadian Museums Association [English & French]
http://www.museums.ca/
The professional group for the field since 1947.

Links to Your Canadian Past
Québec

ICOMOS Canada
http://www.icomos.org/canada/
The Canadian National Committee of the International Committee on Monuments and Sites. The site features news and events, mailing lists, papers, articles and publications.

Military, Native and Historic Groups

Military and Mounted Police
Black Watch (Royal Highland Regiment) of Canada
http://www.odyssee.net/~kerra/bwhome.html
Includes a history of the regiment, the Black Watch Association and Battle Honours.

Books of Remembrance
http://schoolnet2.carleton.ca/books/books.htm
Search for the name of a soldier who died in the following six books of remembrance: Newfoundland, South Africa/Nile, Merchant Navy, Korean War, WWI and WWII.

Canada's Air Force: History and Heritage
http://www.achq.dnd.ca/history.htm
Links to numerous articles, photos and memories of over 75 years of history.

Canadian Army Regiments – Index of Web Sites
http://www.du.edu/~tomills/military/america/cargxref.htm
A list – organized by number of unit and also by name of unit – of Canadian army regiments, with links (where available) to regimental Web sites and a description of the content to be found on the site.

Links to Your Canadian Past
Québec

Canadian Casualties in the Boer War
http://www.islandnet.com/~duke/boercas.htm
A list of servicemen who died in the conflict, with name and rank, date and cause of death.

Canadian Expeditionary Force
http://www.archives.ca/db/cef/index.html
This site contains an index to the personnel files of the over 600,000 Canadians who were part of the CEF during World War I. It also contains access to the attestation papers of over 100,000 recruits and a listing of the veterans and casualties from Renfrew, Ontario.

Canadian Military Genealogical FAQ
http://www.ott.igs.net/~donpark/canmilfaq.htm
Provides information on what sources are available and how to contact them.

The Canadian Military Heritage Project
http://www.rootsweb.com/~canmil/1837/battles/battleind.htm
Contains information and resources on all aspects of Canadian military involvement, from the French and Indian Wars to World War II, including the Rebellion of 1837, Fenian raids, Red River Rebellion and North West Rebellion.

Canadian Navy of Yesterday and Today
http://www.uss-salem.org/navhist/canada/
A presentation of the ships and aircraft of the navy from World War I to today.

Canadian POW/MIA Information Centre
http://www.ipsystems.com/powmia/
A good deal of information by and about Canadian POWs and MIAs.

Links to Your Canadian Past
Québec

Canadian Vietnam Casualties
http://www.ipsystems.com/powmia/names/names.html
A list of those who lost their lives in the war, with links to extended information on some individuals included in the list.

Canadians Who Served in the Maine State Militia in the Civil War
http://www.geocities.com/Heartland/6625/canmaine.txt
A list of individuals, with full name and company and regiment in which they served.

Commonwealth War Graves Commission
http://www.thecommonwealth.org/links/wargrave.html
Dedicated to maintaining the graves of soldiers who died in defense of the British Commonwealth during the two World Wars.

Honour Roll – Canadian UN Peacekeepers
http://www.islandnet.com/~duke/roll.htm
A list of those "who lost their lives in the service of peace."

Millennia Legacy Project (The Maple Leaf Project)
http://orcn.ahs.uwo.ca/legacy/index1.html
An attempt to put together a collection of photographs of each of the over 110,000 Canadian war graves in 74 countries throughout the world into a sort of virtual National War Cemetery.

Military Records Sources in Canada
http://www.archives.ca/www/svcs/english/GenealogicalSources.html#Military Records
An overview of what records are available through the National Archives for the pre-World War I period and from World War I to the present.

Links to Your Canadian Past
Québec

Montcalm Passenger List 1936
http://mypage.direct.ca/d/dobee/pilgrim.html
A list of veterans and descendants aboard the *Montcalm*, which sailed for Antwerp and London on the "Vimy and Battlefields Pilgrimage" in remembrance of the Canadian army's role in WWI.

Reenactment Units in Canada
http://www.geocities.com/Yosemite/2069/anglais.html
A list from the Museum of Applied Military History of contact information and descriptions of military reenactment groups in Canada. Links to Web pages of individual units, where available.

Royal Canadian Air Force Personnel – Honours and Awards
- **1939-1949**: http://www.achq.dnd.ca/awards/index.htm
- **1947-1970**: http://www.achq.dnd.ca/postwar/index.htm

Both sites offer an alphabetical index to RCAF personnel who received awards or citations for service, with links to text describing the honor(s).

Royal Canadian Legion
http://www.legion.ca/
Canada's largest veterans and community service organization. Links to provincial branches.

Royal Canadian Mounted Police (Facts on Canada) [English & French]
http://www.infocan.gc.ca/facts/rcmp-e.html
This site, presented by InfoCan, presents the history of the RCMP, broken down into Origins, Transitions and The RCMP Today.

Royal Canadian Mounted Police: Historical Highlights
http://www.rcmp-grc.gc.ca/html/history.htm
An overview of the major events and development of the RCMP from the 1870's to the 1990's.

Links to Your Canadian Past
Québec

Royal Canadian Mounted Police: Official History
http://www.trakkerinc.com/rcmp/english/history/histind.htm
The history of the RCMP from The New Frontier, Rebellion and the Iron Road, through Gold Diggers and War, National Growth to the Information Age.

Royal Canadian Mounted Police: A Brief History
http://www.district.north-van.bc.ca/home/history.html
An overview of the RCMP from a 1991 brochure by the RCMP Public Affairs Directorate.

Unofficial History of the Royal Canadian Navy
http://www.gcocities.com/Pentagon/6650/rcn00000.htm
A private citizen's view of the men, women and equipment of the RCN.

World War I Canadian Infantry and Cavalry Index
http://www.bookkeeping.com/rings/genealogy/ww1.html
Lists the unit number, original commanding officer, date of sailing, strength on sailing and headquarters on mobilization. Under construction.

Native and Métis Groups
Assembly of First Nations [English & French]
http://www.afn.ca/
Formerly the National Indian Brotherhood, the AFN is an association of the leaders of First Nations groups throughout Canada. The AFN seeks to devise common strategies on issues of common concern and promote communication and exchanges between nations.

Links to Your Canadian Past
Québec

Canadian Métis Coalition – Moncton, NB
http://www.geocities.com/CapitolHill/Senate/7498/
Created to respond to and serve the national or individual political concerns of Métis living in Canada, regardless of their membership or lack thereof in local or provincial organizations.

Centre d'Études Amérindiennes – Chicoutimi, QC
See Canadian Studies Centers and Programs.

Métis Families
http://www.televar.com/~gmorin/
Information on Métis censuses, marriages, families, stories, etc., presented by Gail Morin.

The Other Métis
http://www.cyberus.ca/~mfdunn/metis/index.html
A comprehensive information source, mainly dealing with Métis and aboriginal peoples who are not represented by the larger Métis organizations of the Prairie Provinces.

Tribes and Bands of the United States and Canada
http://www.hanksville.org/sand/contacts/tribal/US.html
A geographical interface to lists of contact information and (where available) links to Web sites of tribal and native groups throughout the United States and Canada.

Loyalists
Loyalist Sources in the National Archives
http://www.archives.ca/www/svcs/english/GenealogicalSources.html#Loyalist Sources
An overview of what records are available concerning Loyalists and where to find them.

Links to Your Canadian Past
Québec

United Empire Loyalists Association of Canada
http://www.npiec.on.ca/~uela/uela1.htm
Sections include What is a Loyalist?, the Loyalist Gazette, Membership, Branches, Important Loyalist Dates, Reading & References and Loyalist Links.

1791: United Empire Loyalists
http://www.magi.com/~westdunn/1791UniL.html
A brief overview of the Loyalist movement and how it affected Canada at this time.

Orangeism and Oddfellows

Canadian Orangeism – An Historical Retrospect
http://members.tripod.com/~Roughian/
This site covers many aspects of Orangeism in Canada, including Orangeism and the Military, Trade Unionism, articles on several historic Orangemen, Military and Historic Documents and several stories and images of historical events and places associated with Canadian Orangeism.

The Grand Orange Lodge of Canada – Willowdale, ON
http://www.orange.ca/
This homepage of the Orange Association of Canada includes sections on Orangeism, What is the Loyal Orange Association?, History, Qualifications, links to Provincial Grand Lodges and information on *The Sentinel*, the official bi-monthly publication of the Association.

International Order of Odd Fellows – Family History Research
http://norm28.hsc.usc.edu/IOOF/FamilyResearch.html
Details what info is and isn't available from the group, with a link to local lodge addresses throughout Canada and how to request information.

Links to Your Canadian Past
Québec

Orangeism – The Canadian Scene
http://members.tripod.com/~firstlight_2/cdnscene.htm
A brief history of the Orange Association in Canada, with contact information.

National and Regional History and Historic Photos

Exploration and Settlement

Alexander Mackenzie: "A Map of America between Latitudes 40 and 70 North, and Longitudes 45 and 180 West, Exhibiting Mackenzie's Track."
http://www.lib.virginia.edu/exhibits/lewis_clark/ch4-27.html
A map from Mackenzie's book *Voyages from Montreal, on the River St. Laurence, through the Continent of North America to the Frozen and Pacific Oceans; In the Years 1789 and 1793*, with explanatory text on the explorer and his voyages.

European Explorations of America
http://www.vmnf.civilization.ca/reper/r-ch1-en.htm
A presentation from the Virtual Museum of New France on the various European explorers who visited North America between 1492 and 1620. Presented in the form of a timeline.

Henry Hudson: The Life and Times of Henry Hudson, 17th Century Explorer
http://www.georgian.net/rally/hudson/
A great deal of information on Hudson, his explorations and family.

Hypertext Guide to the Exploration of the Canadian Arctic
http://home.navisoft.com/ekkhs/chronlgy.htm
Includes a chronology of events from 1,000 BC to 1819 as well as biographical notes and contributions of individuals from Eric the Red to William Edward Parry.

Links to Your Canadian Past
Québec

Northwest Passage: The Quest for an Arctic Route to the East
http://www.nlc-bnc.ca/north/nor-ii/franklin/fran051e.htm
A chronology of exploration from John Cabot in 1497 to R. Hammond in 1989.

Pier 21 Stories
http://pier21.ns.ca/stories.html
Stories submitted by immigrants who arrived through Pier 21 in Halifax or their descendants. Divided into Immigrants, Guest Children, Refugees, War Brides, World War II and Volunteers.

A Scattering of Seeds: The Creation of Canada
http://seeds.history.ca/~seeds/
A Web companion to the 13-part series of documentaries on the immigration of various cultural groups to Canada. Documents French, Ukrainian, Irish as well as recent Chinese, Japanese, Sikh and other immigrants with historical text, photos and even online video clips from the series.

Sir John Franklin: His Life and Afterlife
http://home.navisoft.com/ekkhs/frank1.htm
A lengthy article on the life and career of the famous explorer and his legacy.

Sir John Franklin
- **Naval Career**:
  http://boulder.earthnet.net/~ambranch/hist01.html
- **First Overland Expedition**:
  http://boulder.earthnet.net/~ambranch/artic.html
- **Second Overland Expedition**:
  http://boulder.earthnet.net/~ambranch/hist02.html
- **Final Expedition**:
  http://boulder.earthnet.net/~ambranch/hist03.html

Links to Your Canadian Past
Québec

The Vikings: They Got Here First, But Why Didn't They Stay?
http://www.nlc-bnc.ca/north/nor-i/thule/thu-020e.htm
A presentation by the National Library of Canada on the Viking Discovery of North America.

General and Social History

1791: Canada Act
http://www.magi.com/~westdunn/1791CanA.html
A brief overview of the need for and effects of the Canada Act.

Canada Facts and Trivia
http://www.geocities.com/Heartland/6625/cgwfacts.html
Geographical, historical and personal tidbits, anecdotes and superlatives.

Canadian Economic History
http://web.arts.ubc.ca/cliocan/Clionet.html
A server dedicated to maintaining and exchanging information on the economic history of Canada. Includes conferences, notice boards, data banks, information sources, etc.

CanPix Gallery: Great Canadian Image Base
http://www.nelson.com/nelson/school/discovery/images/ncddimag.htm
Over 3,500 audiovisual resources for Canadian studies, including prominent people, events and places; images of Canadian culture; provincial symbols; as well as audio and text files.

Links to Your Canadian Past
Québec

Early Canadiana Online / Notre Mémoire en Ligne [English & French]
http://nlc-bnc.ca/cihm/ecol/
A project to scan primary source historical material from the first European contact to the end of the 19th century, focusing on literature, women's history, native studies and the history of French Canada. To include a searchable database of titles in the collection.

Facts on Canada
http://www.infocan.gc.ca/facts/canadagen-e.html [English & French]
A quick overview of many aspects of Canadian history and society, including geographical, political, social and cultural information presented by InfoCan.

Facts on Canada: History [English & French]
http://www.infocan.gc.ca/facts/history-e.html
Sections of this brief overview of Canadian history include First Colonial Outposts, A Country is Born, Westward Expansion, A Nation Matures and A New Federation in the Making.

Heritage Post Interactive [English & French]
http://heritage.excite.sfu.ca/hpost.html
"The Web's first interactive Canadian history magazine."

Index to Federal Royal Commissions [English and French]
http://www.nlc-bnc.ca/ifrc/index.htm
An author or keyword search of the over 150 commissions since confederation. Documentation includes commission reports, briefs, evidence and other resources.

Links to Your Canadian Past
Québec

Inter.Canada: Canadian History Documents [English & French]
http://www.naccess.com/~inter.canada/docptr.htm
A vast amount of historical and political documents and accords relating to Canada.

The **Walk to Canada: Tracing the Underground Railroad**
http://www.npca.org/walk.html
One historian's tracing of a possible Underground Railroad route from Montgomery County, Maryland to Amherstburg, Ontario, using only the methods available to escaping slaves.

Timelines and "This Week/Day in History"
A Brief Historical Timeline of Canada
http://www.geocities.com/Heartland/6625/cgwhistory.html
Historical highlights from 1000 to 1982 AD.

The **Great Canadian Timeline**
http://www3.sk.sympatico.ca/vavrr/time-1~1.htm
A timeline of events that occurred on Canadian soil from prehistory to 1995.

Important Moments in Canadian History
http://www.arts.ouc.bc.ca/fiar/his_home.html
An historical timeline of notable events, broken down into Prehistory to 1800, 1800-1867, 1867-1918, 1918-1945, 1946-67, 1968-present.

Parks Canada – This Week in History
http://parkscanada.pch.gc.ca/scripts/dbml.exe?Template=/thisweek/thisweeke.htm
Historical vignettes that occurred in the current week at Canadian Historic sites.

Links to Your Canadian Past
Québec

This Week in Western Canadian History
http://www.glenbow.ab.ca/libhtm/thisweek.htm
Historical highlights and events from the Canadian West for the current week. Previous weeks can also be viewed or searched for specific content.

Sympatico News Express: On This Day
http://www1.sympatico.ca/cgi-bin/on_this_day
Find out what historic events occurred in Canada (or by Canadians) on this day in history.

Confederation
Canadian Confederation: Historical Documents
http://www.nlc-bnc.ca/confed/historic.htm
A collection of documents dealing with confederation, presented by the National Library of Canada, including the British North America Act and 1871 Treaty of Washington.

Canadian Confederation – The National Library of Canada
http://www.nlc-bnc.ca/confed/e-1867.htm
Several subjects dealing with confederation that show the influence of the American Civil War on confederation. Contains the full text of historic documents, a timeline, bibliography and other confederation subjects.

The **Road to Confederation**
http://www.canoe.ca/InDepthUnity/confederation.html
An article from the Canadian Global Almanac on the issues and events leading to confederation.

Links to Your Canadian Past
Québec

Military History

The Canadian Great War Homepage
http://www.rootsweb.com/~ww1can/
Sections include a Timeline, Soldier's Biographies, Women in the War, Famous Canadians, Life of the Home Front, Victoria's Cross Winners and sections on the Army, Navy and Air Force.

Courage Remembered: The World Wars Through Canadian Eyes [English, some French]
http://www.schoolnet.ca/collections/courage/splash.html
A presentation of the role of Canadian soldiers in World Wars I and II, based on personal memoirs, photography, the work of Canadian war artists and the documented exploits of Canadian George Cross and Victoria Cross recipients.

The Valour and the Horror: Canada at War
http://www.valourandhorror.com/home.htm
Based on the TV series of the same name, consisting of three two-hour films depicting World War II campaigns: A Savage Christmas – Hong Kong 1941, Death By Moonlight – Bomber Campaign and In Desperate Battle – Normandy 1944. Includes a forum where visitors can post and respond to messages in a bulletin board format.

Valour Remembered: Canada and the First World War
http://www.vac-acc.gc.ca/historical/firstwar/vrww1.htm
An informative look at Canada's role in the Great War from its entrance into the conflict through Canadian participation in various battles and campaigns to the final outcome and memorials.

War of 1812
http://fingon.norlink.net/~jkeigher/1812.html
A fairly detailed introduction to the causes, development and conflicts of the war.

Links to Your Canadian Past
Québec

War of 1812 Web Site
http://www3.sympatico.ca/dis.general/1812.htm
This site presents a good deal of information on the war, including articles on army life, battles, regiments, and other aspects of the war; a chart of British regiments in North America; book reviews; sound clips of fife & drum music and information on reenactments and replicas.

Professional Groups/Commercial History

A Brief History of Canadian Lighthouses
http://members.aol.com/stiffcrust/pharos/index.html
From the 18th through the 20th centuries, with photos. Also includes a bibliography, museums and societies, postcards, stamps and artwork, plus a list of lighthouses in the movies.

The **Bank of Canada: Its History** [English & French]
http://www.bank-banque-canada.ca/english/histor.htm
A look at the historical debate for the creation of a central bank in Canada, the founding and development of the Bank of Canada and a link to the Bank of Canada Act.

Building Canada [English & French]
http://blackader.library.mcgill.ca/cac/bland/building/index.html
A selection of images from the John Bland Collection of Canadian Architecture – a set of digitized images that formed part of Prof. Bland's class on the History of Canadian Architecture.

Canadian National Railway – Corporate Profile
http://www.cn.ca/cn/english/about/corporate/history/
Read "The CN Story" from Canada's first railroad through privatization of CN, browse a Timeline of events in CN History or look through the Historical Photo Library.

Links to Your Canadian Past
Québec

Canadian National Railways Historic Photo Collection
[English & French]
http://www.schoolnet.ca/collections/cnphoto/cnphoto.html
Photos of over 100 years of locomotives, passenger and freight trains, as well as structures and operations of the Canadian Northern, Grand Trunk Railway, Grand Trunk Pacific, Intercolonial Railway, Canadian National Railway and "CN Today."

Canadian Pacific Railway: Feature Articles
http://www.cpr.ca/www/insidecpr/aboutcpr/cparchives/featurearticles/articles.html
Includes the "Steel Wheels" series by Jonathan Hanna on various CPR apparatus and Heritage Columns by Dave Jones on aspects of CPR history.

Cultivating Canadian Gardens: The History of Gardening in Canada [English & French]
http://www.nlc-bnc.ca/events/garden/eintro.htm
This site, presented by the National Library of Canada, takes an in-depth look at the "leisure activity" of gardening in Canada through the books, periodicals and printed materials in the collections of the NLC from the agricultural activities of the Hurons until our time.

Education in Canada (Facts on Canada/InfoCan) [English & French]
http://www.infocan.gc.ca/facts/educ-e.html
An overview of the educational system in Canada, including a look at the provincial responsibilities, the broad federal role and the various levels of education.

High Flyers: Canadian Women in Aviation [English & French]
See Canadian Women's History.

Links to Your Canadian Past
Québec

History of the Canadian Red Cross
http://www.ncf.carleton.ca/ip/health/redcross/crc/history
A brief text on the origins and development of this organization in Canada and the role played by Surgeon-Major George Sterling Ryerson of the Canadian Army Medical Services.

Hudson's Bay Company
- **Main**: http://www.hbc.com/english.asp

Founded in 1670, the HBC is still alive and functioning today. Find out what ventures the company is currently involved in, or read about HBC history.

- **History**: http://www.hbc.com/hbchistory/

From its founding in 1670 through the early explorers, adventurers and *voyageurs* through the 20th century. Learn about what life was like in the early days, before "Canada" existed.

Hudson Bay Company Fur Trading in 1800s
http://gurukul.ucc.american.edu/TED/HUDSON.HTM
Part of the Trade and Environment Database Project of cases, which seek to provide a common basis for researchers and policy makers to understand issues of trade and the environment. This case study looks at the effects of the Hudson's Bay Company's exploitation of the fur trade in the first half of the 18th century and its impact on the environment.

Libraries Today
http://www.uoguelph.ca/~lbruce/
Dedicated to the history of Canadian public libraries and librarians, especially in the province of Ontario, including biography, public library administration; the impact of technological innovation; rural and children's services, the influence of large urban libraries and the professionalization of librarianship.

Links to Your Canadian Past
Québec

Mountain Men and the Fur Trade
http://www.xmission.com/~drudy/amm.html
Aonline resource center dedicated to the history, traditions and way of life of the trappers, traders and explorers engaged in the fur trade. Includes a "library" of online or downloadable books and articles, an online archive of fur trade documents, images of period artifacts, a gallery of artwork, bibliography and links to a mailing list and other resources.

Northwest Brigade Club
http://www.agt.net/public/gottfred/nwbc.html
A group dedicated to the living history of the western Canadian fur trade from 1774 to 1821. Includes an index, sample articles and subscription info on the quarterly *Northwest Journal*.

Significant Dates in Canadian Railway History
http://infoweb.magi.com/~churcher/candate/candate.htm
Important events and accomplishments in rail travel and transportation from 1790 to 1998.

West Coast Shipbuilding
http://www.schoolnet.ca/collections/shipbuilding/wcssp.htm
A multi-faceted history of the Burrand Dry Dock, later known as Versatile Pacific Shipyards, its role in the development of the Canadian West Coast and contribution to both World Wars.

Geographical History and Information
Canadian Geographic Names [English & French]
http://GeoNames.NRCan.gc.ca/
The source for information on over 350,000 official and formerly official place names in Canada. Find the location of a current or historical place, and generate simple location maps.

Links to Your Canadian Past
Québec

Facts on Canada – Geography [English & French]
http://www.infocan.gc.ca/facts/geography-e.html
This site contains an overview of the geographical scope and features of Canada, including a look at each of the seven distinct geographical regions that make up the country.

Historical Atlas of Canada: Data Dissemination Project
http://www.geog.utoronto.ca/hacddp/hacpage.html
Supplemental charts and tabular data to *Volume II: The Land Transformed, 1800-1891*.

Historical Maps of Canada
http://www.sscl.uwo.ca/assoc/acml/faclist.html
A collection of facsimile maps from the Association of Canadian Map Libraries and Archives, from the 1556 "La Nuova Francia" by G. Gastaldi and G.B. Ramusio to a 1920 map of Edmonton West of the 4th Meridian by the Office of the Surveyor General.

National Atlas of Canada [English & French]
http://ellesmere.ccm.emr.ca/english/home-english.html
Contains links to the Resources Atlas, Geography Class, Canadian Community Atlas, BioMap, Spatial Resources and other sources of geographical and demographic data.

Territorial Evolution of Canada
http://www-nais.ccm.emr.ca/schoolnet/issues/terrevol/english/eTerrEvol.html
Maps, from 1867 to 1949, showing the evolution of Canada's international, provincial and territorial boundaries.

Links to Your Canadian Past
Québec

Regional History

Acadiensis
http://www.unb.ca/web/arts/History/Acadiensis/index.html
A scholarly journal devoted to research in the history of Atlantic Canada. The journal publishes articles on History, Geography, Political Science, Folklore, Literature, Sociology, Economics and other areas. Information on subscriptions, submissions and the scope of the publication.

For the Life of the World: Charisma and Service of the Missionary Oblates
http://www.pma.edmonton.ab.ca/human/folklife/oblates/cover.htm
An online presentation by the Provincial Museum of Alberta on the life, service and impact of the Oblates of Mary Immaculate on the colonization and culture of the Canadian West.

North: Landscape of the Imagination [English & French]
http://www.nlc-bnc.ca/north/
An online presentation from the National Library of Canada on the history and evolution of the Canadian North, including the pre-contact period, early history, the first half of the 20th century and the modern era.

Cultural Groups

African Canadian Historical Web Site ("Historical Connexion")
http://www.torweb.com/histcon/main.html
Sections include Historical Feature, Genealogy, Historical Images, Books & Videos, Kids & Teachers Corners and more, all showcasing the contributions of African men and women.

Canadian Quaker History
http://home.interhop.net/~aschrauwe/CanHis.html
An historical overview, abridged from the "Canadian Yearly Meeting Discipline."

Links to Your Canadian Past
Québec

Cartes des Origines Ethniques des Canadiens, 1901 [French only – maps]
http://www.uottawa.ca/~fgingras/doc/c1901index.html
A series of maps from the 1901 Atlas of Canada, presented in French, showing the ethnic origins of Canadians. Includes maps for Nova Scotia, Cape Breton Island, Prince Edward Island, New Brunswick, three maps for Québec and four maps for Ontario.

The Chinese in Canada: Past and Present
http://www.interlog.com/~fccs/slides.htm
Sections include Historical Background, Cultural Aspects, The Chinese Community Today, Challenges to the Community and a bibliography for further reading.

Doukhobor Home Page
http://www.dlcwest.com/~r.androsoff/index.htm
A source of information on Doukhobor history and culture. Sections include Who are the Doukhobors?, Timeline of Doukhobor History, Culture and Tradition, Events Calendar, etc.

The French Presence in Canada and in British Columbia
http://www.corp.direct.ca/news/french/french1.shtml
An overview of the French and francophone contributions to and achievements in Canada, from Jacques Cartier and Acadia through New France and expansion of the country to the West.

Internment of Ukrainians in Canada 1914-1920
http://www.infoukes.com/history/internment/
A series of articles and photographs recounting the story of the internment of thousands of "enemy aliens," including Ukrainians during the World War I period.

Links to Your Canadian Past
Québec

Jewish Communities of the World: Canada
http://www.virtual.co.il/communities/wjcbook/canada/index.htm
A brief look at the demography, history, culture and education, religious life and sites of the Jewish community in Canada.

Mennonites in Canada
http://www.lib.uwaterloo.ca/MHSC/
Includes "Who are the Mennonites," which describes Mennonite beliefs, differences between Mennonite groups, and information on communities in Canada. Also includes The Canadian Mennonite Encyclopedia, a searchable source of information on Mennonite history, statistics, biography, education, the arts and family history.

Métis Development and the Canadian West
http://schoolnet2.carleton.ca/english/ext/aboriginal/metis-de/index.html
A presentation (with text and photos) of the book *Contrasting Worlds*, depicting the Métis' role in the West, from the fur trade and European settlement to the uprisings and confederation.

Testimony of the Canadian Fugitives
http://history.cc.ukans.edu/carrie/docs/texts/canadian_slaves.html
The recorded testimony of escaped slaves in Upper Canada in the mid 1850's.

Ukrainians in Canada: A Selective Bibliography
http://www.civilization.ca/membrs/biblio/bibgrph/ukrbibe.html
Books and articles on Ukrainians available at the Canadian Museum of Civilization's library.

Links to Your Canadian Past
Québec

Canadian Women's History

Canadian Chronology of Women's History
http://142.3.223.54/~maguirec/chron.html
A timeline of important events in the history of women's contributions, achievements and rights in Canada, from the arrival of Jeanne Mance in 1641 through the installation of Lenna Bradbum as Canada's first woman police chief at Guelph, Ontario in 1994.

The **Canadian Suffrage Movement**
http://www.gov.edmonton.ab.ca/parkrec/fort/1905/cansuff.html
A brief look at the effort to secure the right to vote for women in Canada, from the first organized movement in the 1870's and the arguments involved in the historical debate.

Facts on Canada: Women [English & French]
http://www.infocan.gc.ca/facts/women-e.html
This site takes a look at some of the changes in women's rights in Canada since suffrage was won in 1918, including Women and Economy, Women and Government, Women as Activists and Looking Ahead. Presented by InfoCan.

High Flyers: Canadian Women in Aviation [English & French]
http://www.schoolnet.ca/collections/high_flyers/
An online presentation of a past exhibit at the National Aviation Museum featuring the accomplishments of Canadian women in the field of aviation. Features personal photos, memorabilia, archival documents and biographies of 22 women aviators.

Women's Exhibition: Celebrating Women's Achievements
http://www.nlc-bnc.ca/digiproj/women/ewomen.htm
Presentations from the National Library of past Women's History Month exhibitions. Includes women from the Canadian book trade, legislatures, librarianship and music and literature.

Links to Your Canadian Past
Québec

Women in Canadian History
http://www.niagara.com/~merrwill/
Brief historical sketches of women who contributed in various ways to Canada's development.

Women in the War – World War II
http://www.valourandhorror.com/DB/ISSUE/Women/index.htm
This site examines the various roles played by Canadian women in World War II. Sections include Servicewomen, At Home, Overseas, Stories, German Women and Nurses.

Canadian Culture, Traditions and Symbols

Canadian Crests and Coats of Arms
http://www.schoolnet.ca/collections/governor/heraldry/index.html
A description of the tradition of heraldry in Canada, with examples of crests and coats of arms for various provinces, first peoples, municipalities, businesses, churches and other groups.

Canadian Recipe Collection
http://sunsite.auc.dk/recipes/english/cat70.html
A collection of several traditional recipes from all across Canada, including Québec Tourtière, Potato Scones, Cape Breton Oatcakes, Nanaimo Bars, Saskatoon Pie and All-Canadian Coffee.

Heroes of Lore and Yore: Canadian Heroes in Fact and Fiction
[English & French]
http://www.nlc-bnc.ca/heroes/econtent.htm
Biographical and historical information on several Canadian national heroes, both real and fictional. Portraits include Jeanne Mance, Sir Alexander Mackenzie, Madeleine de Verchères, Anne of Green Gables, Terry Fox, Johnny Canuck and even Sasquatch.

Links to Your Canadian Past
Québec

Hold on to Your Hats! History and Meaning of Headwear in Canada
http://www.civilization.ca/membrs/canhist/hats/hat00eng.html
An online exhibit from the Museum of Civilization on the historic and cultural use of hats in Canadian society. Sections include Protection and Practicality, Religion and Ritual, Authority and Status, Identity and Belonging, Fashion and Image, Hat Lore, a Photo Gallery and Game.

Our National Anthem [English & French]
http://www.infocan.gc.ca/facts/anthem.html
The text and a brief history of "O Canada!" Presented by InfoCan: Facts on Canada.

Family Associations & Surnames

Ancestors Found! Surname Registry
http://members.xoom.com/mygenes/lost/resc.htm
A browseable list of surnames that others are researching or posting queries about.

Canada GenWeb Queries
- **Archived**: http://www.rootsweb.com/~canwgw/queryweb/
- **Post/Current**:
  http://www.geocities.com/Heartland/6625/cgwquery.html

Canada's Query Web
http://www.rootsweb.com/~canwgw/queryweb/
An archive of all queries that have been posted on Canadian GenWeb sites for three months.

GEchanges [English & French]
http://GEchanges-Canada.hypermart.net/index_en.html

Links to Your Canadian Past
Québec

A "genealogical classified ads service" for each province in Canada.

Gendex WWW Genealogical Index
http://www.gendex.com/gendex/
This site claims to index genealogical information from hundreds of databases containing information on over five million individuals.

Genealogical Database Index
http://www.gentree.com/
An index of searchable databases on the Web dealing with specific surnames or families.

Northeast Surnames
http://members.mint.net/mdenis/surnames.html
A query bulletin board for surnames of families located in the New England states of the United States and eastern provinces of Canada, including the Maritimes and Québec.

RootsWeb Surname List
http://www.rootsweb.com/rootsweb/searches/rslsearch.html
An index of submitted surnames being researched by amateur genealogists, containing dates and places and contact information for the person submitting the information.

Surname Helper Home Page
http://cgi.rootsweb.com/surhelp/
Surname-indexes participating genealogy Web sites, allowing users to search for a particular surname and its Soundex variants.

Links to Your Canadian Past
Québec

Nationalities and Cultural Groups

Hutterite Genealogy: Founding Families: Churchbook Extractions
http://feefhs.org/hut/hff-2.html
Genealogies of some of the founding families of Hutterites that settled in Manitoba, Saskatchewan, Alberta and the western United States.

Irish-Canadian Surname List
http://www.bess.tcd.ie/roots/irishcan.htm
A compilation of submitted data with names of Irish immigrants and locations in Ireland and Canada. Searchable by surname, date and location in Ireland and Canada.

Irish Ancestors
http://www.irish-times.com/ancestor/
Sections on surnames, place names, emigration and a guide to available records.

Individual Surnames and Family Associations

Derrick: http://www.labs.net/ATTFIELD/DERRICKS/

Clan **Fraser** Society of Canada:
http://www.canlinks.com/cdnclanfraser/

Clan **Gunn** Society of North America:
http://www.citynet.net/personal/gunn/clan.html

Harmer Family Association:
http://www.angelfire.com/wa/harmer1/index.html

Lacombe: http://www.cpcug.org/user/jlacombe/

Clan **Macrae**: http://calgary.shaw.wave.ca/~lmcrae/

Links to Your Canadian Past
Québec

Clan **Menzies** Society of Canada:
http://home.sprynet.com/sprynet/cmsoc/

Chat Rooms and Mailing Lists
(See Notes section for mailing list instructions)

American-Revolution Mailing List (Also includes French & Indian Wars)
- **all**: american-revolution-l-request@rootsweb.com
- **digest**: american-revolution-d-request@rootsweb.com

Atlantic-Province Mailing List:
majordomo@listserv.northwest.com
all: subscribe atlantic-province@listserv.northwest.com
digest: subscribe atlantic-province-digest@listserv.northwest.com

Brother's Keeper (Software) Mailing List: BK5L-REQUEST@EMCEE.COM

Canada-L: (political, social, cultural, economic)
listserv@vm1.mcgill.ca
```
SUBSCRIBE CANADA-L firstname lastname
```

Canada Orange Mailing List (Orangemen History, Genealogy, Culture)
http://members.tripod.com/~firstlight_2/canorange.htm

Canadian Archives Mailing List (ARCAN-L):
majordomo@majordomo.srv.ualberta.ca
```
subscribe ARCAN-L firstname lastname
```

Canadian Roots-L: listserv@listserv.indiana.edu
```
SUB CANADIAN ROOTS-L firstname lastname
```

Links to Your Canadian Past
Québec

Colonial-America Mailing List (Early Canadian history also an appropriate topic.)
majordomo@listserv.northwest.com
all: `subscribe Colonial-America`;
digest: `subscribe Colonial-America-digest`

Dutch Heritage Mailing List (SHAKEL-NL):
majordomo@esosoft.com
`subscribe schakel-nl`

Genealogy Forum Channel on IRC
http://GEchanges-Canada.hypermart.net/index_en.html
A genealogy chat room on Internet Relay Chat, complete with instructions on installation and use, etiquette, lists of surnames and tips on how to find ancestors and exchange info.

German-Canadian Mailing List
- **all**: german-canadian-l-request@rootsweb.com
- **digest**: german-canadian-d-request@rootsweb.com (digest mode).

Huguenot Mailing List
- **all**: huguenot-l-request@rootsweb.com; **digest**: huguenot-d-request@rootsweb.com

Indian Roots Mailing List: maiser@rmgate.pop.indiana.edu
`sub indian-roots`

Irish-Canadian Mailing List
- **all**: irish-canadian-l-request@rootsweb.com
- **digest**: irish-canadian-d-request@rootsweb.com

Links to Your Canadian Past
Québec

H-Canada Discussion List (Canadian History)
- **info**: http://www.h-net.msu.edu/~canada/
- **English subscription**: http://www.usask.ca/history/form4.html
- **Abonnement français**: http://www.usask.ca/history/form5.html

Loyalists-In-Canada Mailing List:
maiser@rmgate.pop.indiana.edu
sub LOYALISTS-IN-CANADA

Surnames-Canada
- **all**: surnames-canada-m-request@rootsweb.com
- **digest**: surnames-canada-l-request@rootsweb.com
- **index**: surnames-canada-i-request@rootsweb.com

20th Century Wars Genealogy Mailing List:
listserv@listserv.indiana.edu
SUB WW20-ROOTS-L firstname lastname

Québec

Genealogical and Historical Societies

Directories

Fédération Québécoise des Sociétés de Généalogie – Liste des Membres
http://www.federationgenealogie.qc.ca/fqsg4.htm
Contains contact information for several societies without their own Web sites.

Fédération des Sociétés d'Histoire du Québec – Répertoire des Membres
http://www.mcc.gouv.qc.ca/pamu/organis/fshq/fshq3.htm
Lists contact information for member societies by administrative region.

Sociétés [French only – lists]
- **Généalogie**: http://www.total.net/~benoitp/soc_geo.htm
- **Généalogie et Histoire**: http://www.total.net/~benoitp/soc_gh.htm
- **Histoire**: http://www.total.net/~benoitp/soc_h.htm
- **Clubs de Généalogie**: http://www.total.net/~benoitp/clubs.htm

Contact information for genealogical, historical and "combined" genealogical-historical societies in the province, many of which don't have their own Web sites or Internet presence.

Genealogical and Historical Societies

Centre de Recherches Généalogiques du Québec – Montréal, QC [English, some French]
http://www.cam.org/~cdrgduq/english.html
Actually a professional service that will research your direct lineage for a fee and present you with two parchment certificates. For a smaller fee, a certificate on the origin of your French-Canadian family name is available in French or English.

Links to Your Canadian Past
Québec

Club de Généalogie d'Hydro-Québec [French only]
http://www.cybertechs.qc.ca/priv/dubucj/club.html
A genealogy society for the employees and families of Hydro-Québec. At press time, not much information was available, except links to past issues of the journal *La Lignée*.

Club de Généalogie de Longueuil – Longueuil, QC [French only]
http://www.club-genealogie-longueuil.qc.ca/
Ample information on this society, including library hours, publications, the bulletin *Entre Nous* (with index) and an activities calendar. Links to zipped versions of local notarized acts.

Genealogy Society of Bay Chaleur – New Richmond, QC [English & French]
http://members.xoom.com/gaspegal/gsbc/gsbc.htm
Basic contact information and membership, library location and overview of holdings.

Heritage Gaspé
http://www.heritage-gaspe.org/
A non-profit organization dedicated to promoting heritage conservation and genealogy on the Gaspé peninsula, with a focus on the contributions of English settlers to the area. The site includes old photos, a history quiz, family histories and a virtual museum.

Morin Heights Historical Association – Morin Heights, QC
http://www.obds.ca/mhha/
Seeking to foster the appreciation and preservation of the local history and culture of this Argenteuil County town. Includes articles and photos on local people and places.

Links to Your Canadian Past
Québec

Québec Family History Society – Société de l'Histoire des Familles du Québec [English & French]
http://www.cam.org/~qfhs/index.html
This society seeks to foster an interest in genealogy among the English-speaking population of Québec. The site offers society news, a list of resources, contact information for paid research, a list of members' research interests and selected articles from their quarterly journal *Connections*.

Richmond County Historical Society – Melbourne, QC
[English & French]
http://www.interlinx.qc.ca/~e-dhealy/
The society operates a museum and archives (see *Archives*) dedicated to the history of Québec and the county of Richmond. A list of societal publications is available.

Société de Conservation et d'Animation du Patrimoine du Trois-Rivières, Inc. – 3-Rivières, QC
[French only]
http://sites.cgocable.ca/crc/CRC_pgs/P_Organs/SCAP.html
This independent, private organization groups together the various organizations seeking to preserve and promote the heritage of Trois-Rivières and the surrounding area. It is active in the restoration of built heritage, historical research, conferences, exhibits and publications.

La Société des Filles du Roi et Soldats du Carignan, Inc.
See Military, Native and Historic Groups / The Carignan-Salières Regiment.

Société Généalogique d'Argenteuil – Lachute, QC
http://www.letanu.on.ca/sga.htm
Basic information on membership, publications, library hours and contacting the society.

Links to Your Canadian Past
Québec

Société Généalogique Canadienne-Française [English & French]
http://www.sgcf.com/index.html
Formed by the venerable Father Archange Godbout, this society describes its extensive library holdings, upcoming events and conferences, provides an index to and selected articles from its bulletin, *Mémoires* and describes membership advantages.

Société de Généalogie des Cantons de l'Est – Sherbrooke, QC
[English & French]
http://www.genealogie.org/club/sgce/sgce.htm
You'll find information on becoming a member, research center hours, society publications for sale, monthly activities, introductory courses and contact information for the society.

Société Généalogique de l'Est du Québec – Rimouski, QC
[French, English intro only]
http://www.genealogie.org/club/sgeq/sgeq.htm
This site provides information on the society's research center, publications, the quarterly journal *l'Estuaire Généalogique* (w/ multi-year index), Internet and computer courses given by the society and upcoming conferences and activities.

Société de Généalogie de Lanaudière – Joliette, QC [English & French]
http://www.genealogie.org/club/sgl/sgl.htm
Basic information on the society, a list of publications and a membership e-mail directory.

Links to Your Canadian Past
Québec

Société de Généalogie des Laurentides – St. Jérôme, QC
[French only]
- http://societe-genealogie-laurentides.qc.ca/
- [same site] http://members.xoom.com/s_g_l/

This society focuses on the former counties of Argenteuil, Deux-Montagnes, Labelle and Terrebonne. Lists repertories for sale and provides basic information on the society.

Société de Généalogie de la Mauricie et des Bois-Francs – Trois-Rivières, QC [French only]
http://www.genealogie.org/club/sgmbf/sgmbf.htm
This site provides basic information on the society, library hours, an index of articles in recent editions of the monthly publication *l'Héritage*, and a list of member Web sites and e-mail.

Société Généalogique de l'Outaouais – Hull, QC [French only]
- http://www.bvx.ca/sgo/
- [same site] http://Vector.inexpress.net/~sgo/

Information on this society and its publications and back issues of articles that appeared in the newspaper *Le Droit*. Also includes a directory of member e-mail addresses and Web sites, a "Question Box" and the society's bulletin, *l'Outaouais Généalogique*.

Société de Généalogie de Québec – Ste-Foy, QC
- **English**: http://www.genealogie.org/club/sgq/socfr1e.htm
  [*Note: more info on French site.*]
- **French**: http://www.genealogie.org/club/sgq/index.htm

Describes the aims and activities of this society and provides a description of their library holdings, research services, publications and genealogical database. Also provides a list of members with homepages and e-mail addresses.

Links to Your Canadian Past
Québec

Société Généalogique du Saguenay, Inc. – Chicoutimi, QC
[French only]
http://vr3d.cybernaute.com/sgs/
Provides information on membership, the research library, society publications and a directory of members' e-mail addresses.

Société Généalogique et Historique de Trois-Pistoles – Trois-Pistoles, QC [French only]
http://www.icrdl.net/~basques/paba4.htm
Information on the research holdings of this society, which specializes in the local history and genealogy of Trois-Pistoles and the history and culture of Basque immigrants to Québec.

Société d'Histoire de Buckingham – Buckingham, QC [French only]
See Museums and Historic Sites

Société d'Histoire de Coaticook – Coaticook, QC [French only]
http://www.cscoaticook.qc.ca/lepont/shc/
Dedicated to collecting, documenting, preserving and promoting the history and heritage of Coaticook and surrounding towns by forming an archive and conducting research on local history, genealogy, heritage and culture.

Société d'Histoire du Coteau-du-Lac – Coteau-du-Lac, QC
[French only]
http://www.rocler.qc.ca/hbesner/
Contact information for this society, with a brief history of the town of Coteau-du-Lac and a list of the society's publications for sale.

Links to Your Canadian Past
Québec

Société d'Histoire de Drummondville – Drummondville, QC
[French only]
http://histoire-drummond.qc.ca/
This site provides information on the society's membership, activities, publications, collections, hours and a description of a walking tour of Drummondville produced by the society.

Société d'Histoire de la Haute-Yamaska – Granby, QC [French only]
http://www.endirect.qc.ca/~shs/
This society covers the region of the MRC of Acton, La Haute-Yamaska and Brome-Missisquoi, and more specifically the eleven municipalities that make up the MRC of La Haute-Yamaska. The site contains a detailed list of archival fonds by category, lists of available genealogical and local history resources, the society's publications and a "virtual exhibit" of old photos.

Société d'Histoire et de Généalogie de l'Île-Jésus – Laval, QC
http://w2.lavalnet.qc.ca/shgij/
This society collects, documents and preserves the heritage of the town of Laval and surrounding area, including documents, artifacts, photographs, handcrafts and genealogical records.

Société d'Histoire du Lac-Saint-Jean – Alma, QC [French only]
http://www.digicom.qc.ca/~rmlavoie/museelsje_info.html
This society is dedicated to preserving documentation and artifacts relating to the history of the region and the daily life of its inhabitants. It operates the Musée d'Histoire du Lac-Saint-Jean and the Centre d'Archives Lac-Saint-Jean-Est (*See Archives*).

Links to Your Canadian Past
Québec

Société Historique de La Prairie de la Magdeleine – La Prairie, QC [French only]
http://pages.infinit.net/shlm/
Dedicated to historical research, preservation and publications pertaining to the town of La Prairie and the surrounding area. Information on the archives, genealogies, archaeology, built heritage, tours, conferences, and an online version of the society's bulletin *Au Jour le Jour*.

Société d'Histoire et de Généalogie Maria-Chapdelaine – Dolbeau, QC
http://www.destination.ca/~francois/shg/societe.html
Focusing on research in the Saguenay/Lac-St-Jean region and the MRC of Maria-Chapdelaine in particular. This site presents membership and contact information and excerpts from several issues of the quarterly publication *La Souvenance*.

Société Historique du Marigot – Longueuil, QC [French only]
http://pages.infinit.net/marigot/
Dedicated to the research and publication of the history of the southern shore of the Saint Lawrence, particularly in the area of Longueuil. This site offers the full text of the society's recent bulletin, a catalogue of their publications, and much info on the town of Longueuil.

Société d'Histoire et de Généalogie du Rivière-du-Loup – Rivière-du-Loup, QC [English & French]
http://icrdl.net/~mlagace/shgrdl.htm
Preserving the history, genealogy and cultural heritage of Rivière-du-Loup and the surrounding area. The site lists information on membership, the society's research center and provides a calendar of activities and list of publications for sale.

Links to Your Canadian Past
Québec

Société d'Histoire de la Rivière-du-Nord – Saint-Jérôme, QC
[French only]
http://laurentides.net/shrn/accueil.htm
Collecting archival material pertaining to the MRC of Rivière-du-Nord, which includes the towns of Saint-Jérôme, Lafontaine, Saint-Antoine, Bellefeuille, Sainte-Sophie, New Glasgow, Saint-Hippolyte, Prévost and Saint-Colomban. The site presents information on their archives, membership, activities, journal and a "virtual museum."

Société d'Histoire de Sainte-Anne de la Pérade [French only]
http://sites.cgocable.ca/crc/CRC_pgs/P_Organs/hsteanne.htm
Basic contact information on this society, which seeks to study, publish and popularize the local history, genealogy and heritage of the town of Sainte-Anne de la Pérade.

Société Historique et Culturelle de Saint-Antoine-sur-Richelieu – St.-Antoine-s/-Richelieu, QC
[French only] http://www.aei.ca/~barcelof/SHEC.html
Online versions of the society's *Bulletin*, a membership list and links to information on notable past and present citizens of the town.

Société d'Histoire et de Généalogie de Saint-Casimir – Saint-Casimir, QC [French only]
http://www.genealogie.org/club/shgsc/shgsc.html
Information on the society's aims, membership, bulletin, publications and officers.

Société d'Histoire de la Seigneurie de Chambly – Chambly, QC
[French only]
http://www.bassin-chambly.qc.ca/membres/page_individuelle/1890.html
At press time, all this site provided was contact information and an e-mail link to the society.

Links to Your Canadian Past
Québec

Société du Patrimoine et d'Histoire de la Côte-de-Beaupré – Ste-Anne-de-Beaupré [French only]
http://www.genealogie.org/club/sphcb/sphcb.htm
This society brings together those with an interest in the history and heritage of the Beaupré coast. It supports historical conservation, research and publications.

Société Québécoise des Ponts Couverts – Anjou, QC [French only]
http://www.mcc.gouv.qc.ca/pamu/organis/sqpc/sqpc.htm
A society dedicated to the identification, restoration, preservation and history of wooden covered bridges in Québec. Includes some history and photos of covered bridges and membership info.

Web-based Directories, Societies and Resources
Annuaire Généalogique Internet: [French]
http://www.chez.com/agi/intro.htm

Genealogical Internet Directory: [English]
http://agi.hypermart.net/
A directory of Francophone genealogy sites on the Web: societies, family associations, history sites, family history, paleography, and other related subjects and resources.

Centrale Internet de Généalogie [French only]
http://cafe.rapidus.net/genealogie/
A comprehensive site containing links to federations, associations, societies, personal pages and other groups and sources of information for French-Canadian genealogy, history and related subjects, including heraldry and paleography.

Links to Your Canadian Past
Québec

Centre de Généalogie Francophone d'Amérique [French only]
http://www.genealogie.org/accueil.htm
This isn't a genealogy society in the traditional sense, but it is probably the best introduction (on-line, at least) to doing genealogy in Québec. Everything from how to get started to the printed material available, how to use it and doing genealogy on the Web. Plus, there's lots of great information on terms, tools and techniques. And when you've gotten something down on paper, there's even a section on putting your genealogy on the Internet.

Francogene (formerly Francêtres)
http://www.cam.org/~beaur/gen/welcome.html
A collection of information about non-Internet French-Canadian genealogy sources and links to many sources on the Web.

Québec GenWeb Project [English & French]
http://www.rootsweb.com/~canqc/index.htm
Links to genealogical information for the entire province, broken down into regional/county-level sites. Most information is catalogued in the appropriate category below.

Professional Groups and Federations
Conseil Québécois du Patrimoine Vivant – Québec, QC
[French only]
http://www.mcc.gouv.qc.ca/pamu/organis/cqpv/cqpv.htm
The "Québec Council of Living Heritage" seeks to study, record and preserve examples of cultural traditions in the province, whether they are francophone, anglophone, native or other. Oral histories and legends, music, artistic expression and traditional crafts and trades all fall within its mandate. The CQPV also lobbies government and publishes its research.

Links to Your Canadian Past
Québec

Fédération des Communautés Francophone et Acadiennes du Canada – Ottawa, ON & Québec, QC
[French only] http://w3.franco.ca/fcfa/
A nationwide organization dedicated to promoting and preserving the rights and culture of French-speaking communities in each province and territory of Canada. The site offers a francophone discussion forum, with other forums for members.

Fédération des Familles Souches Québécoises, Inc. (Federation of Québec Founding Families)
http://www.mediom.qc.ca/~ffsq/
A non-profit organization grouping 130 family associations from throughout Québec to help promote concerted action, organization, activities and representation in the government. Helps with organization of associations and reunions, the publication of newsletters, conservation of genealogical information and much more. Also publishes a newsletter and holds conferences and workshops.

Fédération Québécoise des Sociétés de Généalogie – Ste-Foy, QC [French only]
http://www.federationgenealogie.qc.ca/
This organization seeks to provide communication and coordination between French-Canadian genealogy societies both within and outside Québec. This is achieved through member services, lobbying, conferences, workshops, the training and certification of Québec genealogists and through the federation's bulletin *Info-Généalogie* and other publications.

Links to Your Canadian Past
Québec

Fédération des Sociétés d'Histoire du Québec – Montréal, QC
[French only]
http://www.mcc.gouv.qc.ca/pamu/organis/fshq/fshq.htm
The FSHQ provides communication to and between local member societies, acts as an intermediary to various government departments, sponsors training workshops, conferences, and generally encourages historical research in Québec and the publication of the results.

Institut Historique de l'Amérique Française – Outremont, QC
[French only]
http://www.cam.org/~ihaf/accueil.html
The IHAF is an association of professional historians, professors and amateur historians dedicated to the study of francophone North America, with a natural focus on Québec. Its committees work towards the promotion of history, the safeguard of research access and conditions, archival laws and issues and other concerns to francophone historians. The site also provides information on the *Revue d'Histoire de l'Amérique Française*, with indexes.

Société de Recherche Historique Archiv-Histo – Montréal, QC
[French only]
http://www.mcc.gouv.qc.ca/pamu/organis/srhah/srhah.htm
Archiv-Histo is a non-profit society whose main focus is to provide a base of historical and archival documents in accessible and modern formats for the research public, including amateur and professional genealogists and historians. A list of their databases and publications is available on this Web site.

Links to Your Canadian Past
Québec

Archives

Directory

Canadian Archival Resources on the Internet – Québec
http://www.usask.ca/archives/car/qcmenu.html
A service of the University of Saskatchewan, this site is a directory of archive centers throughout the province of Québec, listed alphabetically, with links to individual archive centers.

Archive Centers

Archives des Filles de Jésus - Trois-Rivières, QC [French only]
http://sites.cgocable.ca/crc/CRC_pgs/P_Organs/FillesJe.htm
Archives and exhibits pertaining to this order of nuns (and the parishes where they served) who came to Canada in 1902 and taught throughout Québec, the Maritimes and the West.

Archives National du Québec (National Archives of Québec) – various locations [French only]
http://www.anq.gouv.qc.ca/
This site provides an overview of the services offered by the National Archives of Québec, including in the areas of genealogy and family history, and contains a list of the addresses, hours and contact information for the regional centers of the archives.

Archives Nationales de France: Archives des Colonies Françaises 1600-1815 – Aix-en-Provence, France
[French only]
http://www.culture.gouv.fr/culture/nllefce/fr/rep_ress/an_13090.htm
Describes the holdings of the French National Archives concerning the overseas colonies until 1815. The fonds series includes Acts of the Sovereign Power, Correspondence Sent to the Colonies, Correspondence Received From the Colonies, Colonial Troops, Colonial Administrators, Depository of Fortification Maps and Depository of Public Colonial Papers.

Links to Your Canadian Past
Québec

Archives du Séminaire de Québec – Québec, QC [French only]
http://www.mcq.org/objets/fonds_archives/index.html
This site presents the history and background of the Archives of the Québec Seminary, and gives a detailed list of the various fonds that make up the vast collection of materials.

Archives du Séminaire de Trois-Rivières - Trois-Rivières, QC [French only]
http://sites.cgocable.ca/crc/CRC_pgs/P_Organs/SemiTR.htm
Basic information on these archives, which contain over 660 private and institutional collections.

Centre d'Archives du Lac-Saint-Jean Est – Alma, QC [French only]
http://www.digicom.qc.ca/~rmlavoie/museelsje_info1.html
Contact information, hours and a brief description of the genealogical and local history materials found in the archives of the MRC of Lac-Saint-Jean-Est.

McGill University Archives – Montréal, QC [English & French]
http://www.archives.mcgill.ca/
The McGill archives houses material relating to the university as well as fonds of alumni and subjects related to teaching at the university. An online guide to the archives is available and searches of its photo, film audio and text databases are possible through this site.

Montréal – Archives de Montréal [French only]
http://ville.montreal.qc.ca/archives/archives.htm
In addition to contact information and summary descriptions of the various divisions of the city's archives, this site provides an online guide to the archives, FAQ and online exhibits.

Links to Your Canadian Past
Québec

Richmond County Historical Society Archives – Melbourne, QC
http://www.interlinx.qc.ca/~e-dhealy/archives.htm
Includes paper documentation (private and published), photographs, maps, architectural records, audio-visual and other historic material pertaining to Richmond County. This site also lists the genealogical materials available and allows visitors to fill out an initial search request form.

Université de Montréal, Service des Archives – Montréal, QC
http://brise.ere.umontreal.ca/~champagm/saum
Information on the scope, contents and services of the Archives of the University of Montréal, including a list of the fonds and collections and a description of the divisions of the archives.

Université de Québec à Montréal, Service des Archives – Montréal, QC [French only]
http://www.unites.uqam.ca/archives/
The Archives Service of UQAM houses collections of archives pertaining to the history of the university as well as private archives pertaining to subjects studied at the university. Lists of the archival fonds by subject, name and accession number are also provided.

Université de Québec à Rimouski, Archives Régionales – Rimouski, QC [French only]
http://wwwb.uqar.uquebec.ca/archives.htm
The regional archives at the University of Québec at Rimouski houses nearly sixty fonds-level collections pertaining to the eastern part of the province, in particular in the areas of agriculture, forestry, cooperatives, unionism and regional development.

Links to Your Canadian Past
Québec

Untied Church Archives Network – Montréal and Ottawa Conference Archives (various locations)
http://www.uccan.org/archives/montreal.htm
Includes records of most of the Methodist, Presbyterian and Congregational Churches prior to 1925 and of The United Church of Canada after 1925, except those in the Gaspé Peninsula (see below) and three congregations that fall within Ontario's Manitou Province Archives (St. Paul's Church, Temiscaming; All Saints Church, Noranda and Val d'Or Church, Val d'Or).

United Church Archives Network – Maritime Conference Archives (Sackville, NB)
- http://www.uccan.org/archives/maritime.htm
- http://www3.ns.sympatico.ca/don.macqueen/ARCHIVES.HTM

Includes records of the Methodist, Presbyterian and Congregational Churches in the Gaspé Peninsula of Québec prior to 1925 and of The United Church of Canada after 1925.

Professional Organizations
Association des Archivistes du Québec – Sillery, QC [French only]
http://brise.ere.umontreal.ca/~champagm/saum
The AAQ serves as a means of communication between member societies in Québec, offering French-language services, such as training, certification, lobbying, conferences and workshops. An index of the journal *Archives* is available, with French and English article abstracts. This site also presents online versions of position papers and letters of intervention written by the society.

Links to Your Canadian Past
Québec

Collectif des Archivaires, Université de Montréal – Montréal, QC
http://www.fas.umontreal.ca/ebsi/archivaires/
The archival interest group of the students of the *École de Bibliothéconomie et des Sciences de l'Information* (EBSI) of the University of Montréal. Its aims are to improve relations between students and archivists and to promote the profession of archivist among students of the EBSI.

Réseau des Archives du Québec (Québec Archives Network) – Montréal, QC [French only]
http://www.raq.qc.ca/
The RAQ seeks to promote the development of archives in the province, be a communications network among members and a political force with national groups and government agencies. This site presents membership info and texts from conferences and position papers of the RAQ.

Table des Archives de l'Estrie – Sherbrooke, QC [French only]
http://www.cscs.qc.ca/archives/tablestrie/
A regional group working for the coordination of archive policies, practices and priorities in the Estrie region of Québec.

Libraries and Research Centers

Directories and Catalogues
Bibliothèques
http://www.cvfa.ca/Accueil/Publications/R_pertoire/Division_Th_matique/Communication_et_Culture/biblioth_ques.html
A list of French-language libraries in Québec and throughout Canada and the United States.

Links to Your Canadian Past
Québec

Canadian Library Index – Québec
http://www.lights.com/canlib/canlibpq.html
Links to the Web pages and/or online and telnet catalogues of public, private and university libraries throughout the province, listed alphabetically.

Hytelnet Library Catalogues – Québec
http://library.usask.ca/hytelnet/ca0/PQ.html
A listing of links to telnet catalogues of libraries from across the province.

Library and Website Catalogues – Québec
http://www.nlc-bnc.ca/canlib/equebec.htm
Links to Web sites and online catalogues for public, private and university libraries throughout the province of Québec.

Libraries and Research Centers
Bibliothèque National du Québec – Montréal, QC [French, English summary]
http://www2.biblinat.gouv.qc.ca/
Links to the multimedia catalogue Iris, a database of old post cards, Québec government publications, new Québec books and a database of information on France-Québec relations. Also includes information on the library's full collections, exhibitions and services.

Bishop's University Old Library (McGreer Hall) – Lennoxville, QC
http://www.ubishops.ca/library_info/lib-old.htm
The Old Library houses books and archival materials pertaining to the history of Canada and the Eastern Townships in particular. Collections include town and parish histories, birth/marriage/death registers and microfilms of census, civil status registers and

newspapers. The library houses the archives of the Eastern Townships Research Centre and the Québec Diocesan Archives of the Anglican Church of Canada.

Centre de Documentation de Tourisme Québec – Québec, QC
[French only]
http://dses.grics.qc.ca/regard/3/regard.htm
Contact and holdings information for this "library" of documentation on the tourist industry and sites throughout the province of Québec. The collection consists of over 7,000 individual volumes, reports, tourist guides, reference works, CD-ROMs, videos and periodicals.

Concordia University Special Collections – Montréal, QC
http://juno.concordia.ca/collections/spec.col.html
Collections include Antique Maps, the Quinn Collection of Canadian political pamphlets, Participation Québec Collection, the Masonic Collection of over 500 books on Freemasonry and the Rudnyckyj Archives of the 1963-71 Royal Commission on Bilingualism and Biculturalism.

McGill University Department of Rare Books and Special Collections – Montréal, QC
http://www.library.mcgill.ca/rarebook/cube.htm
Collections in the department include maps and prints dating from the 16th to 20th centuries and books on architecture, Canadiana, French Canada, history, social history, travel and exploration.

Links to Your Canadian Past
Québec

Montréal – Bibliothèque de Montréal – Montréal, QC [mostly French]
http://www.ville.montreal.qc.ca/biblio/pageacc.htm
Home of the infamous Salle Gagnon, the Mecca for French-Canadian genealogists. This site provides information on the library's services and collections, access to the online Merlin catalogue [French & English] and other databases and library hours and locations.

Québec and French-Canadian Studies Programs
Directory of Québec Studies Programs [French only]
http://www.aieq.qc.ca/centres.htm
A list of contact information for Québec Studies programs throughout the world.

American Council for Québec Studies – Urbana, IL (USA)
- **Official Site**: http://acqs.plattsburgh.edu/acqs/acqsindx.htm
- **French Overview**: http://www.iccs-ciec.ca/info/assoc/f-aqs.html

A group of individuals from academia, the business world, legal and government circles who are interested in Québec and francophone Canada. The council publishes the journal *Québec Studies*

Association Internationale des Études Québécoises – Québec, QC [French only]
http://www.aieq.qc.ca/
A group for those studying, teaching or publishing about Québec society– its culture, history and development.

Links to Your Canadian Past
Québec

Bishop's University: Département d'Études Françaises et Québécoises – Lennoxville, QC
[French only] http://www.ubishops.ca/ccc/div/hum/fre/
The department offers a minor, major and honors program with courses in French language and literature, Québec literature and civilization and Acadian literature.

Centre d'Études sur le Canada Français et la Francophonie – Regina, SK [French only]
http://www.fl.ulaval.ca/CEFAN/cecff.html
An interdisciplinary program of the University of Regina, the CECFF seeks to study, promote and popularize the francophone presence in Saskatchewan, particularly through its extensive project "Pratiques Culturelles de la Saskatchewan Française," described on this site.

Centre d'Études Franco-Canadiennes de l'Ouest – Winnipeg, MB [French only]
http://www.ustboniface.mb.ca/cusb/jlafonta/colloque/cefco.html
This center, located at the Collège Universitaire de Saint-Boniface, seeks to study, document and publish research pertaining to the French presence and culture in the Canadian West.

Centre d'Études Interdisciplinaires sur les Lettres, les Arts et les Traditions des Francophones en Amérique du Nord (CELAT) – Québec, QC [French only]
http://www.fl.ulaval.ca/celat/
The CELAT is an interdisciplinary program of the University of Laval which seeks to pursue and publish scholarly research on the francophone culture of North America and around the world. The site provides a catalogue of publications and a list of current and recent research projects.

Links to Your Canadian Past
Québec

Centre Interuniversitaire d'Études Québécoises – Ste-Foy & Trois-Rivières, QC
[French only] http://www.ggr.ulaval.ca/cieq/cieq.htm
A joint project of the Laboratoire de Géographie Historique of the Université Laval and the Centre d'Études Québécoises of the Université du Québec à Trois-Rivières. It is dedicated to the study of Québec society from colonization to today in many disciplines, such as geography, history, literature, philosophy, sociology, ethnology and religious studies.

Centre de Recherche en Civilisation Canadienne-Française – Ottawa, ON [French, English intro]
http://www.uottawa.ca/academic/crccf/
Part of the University of Ottawa, the CRCCF maintains an archives/research center with printed and manuscript materials relating to francophone Canada and French America. It also undertakes various research and publishing projects in history, sociology, translation, education and other liberal arts domains. An online guide to the archives and its fonds is available.

Concordia University: Québec Studies Cluster – Montréal, QC
http://artsci-ccwin.concordia.ca/inte/clusters/clust.htm#QS
Includes the list of language, culture, history and politics courses in this cluster.

Globe: **Revue International d'Études Québécoises – Montréal, QC** [French only]
http://www.cam.org/~inuk/
The journal of the Québec Studies Program at McGill University. *Globe* presents articles pertaining to history, economy, native studies, demography, culture, literature, etc.

Links to Your Canadian Past
Québec

McGill University Québec Studies Program – Montréal, QC
[English & French]
http://www.arts.mcgill.ca/programs/qs/
The Québec Studies Program at McGill seeks to "define Québec's reality in its diversity," and to "open new research paths within the arts and social sciences domains." Both major and minor programs are offered.

Le Québec et l'Amérique Française (Université de Laval) – Ste-Foy, QC [French only]
http://www.fl.ulaval.ca/CEFAN/syllabus.htm
The online description of this course, designed to study the diaspora of North American francophone culture and communities and the role played by Québec. Includes the course syllabus, objectives and reading list, which may be beneficial for interested individuals.

Télé-Université: Programme Court d'Initiation au Québec Contemporain – online
[French only]
http://www.teluq.uquebec.ca/Alice/programm/0083.htm
Description of this distance learning program, giving students a basic knowledge of Québec society – its evolution, main components and present situation. Descriptions of the three component courses in politics, society and economy are included.

Birth, Marriage, Death, Census and Other Data Online

Centre de Généalogie Francophone d'Amérique – Centre de Documentation [French only]
- **Databases**: http://www.genealogie.org/doc.htm
- **Become a Member**: http://www.genealogie.org/membre.htm

This online research center, overseen by the *Société Généalogique de l'Est du Québec*, contains various searchable databases. There is the "central" database, with allows you to search (or add to) an integrated GEDCOM database for the entire province. There's also a census database, and various other databases dealing with specific families or themes. To use them, however, you'll first have to become a member (free) and create an online profile.

Sources in Québec (Francêtres/Francogene) [English & French]
http://www.cam.org/~beaur/gen/qc-src-e.html
A list of non-Internet sources used in Québec and French-Canadian genealogy, listed by time period covered by the resource. Presented by Denis Beauregard of Francogene.

<u>*Vital Statistics and Parish Records – Province-wide*</u>
Dictionnaire Généalogique des Familles du Québec – **Explanations**
http://www.geocities.com/Heartland/Ranch/6210/E5jette.html
An English-language explanation to the format and abbreviations used in the DGFQ by René Jetté. Includes translations for abbreviated terms.

Dictionnaire Généalogique de Nos Origines – **Complément à Jetté** [English & French]
http://www.cam.org/~beaur/gen/dgo.html
This work by Denis Beauregard is meant to be a complement to the *Dictionnaire Généalogique des Familles du Québec* by René Jetté. It includes information not found in the DGFQ, corrections and additions. This work's focus is those families that arrived in Québec before 1800, with particular attention to founding families that settled in New France before 1730.

Le Directeur de l'État Civil [French only]
http://www.riq.qc.ca/etatcivil/pages/menu.html
This site, from the official vital statistics department of the Québec government, includes sections on vital records dealing with birth, marriage, death, change in civil status, the different documents available and how to obtain them.

Links to Your Canadian Past
Québec

Fichier Origine [French, some English]
\\\http://www.cam.org/~beaur/origine/
An ongoing project to create an online repertoire of birth and baptism records for French immigrants to Québec from its origins to 1865, compiled by researchers in France and Québec. For English, click on the link *Ordre alphabétique des pionniers*. *Note*: The names given are only the first names on each page. The actual records are much more extensive.

Francogene: Marriage Index
http://www.cam.org/~beaur/imfa/index.html
A compilation of marriage records from throughout the province from the eighteenth through the twentieth centuries.

Hebridean Scots Church Records on Microfilm
http://www.geocities.com/~hebridscots/church.htm
This table shows the towns and parishes in Québec with microfilmed records of Hebridean Scot parishioners, with film numbers for various archival and genealogical groups.

List of Parishes in Québec, by County [French only – list]
http://societe-genealogie-laurentides.qc.ca/comtes.htm
A clickable table of the counties of Québec, with a list of parish churches with founding date.

Place Names and Répertoire Locations
http://ourworld.compuserve.com/homepages/lwjones/place.htm
A list of many Québec parishes and the corresponding repertories (usually for the county) in which the records for that particular parish may be found.

PRDH Place Name Index
- **French**: http://www.genealogie.org/manuel/rabmsr.html
- **English**:
  http://ourworld.compuserve.com/homepages/lwjones/prdh.htm

Links to Your Canadian Past
Québec

Two indexes of place names, their corresponding numeric codes and their locations in the different volumes of the *Répertoires des Actes de Baptêmes, Mariages, Sépulture et des Recensements du Québec Ancien*, published by the Programme de Recherche en Démographie Historique (PRDH) of the University of Montréal.

Québec Vital Records
http://www.familytreemaker.com/00000163.html
Addresses for obtaining records from the colonial and modern periods of the province.

Québec Vital Statistics
ftp://ftp.cac.psu.edu/pub/genealogy/roots-l/genealog/genealog.vican-qu
A text file describing the extent and location of vital statistics records in Québec. Divided into the following sections: Overview/Generalities, French Regime (1621-1765), British Regime (1760-1899), 1900-1992, 1993-present, list of courthouses and archive centers and a description of the National Archives of Québec.

Vital Statistics and Parish Records – Local
Bonaventure County Vital Statistics Indexes
http://members.tripod.com/~gasperoots/bmdcemet.htm
This site contains links to indexes of parish records for New Carlisle and Paspébiac Anglican Church 1811-1884 (partial) and a complete index for the records of Port Daniel & Hopetown Anglican Church 1858-1884.

Château-Richer Confirmations [French only – list]
http://www.fun-move.com/Noella/listes.htm#listes
A list of those people confirmed at Château-Richer by the "Illustrious and Most Reverend Bishop" on 11 April 1662. *Note*: individuals listed vary in age from seven to 26 years old, with the French town of origin listed for some confirmants.

Links to Your Canadian Past
Québec

Île d'Orléans - Réperoire de Mariages [French only]
http://members.tripod.com/~efortier/
Extracted information from the parish registers of the Île d'Orléans for the eighteenth century. Browseable by time period, with an index of both grooms' and brides' names, linked to records.

Lanaudière County – Marriage Database Request
http://www.rootsweb.com/~qclanaud/sourcesa.htm#ferland
The creators of this database of 200,000 Lanaudière marriages claim to be able to provide a list of all the ancestors of a couple married in the Lanaudiere region (Berthier, Joliette, Montcalm and L'Assomption).

Lanaudière County – Parish Repertories and Local Histories
http://www.rootsweb.com/~qclanaud/paroisse.htm
A list of the parishes in this county and the birth/marriage/death registers or local histories available, with the time period and records covered by the register.

Ste-Anne de Restigouche Parish Registers, 1842-1867
http://members.tripod.com/~CyberBart/steann.htm
An extraction of baptisms, marriages and burials for this parish, which included many Acadian refugees from the Campbellton and Dalhousie area of New Brunswick.

Cemetery Data

Cemeteries as a Research Tool
http://www.virtuel.qc.ca/simmons/CEMETERY.HTM
An article by Marlene Simmons on using cemeteries to aid in your Québec research and the challenges and particularities involved in using cemetery info in Eastern Townships research.

Links to Your Canadian Past
Québec

Association of Jewish Genealogical Societies Cemetery Project – Québec
http://www.jewishgen.org/cemetery/canquebe.htm
Contact and cemetery information for this project to catalogue Jewish burial sites in the province of Québec. Information is provided for the known Jewish cemeteries in the province.

Dundee – Zion Church Burials
http://members.tripod.com/~GLENGARRY/zionbur.html
Includes a list of the elders of Zion Church 1833-1956, an index of burials in the cemetery 1833-1965, a list of supplementary burial information and a list of local residents 1966-1980.

Grenville (Argenteuil County) – Scotch Road Cemetery
http://members.tripod.com/~GLENGARRY/ScotchRdCem.html
Transcriptions of the (anglophone) gravestones in this cemetery.

Montréal and Rawdon – St-Seraphim Cemetery
http://www.oca.org/OCA/pim/oca-ca-rawssc.html
At press time, only contact information available for this Orthodox Church of America cemetery.

Pontiac County Cemeteries in the Ontario Cemetery Finding Aid (OCFA)
http://www.islandnet.com/ocfa/cemlist3.html#Pontiac
A list, by township, of the cemeteries of Pontiac County, Québec included in the OCFA online database. Use the links at the bottom of the page to access the rest of the OCFA.

Soulanges/Vaudreuil County Cemetery List
http://members.tripod.com/~GLENGARRY/Cemlist-SoulVaud.html
A list of cemeteries in the county, with church affiliation, location and information on published transcriptions and links to online headstone transcriptions for some of the cemeteries listed.

Links to Your Canadian Past
Québec

Census Information
Census List for Québec Province, 1640-1851, With Film Numbers
- **Part 1**: http://www.oz.net/~johnbang/genealogy/quebcens.txt
- **Part 2**: http://www.oz.net/~johnbang/genealogy/quebcen2.txt
- **Part 3**: http://www.oz.net/~johnbang/genealogy/quebcen3.txt
- **Part 4**: http://www.oz.net/~johnbang/genealogy/quebcen4.txt

A list of censuses available for the province of Québec, with area covered and microfilm numbers for finding actual records. These pages may take some figuring out, as there are no column headings to specify which film numbers are from which organization, and the censuses are not listed chronologically from page to page.

Censuses of New France –17th Century
http://www.gel.ulaval.ca/~senecal/sharefe.htm
Download zipped versions of the 1666, 1667 and 1681 censuses from this site (Word 97 format).

1666 Census Overview
http://www.vmnf.civilization.ca/une/p-un5-en.htm
This article on the 1666 census of Québec by Intendant Talon gives an overview of the number of individuals in each town or seigneurie and also a look at the division of professions.

1871 Québec Census Head of Household Index
Listed by cities and towns beginning with the letters:
- **A-C**: http://www.oz.net/~johnbang/genealogy/quebecac.txt
- **D-L**: http://www.oz.net/~johnbang/genealogy/quebecdl.txt
- **L-M**: http://www.oz.net/~johnbang/genealogy/quebeclm.txt

Remember what this is, because there are no headings or titles on these pages. What you will find is a list of heads of household, with town of residence and an occasional reference to a title.

Links to Your Canadian Past
Québec

Berthier-en-Haut (Berthierville) Census, 1681
http://www.geocities.com/Heartland/Ranch/6210/E11_census1681_Villemur/EVillemur1681_1.html
Transcriptions from the 1681 census of Canada for the Seigneurie of Villemur and the Seigneurie of d'Autray, with corresponding entries from the DGFQ, where available. The table includes name and age, occupation, arms, livestock and cultivated land.

Laurentides – Colonisation des Laurentides [French only]
http://207.253.234.2/pilon/colonisa.htm
This page presents a "List of colonists present at the time of the arrival of Father Labelle in the autumn of 1877" for the communities of Salaberry (or St-Jovite or the Mission of Grand-Brulé), Wolf (or St-Faustin or Mission la Repousse), Clyde (or La Conception), Howard, St-Adolphe, Grandmaison, Lac Tremulant, Lac Mercier, Arundel Village, Amherst, St-Rémi, Montcalm and Lac des Écorces. There is a description of each community and list of settlers, with origins.

Longueuil – Dictionnaire Historique de Longueuil: Aveu et Dénombrement [French only]
http://pages.infinit.net/marigot/A.html#aveu
A list of various censuses and "Aveux et Dénombrements" (Vows and Enumerations) for the town of Longueuil. Includes the Aveu et dénombrement for 1677, 1681, 1695, 1723, census of 1765 and entries for Lovell's directory of 1887.

Mille Isles Census – 1861
See Morin Township, below.

Links to Your Canadian Past
Québec

Montréal – 1666 Census of Montréal [French, some English]
- http://www.geocities.com/Heartland/Estates/4162/recensm.htm
- http://www.geocities.com/Heartland/Acres/5571/montr1666cen.htm

A transcription of this census as recorded (therefore not alphabetical). Lists the entire population of 627 people, not just heads of household, along with age and family status or profession.

Montréal – 1731 Census of Montréal
- **First Section, East**:
  http://www.geocities.com/Heartland/Ranch/6210/E6mtl1.html
- **Second Section, East**:
  http://www.geocities.com/Heartland/Ranch/6210/E8mtl2.html

A map of residents' lots taken from the 1731 "census," of the *seigneurie* of Montréal, known as the *Aveu et dénombrement des Messieurs de Saint-Sulpice*. Includes the names of those landowners holding rights from the Congregation of the Sulpicians within the walled city.

Morin Township (now Morin Heights) and Mille-Isles Census – 1861
http://www.obds.ca/mhha/Censuscover.htm

The actual census pages are quite large – be patient. Data presented includes first and last name, occupation, origin and age. You can also read the 1861 enumerator's report.

Québec (City) – Index to the 1744 Québec City Census
http://www.oz.net/~johnbang/genealogy/1744indx.txt

A nominal list of individuals included in the census, with name, age and occasional notes.

Sorel (Seigneurie de Saurel) Census, 1681
http://www.geocities.com/Heartland/Ranch/6210/E10_Rec1681/ESorel1681_1.html

Links to Your Canadian Past
Québec

Transcriptions from the 1681 census of Canada for the "Seigneurie de Saurel," with corresponding entries from the DGFQ (Jetté), where available. The table includes name and age, occupation, arms, livestock and cultivated land.

Passenger Lists/Immigration Data and Origins
1832 Emigrants Handbook for Arrivals at Québec
http://www.ist.uwaterloo.ca/~marj/genealogy/emigrants1832.html
The reprinted text of a handbook given to new arrivals in Québec, published by His Majesty's Chief Agent For the Superintendence of Settlers and Emigrants in Upper and Lower Canada.

***British Queen* Passenger List, 1790**
http://www.isn.net/~dhunter/british_queen.html
The passenger list of this vessel, which sailed from Arisaig, Scotland and arrived at Québec City. The passengers then traveled to Montréal for a year before settling in Upper Canada.

Les Calvinistes Suisses en Nouvelle-France [French only – list]
http://pages.infinit.net/barbeaum/suisses.htm
A list of 21 Swiss Calvinists (Protestants) who came to New France, and the date and place of each individual's renunciation of Calvinism. Some also include the place of origin.

***Corsican* Passenger List, 1915**
http://listserv.northwest.com/~haight/Ships.htm#The Corsican 1915
The passenger list for this vessel, as given to one of the passengers. The *Corsican*, part of the Allan Royal Mail Line, sailed from Glasgow, Scotland on May 8, 1915 to Québec and Montréal.

Links to Your Canadian Past
Québec

Liste Provisoire des Huguenots en Nouvelle-France [French only]
http://pages.infinit.net/barbeaum/listem.htm
This "Provisional List of Huguenots in New France" includes the names of 297 individuals, the date of their marriage and name of their spouse (when these are known).

Origin of Immigrants from the Pyrénées-Atlantiques [French only – table]
http://www.world-address.com/cgpa/ge64cgpk.htm
A table of data on the vital statistics and origins of immigrants to Québec before 1825 from the present-day French department of Pyrénées-Atlantiques, which included parts of the former provinces of Béarn and Gascogne. Taken from the *Dictionnaire Généalogique de Nos Origines* by Denis Beauregard. Includes date of birth/baptism, place of origin, parents' names, etc.

Québec Genealogy: Immigration [English & French]
http://www.cam.org/~beaur/gen/qcimmi-e.html
A bibliography of printed sources of Québec immigration data, broken down into recent and older books on French immigration and a section of books on non-French immigration.

Québec Ship Arrivals, 1908
http://pixel.cs.vt.edu:70/0/GRG/Ships/quebec.txt
A table of data for ships that arrived in this year. Shows name of ship, date and place of departure and arrival, name of individual passengers, with (where known) age, marital status, occupation and destination of passengers.

***Saint-André* Passenger List, 1659**
http://www.geocities.com/Heartland/Ranch/6210/E7standre.html
A list of the passengers recruited in France during the autumn of 1658 by Jeanne Mance and Marguerite Bourgeoys for the colony of Montréal. The ship sailed in 1659.

Links to Your Canadian Past
Québec

Ships Arriving at Québec in 1866
http://www.ist.uwaterloo.ca/~marj/genealogy/ships1866.html
A table of data on ships arriving at Québec City that were checked at the Grosse Île quarantine station from 28 April to 31 October 1866. Includes name of ship and master, date and port of sailing, cargo, passengers in cabin and steerage, number of sick and dead, date discharged, etc.

Ships that Landed in Canada, 1633-1662
http://www.geocities.com/Heartland/Ranch/6210/E1navires.html
A table of ship arrivals in Canada during the period in which the colony of Canada was maintained and supplied by the *Compagnie des Cents Associés*. The table shows the ship name, tonnage, notes and captain's name.

Ships that Landed in Canada, 1666-1754
http://www.geocities.com/Heartland/Ranch/6210/E14navires1666.html
A table of ship arrivals in the colony of Canada for this given period, after the monopoly of the *Compagnie des Cents Associés* was rescinded and the market opened for commerce. The table shows the ship name, tonnage, notes and captain's name.

Vessels Arriving at the Port of Québec in 1793
http://www.ist.uwaterloo.ca/~marj/genealogy/quebec1793.html
A table of data on ships that arrived at Québec City in 1793. Data includes date of arrival, ship name, master's name, place of sailing and registry, days passage, number of men, cargo, etc.

Land Records
Hatley Lot Assignments 1837
http://www.rootsweb.com/~canqc/hatley.htm
A list of individuals "who have completed the Settlement Duties in Hatley, Ascot, Orford and Dodswell," showing name, lot, range and acres. Taken from British parliamentary papers.

Links to Your Canadian Past
Québec

Lower Canada Land Records Index
http://www.archives.ca/www/svcs/english/INDEXRG1_E.html#Lower Canada
A finding aid for the Land Petitions for Quebec and Lower Canada, c. 1764-1841 and the Gaspé Land Commission records volumes 79-80.

Montréal – Adhémar Database [French only]
http://cca.qc.ca/adhemar/
Adhémar is a database compiled by the Groupe de Recherche sur Montréal, part of the Centre Canadien d'Architecture (*See National / Museums and Historic Sties*). This site presents maps of the city (city-wide and land parcels by sector), several timelines pertaining to the city (history, governors, mayors, priests, etc.) and a database of architectural, land grant and usage information. The database, which requires free registration, is a powerful tool for tracing information on land parcels or purchase/rental history.

Adoption Information and Groups
Adoption in Québec: The Right to Know [English & French]
http://www.total.net/~adoption/english_files/englishv.htm
Information on this group, which seeks to change the adoption laws in Québec, and information on the current and proposed legislation the group is seeking to change or implement.

Civil Code of Québec: Adoption Laws [English & French]
http://www.droit.umontreal.ca/doc/ccq/en/l2/t2/c2/index.html
Browse the various sections of the Québec civil code pertaining to adoption procedures, rights and information or search the articles pertaining to adoption (or entire civil code) by keyword.

Links to Your Canadian Past
Québec

Mouvement Retrouvailles [French only]
http://www.total.net/~elancom/MRETROUVAILLES.html
This francophone organization seeks to inform, support and guide all members of the adoption triad in contacting other registered members. Their services are detailed on this site. An online forum is also available

Parent Finders Montréal [English & French]
http://www.pfmtl.org/
A volunteer-run support group and registry seeking to reunite family members separated by adoption. The site provides a good deal of information about the group as well as legal and other adoption issues in Québec and the other provinces of Canada.

Peacock Babies of Québec
http://members.home.net:80/bjq/
A site dedicated to assisting those people born at the Brome Missisquoi Perkins Hospital in Cowansville, Québec who were placed in adoptive homes by the Reverend Peacock.

Legal and Other Data

Chronica [French only]
http://www.total.net/~benoitp/chronica.htm
Information on this CD-ROM research tool produced by the Archiv-Histo group. Chronica-1 presents the complete text of the *Jugements et délibérations du Conseil Souverain de la Nouvelle-France (1663-1716)*. Chronica 2 includes the *Jugements et délibérations ... (1717-1760), Inventaire des Insinuations de la prévôté de Québec (1640-1760) et Inventaire des Insinuations du régime militaire (1760-1764), Inventaire du Conseil Souverain de la Nouvelle-France (1663-1760), Inventaire d'une Collection de pièces judiciaires, notariales, etc.* Other Chronica editions are being planned or prepared.

Links to Your Canadian Past
Québec

Ferrymen, Innkeepers and Merchants at Trois-Rivières
http://www.rootsweb.com/~canqc/document.htm
A list of ferrymen in the district of Trois-Rivères in 1826 and those who had received licenses to be a merchant or innkeeper for the year 1836.

Longueuil: Actes Notariés (Notary Records) [French only]
http://pages.infinit.net/marigot/notaires.html
Transcriptions of the notarized records of Pierre Brais (1871-1905), Isidore Hurteau (1839-1878) and Louis Lacoste (1821-1871) pertaining to the residents of Longueuil. Also provides links to records of notaries A. Adhémar, J-B Adhémar, B. Basset, P. Cabazié, D. de Blanzy, J. Dufresne, Hodiesne, M. Lepailleur, F. Lepailleur, C. Maugue, Raimbeau (père & fils), F. Simonet and M. Tailhandier, viewable with the Adobe Acrobat Reader.

Parchemin Database [French only]
http://www.cdnq.org/cnq/origines/framorig.html
A searchable database of 30,000 notarized records (out of 3,500,000) from Québec between 1635 and 1800. Maintained by the notaries of Québec and the Archiv-Histo group. Searches return a summary of the record, with its location in the National Archives of Québec.

Prévôté de Québec: Régistres [French only]
http://www.jctca.com/jct/paleographie.html
Links to page-by-page transcriptions of the registers of the prévôté de Québec, each with an index of names and places included in the register. Includes the years 1676-1686.

Links to Your Canadian Past
Québec

Themis Collection [French only]
http://www.total.net/~benoitp/themis.htm
Another research tool from the Archiv-Histo group. Themis is a CD-ROM collection of legal and judicial records that includes the *Cour du banc du Roi (1791-1827+) du district de Montréal, en matière civile* and the *Cour des Sessions de la Paix (1800-1900) du district de Québec, en matières civile et criminelle*. Other versions are being planned or prepared.

Museums and Historic Sites

Directory
La Société des Musées Québécois Directory [French only]
http://www.unites.uqam.ca/musees/fr/repertoire.html
A searchable directory of museums in the province. You can select by region (list or clickable map), type of institution and type of collections. Search results provide information on many museums in the province that don't have their own Web sites.

Museums and Historic Sites
Artillery Park National Historic Site – Québec, QC [English & French]
http://parcscanada.risq.qc.ca/artillery/
Visit historic buildings and other installations that recall the military and industrial history of Québec City at the site of the first military quarters built in Québec in the 17th century.

Basilique-Cathédrale Notre-Dame-de-Québec – Québec, QC
[French only]
http://www.museocapitale.qc.ca/004.html
Guided visits, a *son et lumière* presentation and other exhibits and activities help the visitor appreciate the history of the religious heritage in Québec and the building of its churches.

Links to Your Canadian Past
Québec

Battle of the Châteauguay National Historic Site – Howick, QC
[English & French]
http://parkscanada.pch.gc.ca/parks/quebec/bataille_chateauguay/bataille_chateauguaye.htm
Experience the military life of the War of 1812 era at the site of a battle in which a small Canadian force repulsed an American invasion of Lower Canada.

Battle of the Restigouche National Historic Site – Pointe-à-la-Croix, QC [English & French]
http://parcscanada.risq.qc.ca/ristigouche/en/
The site of the last naval battle between France and England in the Seven Years' War. The interpretation center contains artifacts and vestiges of the frigate *The Machault*, and the Web site provides a good deal of information on the ship, battle and their importance in the war.

Beaulne Museum and Château Norton – Coaticook, QC
[English & French]
http://www.cscoaticook.qc.ca/Lepont/musee/Index.html
Dedicated to the history of the town of Coaticook, the Beaulne Museum is located in the "Château Norton," the beautifully restored 19th century home of a prominent local family.

Carillon Barracks National Historic Site – Carillon, QC
[English & French]
http://parkscanada.pch.gc.ca/parks/quebec/caserne_carillon/caserne_carillone.htm
A military museum now occupies the building that originally served as a barracks during the 1837 Rebellion and was converted to a hotel after 1840.

Links to Your Canadian Past
Québec

Carillon Canal National Historic Site – Carillon, QC [English & French]
http://parcscanada.risq.qc.ca/canaux/canal-de-carillon/aindex.html
This still-operational canal was originally built in 1833 for military purposes, and was used extensively for commercial navigation. The Web site contains a great deal of information on the cultural and natural heritage of the canal, including an online tour and photo gallery.

Cartier-Brébeuf National Historic Site – Québec, QC [English & French]
http://parkscanada.pch.gc.ca/parks/quebec/cartier-brebeuf/cartier-brebeufe.htm
This historic center, at the site of Cartier's wintering camp in 1535-36 includes exhibits on Cartier's early explorations, encounters between the French and natives and also exhibits on the role of the Jesuits in the colonization of New France.

Centre Culturel et Patrimoniale de la Poudrerie de Windsor – Windsor, QC [French only]
http://susan.chin.gc.ca:8016/BASIS/guide/user/search/DDW?M=1&U=1&W=GUIDE_KEY=1377
This museum, housed in an old furniture factory, presents the history of black powder production in Windsor. A walking tour of the remains of the old powder factory is also available.

Centre d'Exposition sur l'Industrie des Pâtes et Papiers - Trois-Rivières, QC [French only]
http://sites.cgocable.ca/crc/CRC_pgs/P_Organs/CEIPP.htm
Exhibits and collections presenting the history and importance of the paper and forest products industry in the local, regional and national economy.

Links to Your Canadian Past
Québec

Centre d'Histoire de Montréal – Vieux-Montréal, QC [French only]
http://ville.montreal.qc.ca/chm/chm.htm
Presenting the history and evolution of Montréal from 1642 until today in the urban, economic, architectural, social and cultural contexts particular to each time period covered.

Centre d'Interprétation Archéo-Topo – Grandes-Bergeronnes, QC [French only]
http://susan.chin.gc.ca:8016/BASIS/guide/user/search/DDW?M=1&U=1&W=GUIDE_KEY=1356
This center "combines archeology, Amerindian culture, nature and adventure." Visitors become researchers in an interactive panorama or can view active archaeological digs in the summer.

Centre d'Interprétation de la Vie Urbaine de la Ville de Québec – Québec, QC [French only]
http://www.museocapitale.qc.ca/002.html
The center presents exhibits, walking tours and other educational programs focusing on urban life in Québec City from the past through today.

Chambly Canal National Historic Site – Chambly, QC [English & French]
http://parcscanada.risq.qc.ca/canaux/canal-de-chambly/aindex.html
Take an online tour of this historic canal along the Richelieu River, which was used extensively in the Québec forest products industry and exporting its products to the United States.

Links to Your Canadian Past
Québec

La Citadelle de Québec – Québec, QC [English & French]
http://www.qbc.clic.net/~citadel/
This "Gibraltar of America" tells the story of military history in Québec, including a visit to the 22nd Regiment Museum in a 1750's French powder magazine and an 1841 British military prison. Take a guided tour or watch one of the military ceremonies at the museum.

La **Cité de l'Or – Val d'Or, QC** [English & French]
http://www.lino.com/~laciteor/
A museum center and mining village at the site of Québec's richest gold mine, extending 300 feet underground. Photos of the village and mine site are available online.

Coteau-du-Lac National Historic Site – Coteau-du-Lac, QC [English & French]
http://parkscanada.pch.gc.ca/parks/quebec/coteau_lac/Coteau_lace.htm
The remains of the first lock canal in North America and defense structures, both of which were important to navigation and trade on the Saint Lawrence in the 18th and 19th centuries.

Domaine Joly-De Lotbinière – Sainte-Croix, QC [French only]
http://www.cmsq.qc.ca/domaine.htm
The manor house and grounds built in 1851 by Pierre-Gustave Joly adjoining the *seigneurie* of Lotbinière are a stunning example of the upper-class lifestyle of the mid to late 19th century.

École du Rang II d'Authier – Authier, QC [French only]
http://susan.chin.gc.ca:8016/BASIS/guide/user/search/DDW?M=1&U=1&W=GUIDE_KEY=1533
This rural schoolhouse, active from 1937 to 1958, presents a restored classroom, mistress' quarters, woodshed and latrines as well as many books used for instruction.

Links to Your Canadian Past
Québec

Forges du Saint-Maurice National Historic Site - Trois-Rivières, QC [English & French]
http://parkscanada.pch.gc.ca/parks/quebec/forges-st-maurice/forges-st-mauricee.htm
The interpretive center at the site of the birthplace of Canada's iron industry tells the story of the 18th and 19th century manufacturing techniques and the industry's impact on society.

Fort Chambly National Historic Site – Chambly, QC [English & French]
http://parkscanada.pch.gc.ca/parks/quebec/fort_chambly/fort_chamblye.htm
The restored and fortified remains of this French fort, built in 1709 on the site of two previous forts. Includes exhibits on the town of Chambly, the fort and artifacts from the previous forts.

Fort Lennox National Historic Site – Saint-Paul-de-l'Île-aux-Noix, QC [English & French]
http://parkscanada.pch.gc.ca/parks/quebec/fort_lennox/fort_lennoxe.htm
The present fort, built by the British between 1819 and 1829, is still intact and is an excellent example of 19th century military architecture.

Fort No. 1 at Pointe-de-Lévy National Historic Site – Lévis, QC [English & French]
http://parkscanada.pch.gc.ca/parks/quebec/fort_no1_pointe_levy/fort_no1_pointe_levye.htm
This fort is the only of three remaining forts built between 1865 and 1872 to guard against American invasion. Its pentagonal shape and view of Québec City add to its interest.

Links to Your Canadian Past
Québec

Fort Témiscamingue National Historic Site – Ville-Marie, QC
[English & French]
http://parkscanada.pch.gc.ca/parks/quebec/temiscamingue/temiscaminguee.htm
The site of an important fur trading post for over two hundred years.

Fortifications of Québec National Historic Site – Québec, QC
[English & French]
http://parcscanada.risq.qc.ca/fortifications_e/
An online tour is available of the 4.6 miles of walls, towers and other structures built from the 17th through the 19th centuries by both the French and English in the defense of Québec City. The fortifications make Québec the only city in North America designated as a UNESCO World Heritage site.

The Fur Trade at Lachine National Historic Site – Lachine, QC [English & French]
http://parkscanada.pch.gc.ca/parks/quebec/fourrure_lachine/fourrure_lachinee.htm
The only remaining Hudson's Bay Company warehouse in the Montréal area includes interactive exhibits on the fur trade in the 18th century at the departure point of many *voyageurs*.

Galerie Historique Lucienne-Maheux du Centre Hospitalier Robert Giffard – Beauport, QC [French only]
http://susan.chin.gc.ca:8016/BASIS/guide/user/search/DDW?M=1&U=1&W=GUIDE_KEY=1439
Exhibits and artifacts presenting the history of Québec's first psychiatric hospital, depicting the history and evolution of the hospital, its first patients and methods of treatment.

Links to Your Canadian Past
Québec

Grande-Gave National Historic Site – Gaspé, QC [English & French]
http://parkscanada.pch.gc.ca/parks/quebec/grande-grave/grande-gravee.htm
Six houses with outbuildings and two commercial buildings are all that remain of this abandoned fishing village typical of Gaspé fishing communities of the turn of the 20th century.

Grosse-Île and the Irish Memorial National Historic Site – Grosse-Île, QC [English & French]
http://parcscanada.risq.qc.ca/grosse_ile/
This site tells the story of Grosse-Île's role as the quarantine station for the port of Québec from 1832 to 1937. It also commemorates the hardships endured by many Irish immigrants. History, photographs and an online tour are available on the Web site.

L'Ilôt des Palais – Québec, QC [French only]
http://www.museocapitale.qc.ca/010.html
This museum is the site of the official residence of the Intendants of New France and the *Conseil Souverain*. Exhibits and artifacts from an archaeological dig of the first *Palais des Intendants* and a model of the site allow visitors to experience over 300 years of history of the city and this site.

Les Jardins de Métis – Grand-Métis, QC [English & French]
http://www.schoolnet.ca/collections/metis/
This Web site presents the history, activities and gardens of Les Jardins de Métis, one of Canada's most historic landscapes, built and tended by Elsie Reford, wife of the photographer Robert Wilson Reford, whose photos of the grounds can be seen online.

Links to Your Canadian Past
Québec

Lachine Canal National Historic Site – Montréal, QC [English & French]
http://parkscanada.pch.gc.ca/parks/quebec/canal_lachine/canal_lachinee.htm
This canal, first built in 1825, was important both in the navigation of the Saint Lawrence and the development of the city of Montréal.

Louis Hébert Monument – Québec, QC
http://www.geocities.com/Heartland/Ranch/6210/E4_F4_MON_HEBERT/E4monument.html
A description of the monument to Louis Hébert and the first families of New France, with photos and a transcription of the names on the monument's plaque.

Louis S. Saint Laurent National Historic Site – Compton, QC [English & French]
http://parcscanada.risq.qc.ca/st-laurent/en/
Photographs, history and an online tour of the birthplace of the former Prime Minister.

Maison du Colon – Ville-Marie, QC [French only]
http://susan.chin.gc.ca:8016/BASIS/guide/user/search/DDW?M=1&U=1&W=GUIDE_KEY=697
The oldest existing house in Ville-Marie, built in 1881, presents the history of the Témiscamingue region.

Maison Dumulon – Rouyn-Noranda, QC [French only]
http://susan.chin.gc.ca:8016/BASIS/guide/user/search/DDW?M=1&U=1&W=GUIDE_KEY=1641
This museum presents artifacts from the first general store in the town, as well as the town's former post office and objects from the Dumulon household from the beginning of the gold rush.

Links to Your Canadian Past
Québec

Maison Henry-Stuart – Québec, QC [French only]
http://www.cmsq.qc.ca/HenryStu.htm
A charming 19th century home in the middle of Québec City. The interior and gardens have been restored to their late 19th-early 20th century appearance.

Manoir Papineau National Historic Site – Montebello, QC [English & French]
- http://parkscanada.pch.gc.ca/parks/quebec/manoir_papineau/manoir_papineaue.htm
- http://w3.franco.ca/petite-nation/manoir.htm

The manor home of Louis-Joseph Papineau, political leader and *seigneur* of the Petite-Nation. The historic site recalls the seigniorial regime in the mid-1800's.

Missisquoi Museum – Stanbridge East, QC [English & French]
http://susan.chin.gc.ca:8016/BASIS/guide/user/search/DDW?M=1&U=1&W=GUIDE_KEY=1601
Three building make up this museum: The Cornell Mill (1830) houses artifacts presenting the history of Missisquoi County, Hodge's General Store is restored to its World War II-era appearance and the Annex houses a collection of farm implements and machinery.

Moulin Michel – Gentilly, QC [French only]
http://sites.cgocable.ca/crc/CRC_pgs/P_Organs/MoulinMi.htm
This restored flour mill stands on the site of one first built in 1739 for the *seigneurie* of Bécancour. Now an historic site, it still grinds grain and recalls the old seigniorial regime.

Links to Your Canadian Past
Québec

Moulin Seigneurial de Pointe-du-Lac – Pointe-du-Lac, QC
[French only]
http://sites.cgocable.ca/crc/CRC_pgs/P_Organs/MoulSeig.htm
This flour mill, which originally dates from the seigniorial regime in the province, together with a nearby sawmill recalls an important part of daily life in 18th and 19th century Québec.

Musée des Abénakis – Odanak, QC [French only]
http://susan.chin.gc.ca:8016/BASIS/guide/user/search/DDW?M=1&U=1&W=GUIDE_KEY=1250
Archaeological remains, tools, hides, manuscripts and other objects help tell the history of the Abenaki tribe and other native peoples of the province of Québec.

Musée Acadien du Québec à Bonaventure – Bonaventure, QC
[French only]
http://susan.chin.gc.ca:8016/BASIS/guide/user/search/DDW?M=1&U=1&W=GUIDE_KEY=1612
This museum depicts the history and culture of the Acadian refugees who came to Québec to settle after the expulsion and their contribution to Québec society. Includes photos.

Musée Amérindien de Mashteuiatsh – Mashteuiatsh, QC
[French only]
http://susan.chin.gc.ca:8016/BASIS/guide/user/search/DDW?M=1&U=1&W=GUIDE_KEY=1677
A center for the presentation, teaching, research and documentation of the Ilnuatsh culture.

Links to Your Canadian Past
Québec

Musée de l'Amérique Française – Québec, QC [English & French]
http://www.mcq.org/maf/aaindex.html
The collections and exhibits of the museum focus on the establishment and spread of the French culture in North America. Permanent exhibits include artifacts and documents relating to the settling of New France, collections of the *Séminaire du Québec* (the site of the museum) and an exhibit on the lives of Louis Hébert and the first settlers in Québec City.

Musée des Arts et Traditions Populaires du Québec - Trois-Rivières, QC
- http://susan.chin.gc.ca:8016/BASIS/guide/user/search/DDW?M=1&U=1&W=GUIDE_KEY=451
- [French only] http://sites.cgocable.ca/crc/CRC_pgs/P_Organs/MATPQ.htm

A museum entirely dedicated to the cultural heritage of Québec. It houses nearly 100,000 objects in its exhibits on the ethnology and archaeology of the province and also includes the old Trois-Rivières prison, with its exhibits on penitentiary life.

Musée de l'Aviation de Brousse – St-Georges-de-Champlain, QC [French only]
http://sites.cgocable.ca/crc/CRC_pgs/P_Organs/aviabrou.htm
This museum houses photographs, artifacts and exhibits relating to the history of bush pilots and commercial aviation in the Saint Maurice Valley region of Québec.

Links to Your Canadian Past
Québec

Musée du Bas-St-Laurent – Rivière-du-Loup, QC [French only]
http://susan.chin.gc.ca:8016/BASIS/guide/user/search/DDW?M=1&U=1&W=GUIDE_KEY=1576
The museum houses over 150,000 artifacts and ethnological objects from the region, as well as local and regional works of art. It also has an extensive collection of photographs of the region from 1894-1980 and houses the Société généalogique et historique du Rivière-du-Loup.

Musée J. Armand Bombardier – Valcourt, QC [English & French]
http://www.ucctech.com/museejab/
This museum is dedicated to the life and work of inventor and businessman J. Armand Bombardier. It also features extensive exhibits on the snowmobile industry in Québec.

Musée Bon-Pasteur – Vieux-Québec, QC [French only]
http://www.museocapitale.qc.ca/011.html
A museum dedicated to the history and works of the *Servantes du Coeur Immaculé de Marie,* known as the *Soeurs du Bon-Pasteur de Québec.* This order was founded in 1850 by Marie Fitzbach, a native of Québec.

Musée de Charlevoix – La Malbaie/Pointe-au-Pic, QC [French only]
http://susan.chin.gc.ca:8016/BASIS/guide/user/search/DDW?M=1&U=1&W=GUIDE_KEY=1218
This museum presents the ethnographic and social history of the region and also mounts exhibits on local and regional arts and crafts.

Links to Your Canadian Past
Québec

Musée du Château de Ramezay – Montréal, QC [French only]
http://susan.chin.gc.ca:8016/BASIS/guide/user/search/DDW?M=1&U=1&W=GUIDE_KEY=1284
The history of Montréal and the entire province is displayed in the historical setting of the former residence of the governor of Québec, built in the 18th century.

Musée Colby-Curtis – Stanstead, QC [French only]
http://susan.chin.gc.ca:8016/BASIS/guide/user/search/DDW?M=1&U=1&W=GUIDE_KEY=975
Exhibits in this museum depict life on the international border between the 18th century and the 1940's and provide a glimpse at daily life in the Eastern Townships during the Victorian era.

Musée des Filles de Jésus
See Archives.

Musée du Fjord – La Baie, QC [French only]
http://susan.chin.gc.ca:8016/BASIS/guide/user/search/DDW?M=1&U=1&W=GUIDE_KEY=1505
An ethno-history museum presenting exhibitions focusing on the maritime and land-based history of the Saguenay fjord. The museum also presents the history of the town of La Baie.

Musée François-Pilote – La Pocatière, QC [French only]
http://www.kam.qc.ca/quoi/musees/mfranpilote/mfp00.html
Take a virtual visit to this four-story museum presenting the history of rural Québec. Exhibits include maple sugaring, agricultural teaching, horse-drawn transportation, reconstructed business offices, rooms from a bourgeois household and a reconstructed farmer's home.

Links to Your Canadian Past
Québec

Musée de Guérin – Guérin, QC [French only]
http://susan.chin.gc.ca:8016/BASIS/guide/user/search/DDW?M=1&U=1&W=GUIDE_KEY=1385
Agricultural, religious and domestic objects from the colonial period are on display in the community's old rectory, church and a restored home.

Musée Historique des Soeurs de l'Assomption – Nicolet, QC [French only]
http://susan.chin.gc.ca:8016/BASIS/guide/user/search/DDW?M=1&U=1&W=GUIDE_KEY=1648
View online photos of this museum, which focuses on the history and daily life of the Sisters of Assumption, a teaching community founded at Saint-Grégoire de Nicolet.

Musée des Hospitalières de l'Hôtel-Dieu de Montréal – Montréal, QC [English & French]
http://susan.chin.gc.ca:8016/BASIS/guide/user/search/DDW?M=1&U=1&W=GUIDE_KEY=1070
This museum presents the intertwined histories of the city of Montréal and the Hôtel-Dieu hospital from their beginnings in the 17th century through the development of the city.

Musée de Kamouraska – Kamouraska, QC [French only]
http://susan.chin.gc.ca:8016/BASIS/guide/user/search/DDW?M=1&U=1&W=GUIDE_KEY=1525
The history of Kamouraska and the surrounding region is presented through old clothes and textiles, artifacts of the fishing, navigation and agricultural industries and religious communities.

Links to Your Canadian Past
Québec

Musée de Lachine – Lachine, QC [French only]
http://www.cum.qc.ca/LACHINE/fr/musee.htm
In addition to permanent exhibits on the furniture, accessories and tools of 19th century Québec and photographs and objects relating to the town's waterfront history, the museum also presents temporary exhibits of historical artifacts and local and regional architecture, artwork and crafts.

Musée Laurier – Victoriaville, QC [French only]
- http://sites.cgocable.ca/crc/CRC_pgs/P_Organs/mulaurie.htm
- http://susan.chin.gc.ca:8016/BASIS/guide/user/search/DDW?M=1&U=1&W=GUIDE_KEY=1675

The restored home of Sir Wilfrid Laurier, including many authentic pieces of furniture and other objects belonging to Laurier and his family.

Musée Maison Saint-Gabriel – Montréal, QC [French only]
http://susan.chin.gc.ca:8016/BASIS/guide/user/search/DDW?M=1&U=1&W=GUIDE_KEY=846
Located in an historic 17th century home, this museum presents the cultural, social and religious history of the province of Québec.

Musée Maritime du Québec, Inc. – L'Islet-sur-Mer, QC
[French only]
http://susan.chin.gc.ca:8016/BASIS/guide/user/search/DDW?M=1&U=1&W=GUIDE_KEY=1598
The maritime history of the Saint Lawrence is presented not only in the waterfront museum building, but also with the icebreaker Ernest Lapointe, the hydrofoil Bras d'Or 400 and a beautiful maritime park along the river.

Links to Your Canadian Past
Québec

Musée Marius-Barbeau – St-Joseph-de-Beauce, QC [French only]
http://susan.chin.gc.ca:8016/BASIS/guide/user/search/DDW?M=1&U=1&W=GUIDE_KEY=485
This regional museum dedicated to Beauce County and the surrounding area contains exhibits on the historical, ethnological, artistic and religious life in the region.

Musée McCord Museum – Montréal, QC [English & French]
http://www.musee-mccord.qc.ca/
Objects, archives and photographs depicting the history of Canada, Montréal and Québec from the 18th century to the present. Collections include ethnology and archaeology objects; paintings, prints and drawings; decorative arts; costumes and textiles; photographic and textual archives.

Musée de la Mer – Îles-de-la-Madeleine, QC [French only]
http://susan.chin.gc.ca:8016/BASIS/guide/user/search/DDW?M=1&U=1&W=GUIDE_KEY=1387
Exhibits presenting the maritime and francophone culture and history of these islands.

Musée Pierre-Boucher - Trois-Rivières, QC [French only]
http://sites.cgocable.ca/crc/CRC_pgs/P_Organs/mupierbo.htm
In addition to presenting works of art by local and provincial artists, the Musée Pierre-Boucher also presents changing exhibits on history and ethnography in its role as a regional museum.

Musée du Québec – Québec, QC [English & French]
http://www.mdq.org/fr/
The province's fine arts museum contains over 20,000 works of art, most of which were created in Québec from its origins through today. As such, it is a visual record of the creative and cultural history of the province. Includes a Library/Documentation Center and Archives.

Links to Your Canadian Past
Québec

Musée Régional de la Côte-Nord – Sept-Îles, QC [French only]
http://www.bbsi.net/mrcn/francais.htm
The permanent exhibit *Un Rivage Sans Fin* ("An Endless Coastline") traces the socio-economic history of the Côte-Nord region in its daily life and major events in its development. Other exhibits focus on the ethnological and archaeological aspects and local art of the region.

Musée Régional des Mines de Malaric – Malaric, QC [English & French]
http://www.lino.com/~museem/
Focusing primarily on minerals and geology, this museum also presents exhibits on the mining industry and the social and cultural life of the men and women who worked the region's mines.

Musée Régional de Rimouski – Rimouski, QC
http://www.museerimouski.qc.ca/
In addition to presenting the works of local, provincial and national artists, this museum also stages exhibits on society, culture and history.

Musée Régional de Vaudreuil-Soulanges – Vaudreuil-Dorion, QC [French only]
http://susan.chin.gc.ca:8016/BASIS/guide/user/search/DDW?M=1&U=1&W=GUIDE_KEY=1413
Focusing on the seigniorial life in old Québec under the French Regime, this museum presents artifacts, such as objects from domestic life, tools and completed works from traditional trades and objects relating to agriculture, clothing, food and shelter.

Musée des Religions – Nicolet, QC [French only]
http://www.itr.qc.ca/~religion/
A number of permanent and temporary exhibitions delve into various aspects of the world's main religions and their traditions, practices and followers in the province of Québec.

Links to Your Canadian Past
Québec

Musée des Soeurs Grises – Montréal, QC [French only]
http://www.sgm.qc.ca/centre/museemy.htm
A museum dedicated to the life and works of Marguerite d'Youville, founder of the Sisters of Charity, known in French as the *Soeurs Grises*.

Musée "Souvenir d'Autrefois" – St-Tite, QC [French only]
http://www.mauricie.net/musees/autrefois/
Dedicated to the hardworking men and women who were the pioneers of this region and cleared its land for future settlement, this museum set in a former residence presents "memories of the past," including the bedroom where 12 children were born, the kitchen where all their meals were cooked, original furniture handmade by our ancestors and old books and toys.

Musée Stewart au Fort de l'Île Sainte-Hélène – Île Sainte-Hélène, QC [English & French]
http://www.mlink.net/~stewart/index.html
The discovery, exploration and development of New France and North America and Canada's relationships with the European cultures from which it was born are presented at the Stewart Museum. The museum houses five collections: the history collection, household objects, antique arms, science and technology and the library collection.

Musée des Ursulines – Trois-Rivières, QC [French only]
- http://sites.cgocable.ca/crc/CRC_pgs/P_Organs/musursul.htm
- http://susan.chin.gc.ca:8016/BASIS/guide/user/search/DDW?M=1&U=1&W=GUIDE_KEY=506

This museum, located in Trois-Rivières' first hospital, presents exhibits on the daily and cultural life of the community of the Ursuline sisters and town of Trois-Rivières.

Links to Your Canadian Past
Québec

Musée de la Ville de Lachine – Lachine, QC [French only]
http://susan.chin.gc.ca:8016/BASIS/guide/user/search/DDW?M=1&U=1&W=GUIDE_KEY=1509
Located in an old fur trading post, this museum presents furniture, textiles, personal objects and correspondence and Amerindian artifacts as well as local and regional works of art.

Museum of Civilization in Québec City – Québec, QC [English & French]
http://www.mcq.org/english/index.html
Extensive permanent and temporary exhibitions on the human history and development of Québec as a society. Includes exhibits on First Nations, pioneer life and artifacts and exhibits on cultures and societies outside the province.

National Battlefield Park (Plains of Abraham) – QC [English & French]
http://futurix.clic.net/com/ccbn/
The site of infamous battles between Montcalm and Wolfe and Lévis and Murray, the National Battlefields Park now houses an interpretive center that presents a multimedia show on the history of the Plains of Abraham and two Martello towers with historic and scientific exhibits.

Naval Museum of Québec – Québec, QC [English & French]
http://www.navreshq.queb.dnd.ca/an/museum.htm
Discover the naval history of Québec City and the Saint Lawrence River, from the Naval Reserve and the Battle of the Saint Lawrence to the role of the Navy in World War II.

Links to Your Canadian Past
Québec

Old Port of Québec Interpretation Centre – Québec, QC
[English & French]
http://parcscanada.risq.qc.ca/oport/
The interpretation center presents the history and importance of the port of Québec, especially in the 19th century during a boom in the commercial shipping and shipbuilding industries. This Web site presents an online visit to the Old Port as well as its history and a photo gallery.

Parc de l'Aventure Basque en Amérique - Trois-Pistoles, QC
[French only]
http://www.icrdl.net/~basques/paba.htm
The permanent exhibitions at the park focus on the history of Basque whaling in the area, with artifacts from the archaeological digs on the facing Île-aux-Basques. The park also hosts various cultural events and productions and contains two 19th century houses with exhibits.

Phonothèque Québécoise/Musée du Son – Montréal, QC
[French only]
http://www.mcc.gouv.qc.ca/pamu/organis/pq/phono.htm
The objectives of this organization are to preserve, document and make accessible the audio heritage of Québec. It collects musical and spoken recordings and playback/recording devices. The Phonothèque also re-issues restored recordings and produces original work.

Place-Royale – Québec, QC [English & French]
http://www.mcq.org/place_royale/aaindex.html
This historic square, which began as a market in the heart of the Lower Town of Québec City, is commonly called the "birthplace of French America" and is one of the oldest districts in North America. This Web site presents its history, places to visit and upcoming activities.

Links to Your Canadian Past
Québec

Plains of Abraham
See National Battlefield Park.

Pointe-à-Callière, Montréal Museum of Archaeology and History – Montréal, QC [English & French]
http://musee-Pointe-a-Calliere.qc.ca/
Located on the site where Father Vimont celebrated mass at the founding of Montréal, the museum preserves architectural structures and artifacts discovered on site, at the nearby Place Royale and throughout Montréal.

Pointe-au-Père Lighthouse National Historic Site – Pointe-au-Père, QC [English & French]
http://parkscanada.pch.gc.ca/parks/quebec/phare-pointe-pere/phare-pointe-peree.htm
This lighthouse, built in 1909 is the second highest in Canada. It is the third lighthouse to be built at this strategic location along the Saint Lawrence River.

Powerscourt Covered Bridge – Elgin/Hinchinbrooke, QC
http://www.rocler.qc.ca/aqk/percy.htm
The oldest covered bridge in Québec and second oldest in all of Canada.

La Pulperie de Chicoutimi – Chicoutimi, QC [French only]
http://www.reseau.qc.ca/pulperie.htm
A restored paper mill depicting the history of paper production and the town of Chicoutimi. Includes a sawmill, 1921 factory and historic circuit showing all aspects of production.

Links to Your Canadian Past
Québec

Québec – Repertory of Commemorative Monuments of Québec City [French, English intro]
http://www.rescol.ca/collections/quebec/
An online presentation of the many statues and monuments found in Québec City. Each monument is presented with an historic text and information on the artist, monuments construction and materials and conservation efforts.

Québec Expérience – Québec, QC [French only]
http://www.museocapitale.qc.ca/020.html
A special effects show on the history of Québec from the arrival of the first explorers up to today. The experience also includes a workshop theater production on various elements of the province's history, including Amerindian life and legends, day-to-day life in New France, the English regime, the life of fur traders, democracy and more.

Sainte-Anne-de-Bellevue Canal National Historic Site – Sainte-Anne, QC [English & French]
http://parcscanada.risq.qc.ca/canaux/canal-de-ste-anne/aindex.html
Opened in 1843, this canal was an integral part of commercial navigation on the Montréal-Ottawa-Kingston inland shipping route. A picture gallery, heritage information and an online tour are all available at this Web site.

Saint-Ours Canal National Historic Site – Saint-Ours, QC [English & French]
http://parcscanada.risq.qc.ca/canaux/canal-de-st-ours/aindex.html
Take an online tour of this canal, opened in 1849 as an extension of the Chambly canal.

Links to Your Canadian Past
Québec

Sir George-Étienne Cartier National Historic Site – Montréal, QC [English & French]
http://parkscanada.pch.gc.ca/parks/quebec/george_e_cartier/george_e_cartiere.htm
Visit the 1848-1871 home of this father of confederation and major player in the transcontinental railway system. Exhibits focus on Cartier's life and work in Victorian Canada.

Sir Wilfrid Laurier National Historic Site – Ville des Laurentides, QC [English & French]
http://parkscanada.pch.gc.ca/parks/quebec/wilfrid_laurier/wilfrid_lauriere.htm
This site, in Laurier's boyhood hometown, not only recalls his life and career as prime minister, but also the traditions of small-town life in the mid 1800's.

Site Historique du Banc-de-Paspébiac – Paspébiac, QC [French only]
http://daryl.chin.gc.ca:8000/BASIS/guide/user/search/DDW?M=1&U=1&W=GUIDE_KEY=1480
This historic site features eleven buildings formerly belonging to the two largest companies from the Jersey Islands: Robin and Boutillier Brothers.

Site Historique de la Maison Lamontagne – Rimouski-Est, QC [French only]
http://susan.chin.gc.ca:8016/BASIS/guide/user/search/DDW?M=1&U=1&W=GUIDE_KEY=1430
A typical home in the architectural style of the French Regime, decorated with authentic objects from the 18th and 19th centuries.

Links to Your Canadian Past
Québec

Site Historique *T.E. Draper*/Les Chantier Gédéon – Angliers, QC [French only]
http://susan.chin.gc.ca:8016/BASIS/guide/user/search/DDW?M=1&U=1&W=GUIDE_KEY=703
Climb on board the boat *T.E. Draper* to experience first-hand the history of lumber transportation on the Témiscamingue. Visit an exhibition space and a sawmill presenting the life of lumberjacks and woodcutters in the 1930's and 40's.

Société d'Histoire de Buckingham – Buckingham, QC [French only]
http://ppp.atreide.net/infocomm/Shb-f.htm
No information on the society beyond its postal address, but a list of 23 historic sites and buildings throughout the town, with links to information capsules on each site.

Tamis de Bois et Jambières de Laine: Traditions Toujours Présentes des Premières Nations du Canada
http://www.xist.com/ROM-MCQ/F/index.htm
An online presentation of traditional Amerindian tools, utensils and everyday objects from the 18th century through today, divided into three categories: Objects made solely from traditional materials, objects made with materials obtained by trade and contemporary objects.

Village du Bûcheron / Lumberjack's Village – Grandes-Piles, QC [English & French]
http://www.villagebucheron.qc.ca/
A visit to this re-created early 20th century lumberjack camp will help you relive the history of La Mauricie and the many villages and towns that sprung up along the St-Maurice River because of the forestry and logging industry.

Links to Your Canadian Past
Québec

Virtual Museum of New France – online [English & French]
http://www.civilization.ca/mnf/mnfeng.html
An online presentation of the French exploration of North America and the founding and development of New France. Sections of this Web site include Collections, Adventures, People, Exhibitions, The Explorers, Maps, Timeline and a Glossary.

Government and Professional Organizations

Amis et Propriétaires des Maisons Anciennes du Québec – Montréal, QC [French only]
http://www.mcc.gouv.qc.ca/pamu/organis/apmaq/apmaq.htm
This society, the Friends and Owners of Historic Houses of Québec, seeks to unite these two groups to exchange information and experiences and promote historic preservation.

Association des Archéologues du Québec – Québec, QC
[French only]
http://www.archeologie.qc.ca/
A professional organization for archaeologists working in Québec. The AAQ seeks to promote archaeological work in the province and the development of scientific research. An online bulletin is available, as are the society's press releases and list of publications.

Association Québécoise pour le Patrimoine Industriel – Montréal, QC [French only]
http://www.mcc.gouv.qc.ca/pamu/organis/aqpi/aqpi.htm
The AQPI seeks to promote the study, understanding, conservation and importance of Québec's industrial heritage. The association works towards the restoration of buildings, machines, artifacts and archival materials, publishes research and organizes conferences and exhibitions.

Links to Your Canadian Past
Québec

Centre de Conservation du Québec – Québec, QC [English & French]
http://www.ccq.mcc.gouv.qc.ca/anglais/aindex.htm
A government institution ensuring the collection and conservation of the province's cultural heritage. The center offers services to museums and heritage institutions, including conservation assessment and work, education, training and communications.

Conseil des Monuments et Sites du Québec – Québec, QC [French only]
http://www.cmsq.qc.ca/
A group of institutions and individuals dedicated to preserving Québec's heritage sites. The CMSQ targets architectural, natural, industrial and scientific sites for preservation, publishes the journal *Coninuité* and other publications, educates the public and professionals and manages several historic sites in the province.

Regroupement des Institutions Muséales de la Région de Québec – Québec, QC [French only]
http://www.museocapitale.qc.ca/index.html
An alliance of museums in the greater Québec City region whose main focus is to bring dynamic and interactive learning experiences to students.

La Société des Musées Québécois [French only]
http://www.unites.uqam.ca/musees/
An association of institutions and individuals who work in the museum field in Québec or are interested in the development of museological professions. The society promotes museum standards and practices, offers professional training, acts as a communications network among institutions and between its members and the public, and lobbies on behalf of museums.

Links to Your Canadian Past
Québec

Military, Native and Historic Groups

The Carignan-Salières Regiment
Carignan-Salières Lineage Regiment
http://fp-www.wwnet.net/~dulongj/Carignan.htm
Background information on the regiment, with a link to a well-done chart showing the "lineage" of the regiment – its origin, composition, evolution, commanders and service.

Carignan-Salières Regiment Soldiers and Officers
http://users.deltanet.com/~ms900/Kings/soldiers.html
The roll of the Carignan-Salières Regiment, showing each man's name, rank, company and dit name, where known. Cross-referenced for spelling variations.

Le Régiment Carignan-Salières [French only]
http://www.geocities.com/Heartland/Plains/6889/
A French-language overview of the regiment, including a brief look at its origins, the makeup of the headquarters staff, a list of officers whose company is not known and men killed in 1666.

Roll of the Carignan-Salières Regiment, 1668
http://www.geocities.com/Heartland/Ranch/6210/E3rollcarignan.html
This list, not a complete roll of soldiers in the regiment, is of those men who elected to remain in Canada in 1668. It is taken from a microfilmed copy of a handwritten list from the French "Archives des Colonies." A copy is available at the National Archives of Canada.

Links to Your Canadian Past
Québec

Ships of the Carignan-Salières Regiment
http://www.geocities.com/Heartland/Ranch/6210/E9nav_car.html
Brief information on the seven ships involved in transporting the regiment to New France: the *Joyeux Siméon, Paix, Aigle d'Or, Saint Sébastien, Justice, Jardin de Hollande* and *Brèse*. Link to a page with more information on the *Brèse* and photos of a scale model of the ship.

La Société des Filles du Roi et Soldats du Carignan, Inc. – Merrick, NY (USA)
http://users.deltanet.com/~ms900/Kings/member.html
A society dedicated to the research and history of the Carignan-Salières Regiment and the women who came to New France as "Filles du Roi." Membership is open to those who are direct descendants or who are just interested in these two groups.

Les Filles du Roi / The King's Daughters

800 Filles à Marier ("800 Marriageable Girls") [French only]
http://205.205.229.3/documents/nouvfrance/article15.html
An article from the newspaper *Le Soleil* that seems to put to rest the question of whether they were courageous pioneers of Québec or questionable outcasts of France.

Les Filles du Roi [French only]
http://www.cam.org/~cdrgduq/filles.html
A brief article in French which seeks to dispel the notion that *filles du roi = filles de joie*.

Links to Your Canadian Past
Québec

Origins of the Filles du Roi
http://204.50.177.183/roots/fillesdu.htm
Several tables, showing the King's Daughters that came from various regions of France, with marriage date and place and name of husband. Lists include Girls from Noble Families, Girls Who "Had Second Thoughts" Before Finally Getting Married and Girls from Île-de-France, Normandy, Other Locations and Unknown Origins. Some links to further genealogical data.

Les Filles du Roy (Musée Virtuel de la Nouvelle-France)
- http://www.mvnf.muse.digital.ca/popul/filles/s-fil-en.htm
- [same site] http://www.vmnf.civilization.ca/popul/filles/s-fil-en.htm

An online presentation from the Virtual Museum of New France on the history of the King's Daughters, with sample images and documents concerning these women.

Il Était Une Fois...Les Filles Venues de France [French only]
http://www.mcq.org/histoire/filles_du_roi/lettre.html
An online presentation by the Musée de la Civilisation du Québec on the history of the Filles du Roi. Follow their story through period documents, beginning with a letter from Intendant Talon to Mgr. Colbert, including several images of documents and artwork concerning these women.

The King's Daughters/Les Filles du Roy
http://members.mint.net/frenchcx/filleroi.htm
An article by Robert Chenard on the need for and background of the King's Daughters. This article originally appeared in the newspapers *Morning Sentinel* and Kennebec *Daily Journal*.

Links to Your Canadian Past
Québec

"Louis Hébert: A Legacy of Tenacity" – The Filles du Roi [English & French]
http://seeds.history.ca/~seeds/episodes/episode-0401/sidebar.html
Historical background for this episode of the History Television series "A Scattering of Seeds: The Creation of Canada."

Repertory of the Filles du Roi
http://users.deltanet.com/~ms900/Kings/daughters.html
An alphabetical list of the Filles du Roi, with marriage date and husband's name.

La Société des Filles du Roi et Soldats du Carignan, Inc.
See Military, Native and Historic Groups / The Carignan-Salières Regiment.

First Nations and Native Groups

Centre de Référence Lithique du Québec [French only]
http://www3.sympatico.ca/crlq/C.R.L.Q.html
The Québec Lithic Reference Center studies the use of stones in pre-historic Amerindian culture for the fabrication of tools and weapons. This site presents the different types of stones used and their distribution throughout the province.

Cree Nation of Mistissini
http://NATION.MISTISSINI.QC.CA/
Here you'll find information on the geography, culture and history, nature, tourism and council of the Cree Nation of Mistissini and a link to a virtual tour of this area of northern Québec.

Genealogy of Québec's Native People and Francophone Métis
http://www.cam.org/~beaur/gen/amerin-e.html
A brief introduction to common sources and problems in native genealogy in Québec, along with a brief bibliography of research materials.

Links to Your Canadian Past
Québec

Grand Council of the Crees
http://www.gcc.ca/
Sections of this official site include Overview of the Crees, News and Headlines, Cree Communities, Cree Culture, Environmental Issues, Political Issues and Education.

Listuguj First Nation
http://www.johnco.com/firstnat/listuguj.html
Brief information on the Cultural Centre and other aspects of this Mi'gmaq First Nation.

Micmac History
http://www.dickshovel.com/mic.html
An informative and thorough look at the history of the Micmac people of Québec and the Maritime Provinces. The author welcomes comments and corrections.

Micmac Nation of Gespeg [English & French]
http://www.gaspesie.qc.ca/gespeg/
This site, from a Gaspé Peninsula native group, provides information on "The Micmac Way of Life," "The Knowledge of the Micmacs," "At Gespeg in the Year 1675" and other information.

The Mi'kmaq Story
http://sae.ca/abt/micmac/micmac09.html
An overview of the customs, history and traditions of this tribe.

Mohawk Nation Council of Chiefs
http://www.slic.com/~mohawkna/home.html
This page for the administrative agency of eight Mohawk territories in the province includes press releases, information on a Mohawk school and magazine and making genealogy requests.

Links to Your Canadian Past
Québec

The Native Trail [English & French]
http://www.autochtones.com/
An online information resource for the First Nations and Inuit in Québec. The site is broken down into Information, Tourism, First Nations, Youth and Arts & Handicrafts. This site also features a chat room and a collection of links to native sites throughout Canada.

Oujé-Bougoumou Cree Nation
http://www.ouje.ca/
Learn about the history of Oujé-Bougoumou, "The Road to Self-Reliance" and other aspects of this innovative village, or watch QuickTimeVR moveable panoramic photos of the village.

Québec's Northern Cree
http://arcticcircle.uconn.edu/HistoryCulture/Cree/
Several articles, maps, tribal and Canadian government policies and agreements about the Cree of northern Québec.

Tribes and Bands of Québec
http://www.hanksville.org/sand/contacts/tribal/QU.html
Contact information and links to Web pages (where available) for various native groups throughout the province of Québec, with links to other provinces and the U.S.

Other Military and Historic Groups
1755 – The French and Indian War Home Page
http://web.syr.edu/~laroux/index.html
This site contains a list of French soldiers from the Languedoc, La Reine, Guyenne, Bearn, Royal Roussillon, La Sarre, and Berry regiments; a bibliography of reference sources; places to visit; description of a work in progress on the war and a "document of the month."

Links to Your Canadian Past
Québec

1837 Les Patriotes [French only]
http://www.1837.qc.ca/
This site, on the Patriote movement of 1837-38, includes sections on a chronology of the period, the battles, condemned prisoners, the historical context of the movement, historical texts and writings of Louis-Joseph Papineau and others associated with the Parti Patriote.

22nd Regiment
See Museums and Historic Sites / La Citadelle de Québec

78th Fraser Highlanders
http://www.mlink.net/~stewart/fraser1.htm
Information on the history of this regiment, which was raised in Scotland, saw action in Québec on the Plains of Abraham and now lives on through a group of historical re-enactors.

Canadian Grenadier Guards
http://www.cgg.ca/
This military unit, stationed at Montréal, was first formed in 1764 for the defense of Canada, making it the nation's oldest military unit. This site presents its history and current activities.

Compagnie Franche de la Marine
- http://www.navreshq.queb.dnd.ca/an/compfran.htm
- *See also United States / Museums and Historic Sites and Groups*

A re-enactment company, commemorating the original Compagnie Franche de la Marine sent to New France in the 17th century. Demonstrations of period maneuvers are performed in summer.

Links to Your Canadian Past
Québec

Compagnie Franche de la Marine de Montréal [French only]
http://www.colba.net/~senkara/
This re-enactment unit presents a photo gallery of their uniforms, re-enactments and activities, as well as an informative history of the original company that came to defend New France.

Milice de Chambly [English & French]
http://www.multi-medias.ca/Milice_Chambly/Jeanplam/
A re-enactment unit participating in living history demonstrations of the militia and civilians living in and around Fort Chambly in the period of the French Regime.

Militia Captains in 1776, District of Québec City
http://www.geocities.com/Heartland/Ranch/6210/E13capitain.html
A transcript of a roll drawn up by the British military government. The table shows the name of each parish, captain in charge, married men, single men, totals and notes.

Les Patriotes de 1837-38 [French only]
http://www.er.uqam.ca/nobel/k14664/pat1.htm
A comprehensive site on the Parti Patriote and the events leading up to and during the Rebellion of 1837-38 against the British government of Québec. This site includes a chronology of preceding events, details of battles, biographies of key players, an atlas of maps covering the period and conflict, pertinent documents, a bibliography of sources and more.

Royal Roussillon Regiment [French only]
http://ww.total.net/~patgal/Geneo/rrintro.htm
A list of compiled military and genealogical data on the members of this regiment from the French and Indian War. Some information is sparse, while other entries include notarized records, names of children, parents, etc.

Links to Your Canadian Past
Québec

Sorel Company Roll, 1760
http://www.geocities.com/Heartland/Ranch/6210/E2sorel1760.html
The roll of this company that started out as part of the Carignan-Salières Regiment, as taken from a microfilm at the National Archives of Canada and augmented with further data.

Troupes de Marine Françaises [French only]
- **17th & 18th Centuries:** http://tdm.vo.qc.ca/histoire/hist002.htm
- **Organization from 1622-1900:**
  http://tdm.vo.qc.ca/histoire/hist003.htm

These two history pages, from a French site about the *Troupes de Marine*, present the European view of these troops during the first two colonial empires and the overall organizations of the troops from their inception to the beginning of the 20th century.

Veterans of the War of 1812
http://www.geocities.com/Heartland/Ranch/6210/1812/E12_1812.html
A list of veterans living on the south shore of Montréal in 1875 who received a pension of $20. The table includes each man's name, ages in 1812 and 1875, home and militia battalion.

Provincial and Local History and Photos

Ancêtres et Histoire [French only]
http://www.genealogie.org/histoire.htm
Sections of this site (part of the Centre de Généalogie Francophone d'Amérique) include Our Ancestors and Their Descendants, History of North America, Parish Histories and a link to the Parchemin database. To access everything but Parchemin, you'll have to register for free with the CGFA. Click on "Devenir Membre" in the lower right corner of the page.

Links to Your Canadian Past
Québec

Nouvelle-France: La Grande Aventure [French only]
http://205.205.229.3/documents/nouvfrance/
A series of articles from the newspaper *Le Soleil* on many of the people, places and events that helped shape the colony of New France.

Timelines / Historical Overviews

A Brief History of New France
http://www.canoe.ca/InDepthUnity/newfrance.html
Brief is the operative word here. A more apt title would be "A Brief History of the Fall of New France," with a look at the first years of British rule over the colony.

Chronologie Historique des Femmes du Québec [French only]
http://pages.infinit.net/histoire/femmes.html
This Historical Chronology of Québec Women is broken down into seven time periods from 1608 until today. Links to other articles, maps, calendars and resources.

Chronologie Historique du Québec [French only]
http://pages.infinit.net/histoire/
A very thorough and easy-to-navigate site on the history of New France/Québec. A left-hand column gives access to major historical events, while the actual abridged but informative accounts link to maps, calendars and other documents relating to the event in question. Includes an index, bibliography and list of Intendants, Governors and Bishops of Québec.

Facts on Canada – Québec
http://www.infocan.gc.ca/facts/quebec-e.html
A brief overview of the history, people, geography and economy of Québec.

Links to Your Canadian Past
Québec

Headlines: Virtual Museum of New France
http://www.vmnf.civilization.ca/une/p-une-en.htm
These historical vignettes are presented as "headlines" from a hypothetical newspaper covering some of the major events in the history of New France from 1604 to 1733.

Histoire du Québec et de l'Acadie [French only]
http://www.total.net/~jtrudel/histoire.htm
A timeline of historical events that occurred in, affected or were produced by people from Québec or Acadia. These events are browseable by time period, place or type of event.

The History of Québec in a Few Paragraphs
http://www.cam.org/~beaur/gen/qcgeog-e.html
Scroll past the geographical information to find this overview of Québec history, written by Denis Beauregard, webmaster of the Francogene site (*See Societies/Online Directories, etc.*)

Un Nouveau Régime: 1760-1867 [French only]
http://www.msq.qc.ca/divers/nregim.html
A brief synopsis of the major events that occurred in this time period in Québec history. Follows the timeline *La Nouvelle France: 1534-1760*, below.

Links to Your Canadian Past
Québec

La Nouvelle-France, Le Bas Canada and Québec [English & French]
- **Nouvelle-France, 1524-1763**:
  http://www3.sympatico.ca/cousture/NVFR2.HTM
- **Bas Canada, 1763-1867**:
  http://www3.sympatico.ca/cousture/BAS2.HTM
- **Québec, 1867-Today**:
  http://www3.sympatico.ca/cousture/QUEB2.HTM

Three timelines, summarizing major historical events that occurred in or shaped the present-day province of Québec from colonization through the French Regime, after the surrender to the British until the Confederation of Canada and post-Confederation history.

La Nouvelle-France: 1534-1760 [French only]
http://www.msq.qc.ca/divers/nfrance.html
A timeline of the major events the contributed to the founding, settlement and development of New France and the French Regime in North America. The timeline continues with *Un Nouveau Régime: 1760-1867*, above.

Exploration, Immigration and Settlement
Acadiens au Québec [French only]
http://www.game-master.com/jleblanc/acad-q.htm
This site examines the Acadian presence in Québec, from the immigration of refugees in the 18th century through the development and contribution of those of Acadian origin in the province. This examination is broken down into the various urban and regional areas of Québec.

Les Basques, Chasseurs de Baleines [French only]
http://www.icrdl.net/~basques/paba1.htm
This brief article takes a look at the presence of Basque fishermen and whalers in the waters off Newfoundland and the estuary of the Saint Lawrence in the 16th century.

Links to Your Canadian Past
Québec

Bibliographie sur la Mobilité au Canada Français [French only – list]
http://mistral.ere.umontreal.ca/~larinr/biblimig.html
This "Bibliography on Mobility in French Canada" presents a list of books dealing with population movements, mobility, family migrations, colonization and family networks.

Les Explorateurs Français et Canadiens [French only]
http://www.nouvellefrance.qc.ca/histoire.htm
Brief biographical information, in the form of timelines, on Nicollet, Des Groseilliers, Radisson, Jolliet, La Salle, La Vérendrye and short entries for other notables of New France.

The Force of Hope: The Legacy of Father McGauran [English & French]
http://seeds.history.ca/~seeds/episodes/episode-0121/index.html
A description of this episode of the History Television series "A Scattering of Seeds: The Creation of Canada," dealing with the Irish immigration during the potato famine of 1847 and the immigrants' arrival and trials at the quarantine station at Grosse-Île. This site presents information on the role of fellow Irish immigrant Father Bernard McGauran and background on the Irish immigration to Canada.

French-Canadian Immigration (from **"Louis Hébert: A Legacy of Tenacity"**)
http://seeds.history.ca/~seeds/episodes/episode-0401/history1.html
Historical background from this episode of the History Television series "A Scattering of Seeds: The Creation of Canada." Follow the next several pages, which present Obstacles and Beyond, Legacy and Related Books.

Links to Your Canadian Past
Québec

Grosse-Île
- **Grosse-Île at a Glance**:
  http://parcscanada.risq.qc.ca/grosse_ile/glance_e.html
- **Grosse-Île History**:
  http://parcscanada.risq.qc.ca/grosse_ile/frame_history_e.html

Grosse-Île at a Glance takes you on a virtual visit of the island and its various monuments and structures, explaining the significance, origin and use of each. Grosse-Île History is broken down into the sections The Evolution of the Historic Role of Grosse-Île, 1847...A Year of Tragedy and Statistics & More Statistics.

L'Immigration en Nouvelle-France Sous le Régime Français [French only]
http://www.jctca.com/jct/Immigration/index.html
An essay on immigration to the colony of New France under the French Regime, written by Jean-Claude Trottier, a graduate student in history at the University of Québec at Montréal.

Louis Dupuis, *Coureur du Bois*
http://www.lanset.com/brennan/LDupuis.htm
The exciting and informative story of this French-Canadian fur trader is a glimpse into the early life of the colony, the fur trade and the men who "ran through the woods" that became Canada.

La Nouvelle-France [French only]
http://www.culture.fr/culture/nllefce/fr/intro.htm
A multi-part introduction to the colonization and development of New France. This site includes an overview (Presentation) and brief sections on Origins, French Presence, Colonization, Exploration, Administration and "Today."

Links to Your Canadian Past
Québec

Population de la Nouvelle-France et du Canada au XVIIe et XVIIIe Siècles [French only]
http://mistral.ere.umontreal.ca/~larinr/popnf.html
This site presents a timeline of the demographic evolution of the various colonies that made up New France, from the first explorations and settlements until 1800.

Population du Québec [French only – graph]
http://www.total.net/~jtrudel/quebecpopulati.htm
This page shows a graphical representation of the population of Québec from 1600-2000.

Origins of the French-Canadians

L'Annuaire des Villes et Villages de France sur Internet [French only]
http://www.histo.com/villes/start.htm
A directory of the official and personal sites for towns and villages of France on the World Wide Web. Browseable alphabetically by town or by a list of departments.

Descendants of Pioneers in Canada [English & French]
http://www.acpo.on.ca/claude/descen-a.htm
An interesting table of some of the earliest pioneers of New France, with links to information on the pioneers, their places of origin, spouses, date of marriage and year of arrival in Canada.

Origine des Pionniers au Canada [French only – table]
http://www.acpo.on.ca/claude/pionnier.htm
A table, with accompanying text, showing the number of immigrants to New France from each region of France for the periods 1608-1699 and 1700-1765.

Links to Your Canadian Past
Québec

Origines des Pionniers Français [French only]
http://www.cam.org/~le_prof/pion/index.html
A listing of almost all pioneers of French origin who settled in Québec before 1825 and other Europeans who settled in Québec before 1765. Each name is accompanied by the individual's place of origin and a reference to a printed source documenting this fact.

Origins of Our Immigrant Ancestors
http://members.mint.net/frenchcx/origins1.htm
In addition to a table showing the origins of ancestors with their wives' names, place of origin and date and place of marriage, this site also includes several useful maps: A four-part map of France, an Ecclesiastical map of France (circa 17th century) showing division of dioceses, a map of modern-day France with departmental divisions, a map showing the medieval names of the regions of France, a map of Paris with *faubourgs* and church locations and a list of the most common notaries from pre-1800 marriage records.

Les Villages de Nos Ancêtres [French only]
http://planete.qc.ca/histoire/villages/
This site, presented by Planète Québec, is a monthly feature by Marcel Fournier focusing on various towns and villages in France where our ancestors came from. Articles present information on both the towns and the ancestors. Links to archived articles from past months.

Voyage au Pays de Nos Ancêtres [French only]
http://www.microtec.net/~ouipie/
A "guided tour" through several of the ancestral villages in the ancient province of Perche, where so many of the early families of New France have their roots.

Links to Your Canadian Past
Québec

Military History/Wars

Arnold Invades Québec
http://www.wcha.org/wcj/wc_v19_n1/arnold.html
A description of Colonel Benedict Arnold's invasion of Québec City by birchbark canoe in 1776. Presented by the Wooden Canoe Heritage Association, this article focuses heavily on the use of canoes and the route the invasion took from Maine.

Dissentions Entre Français et Canadiens Pendant la Guerre de la Conquête [French only]
http://www.er.uqam.ca/nobel/m253625/
This site examines the differences between French-Canadians and soldiers who arrived from France during the "War of Conquest" or Seven Year's War. Sections include Combat Techniques, Conflicts Between Officers, Montcalm and Vaudreuil and Strategies.

French and Indian War Magazine Online
http://members.aol.com/fiwar/directory.html
An online magazine, featuring sections on French and British regiments, forts, music and other aspects of the war.

Historical Documents on the Seven Years War
Several documents from the collection of the Hillsdale College (MI) Department of History pertaining to the war between France and England for the conquest of North America.
** *All URLs begin with*:
http://www.hillsdale.edu/dept/History/Documents/War/Abroad/
- **Account of French Defeat in Canada, 1755**: 1755-Dieskau.htm
- **French Account of Braddock's Defeat, 1755**: 1755-Braddock.htm
- **General Townshend's Report on the Fall of Québec, 1759**: 1759-Quebec-Town.htm

Links to Your Canadian Past
Québec

- **Captain Knox's Account of the Fall of Québec, 1759**: 1759-Quebec.htm

Montcalm and Wolfe: The French and Indian War
http://www.digitalhistory.org/wolfe.html
A comprehensive site on the French and Indian War. Includes sections on British Troops, French Soldiers, A Prelude to War, The Major Battles, French Forts, British Forts, Bibliography, Artillery, British Firearms and British Lake Vessels.

Operation Phips: Archaeological Rescue [English & French]
http://www.mcc.gouv.qc.ca/pamu/champs/archeo/epaphips/wreck01.htm
Extensive textual and photographic information on the discovery of a shipwreck from Phips' expedition to capture Québec City in 1690. Includes historical information on the mission, plus a Journal of Rescue Operations, Journal of Laboratory Operations and Photo Album.

Organisation Militaire de la Nouvelle-France [French only]
http://www3.sympatico.ca/dis.general/nfrance.htm
This article on the military organization in defense of New France takes a look at the main components of this defense: the Canadian Militia, the *Compagnies Frances de la Marine* and French regular regiments.

Propagande et Milice au Québec Durant la Guerre de 1812 [French only]
http://www3.sympatico.ca/dis.general/propand.htm
An article on the use of propaganda in and by the francophone militias of Québec during the war of 1812 in order to rally the French population to the British – not American – cause.

Links to Your Canadian Past
Québec

The Seven Years War Website (French & Indian War)
http://www3.sympatico.ca/dis.general/7yrswar.htm
This site contains articles on various aspects of the war, lists and information on British and French Regiments, information on reenactments, military replicas and sound clips.

Professional Groups/Commercial History

Annals of the Port of Québec
http://www.ist.uwaterloo.ca/~marj/genealogy/quebecport1901.html
Excerpts from this 1901 publication, including a list of the dates of the arrival of the first vessel at the port of Québec from 1855-1866, dates for the last trip of steamers to Montréal from 1854-1873 and advertisements for two passenger ship companies and the Great Northern Railroad.

Histoire de la Navigation au Témiscamingue [French only]
http://www.abitibi.tcpip-consultant.com/temis/navig.html
A timeline of the major events and accomplishments relating to navigation on Lac Témiscamingue, Lacs des Quinze and Simard and Lac Kipawa.

History of Dentistry in Québec [English & French]
http://www.odq.qc.ca/english/history.htm
This article, presented by the Ordre des Dentistes du Québec, examines the early beginnings of the treatment of teeth in the province, the arrival of the first actual dentist and development of the profession and dental education in Québec.

L'Iconographie Botanique en Amérique Française du 17e au Milieu du 18e Siècles
[French only]:
http://www.uqtr.uquebec.ca/arts/histoire/botanique/intro.html
This doctoral thesis is a look at the scientific knowledge and botanical history of French North America in the 17th and 18th centuries through the examination of period texts and treaties.

Links to Your Canadian Past
Québec

Les Infirmières du Québec [French only]
- **Les Infirmières de Colonie**:
  http://www.oiiq.org/pratique/prat_colonie.html
- **Les Infirmières en Santé Communautaire**:
  http://www.oiiq.org/pratique/prat_sante.html

The first article takes a look at the courageous and adventurous women who became nurses or *dispensaires* from 1921 until the present day in the outposts of new colonization and development in Québec, while the second article examines the role played by nurses in the various regional community health centers in the 19th and 20th centuries.

A Look at 350 Years of Physicians' Fees in Québec
http://www.cma.ca/cmaj/vol-157/issue-7/0874b.htm
This article from the Canadian Medical Association Journal takes a look at what physicians in Québec have been paid, from Étienne Bouchard in 1653 through the author in 1997.

Métiers Insolites Du Passé [French only]
http://perso.wanadoo.fr/chatry/dcy005_f.htm
A list of professions from the past which have either disappeared, changed meaning or are now extremely rare or uncommon. Lists name of old profession with its description or definition.

Le Patrimoine Ferroviaire du Québec [French only]
http://pages.infinit.net/urba/rail/index.html
This site presents information on the various aspects of Québec's railway heritage. Sections include Old Stations of Québec, Converted Railway Trunks, Local Interest Railways, Main Active Trunks in Québec, Active Regional Trunks, Former Trunks and Railway Bridges.

Links to Your Canadian Past
Québec

Pilots and Lighthouse Keepers on the Saint Lawrence, 1866
http://www.ist.uwaterloo.ca/~marj/genealogy/pilots.html
An excerpt from the report of the Department of Public Works (1866) relating to river pilots on the St. Lawrence, and various tables pertaining to the Decayed Pilots Fund, showing pensioners, widows and children of pilots. Also includes a list of "Keepers of Light Houses and Provision Depots, under the Superintendence of the Trinity House of Québec" and other similar lists.

La Vie Maritime Dans le Kamouraska [French only]
http://www.kam.qc.ca/portrait/ancetres/maritk.html
Several articles on the nautical and maritime industries and history of this area, including articles on fishing, crossing the Rivière-Ouelle, shipping, shipbuilding, pleasure boating and more.

Religious History

Les Communautés Hospitalières Religeuses [French only]
http://www.oiiq.org/pratique/prat_religieuse.html
A look at the history of religious communities in Québec that have seen to the administration of hospitals and health care in the province, from the Augustines who founded the Hôtel-Dieu de Québec in 1639 to the institution of new health laws favoring the state in the 1960's.

Histoire du Grand Séminaire de Québec [French only]
http://WWW3.sympatico.ca/grand.seminaire/hist.htm
Includes an overview of the founding of the seminary, the text of the founding charter, statistics on the number of seminarians over the years, photos and descriptions of the seminary buildings and grounds, and other texts and information on the administration and life of the seminary.

Links to Your Canadian Past
Québec

The Huron Relation of 1635
http://www.sfo.com/~denglish/relations/1635/intro.html
This text, written by Father Jean de Bréboeuf, recounts the trials and daily tasks he and other Jesuit missionaries endured while ministering to the Hurons of Québec and also gives an insight into the customs and beliefs of the Amerindians they visited and lived among. Includes an introduction and background on the *Jesuit Relations*, of which this is a part.

The *Jesuit Relations* and Allied Documents, 1610-1791
http://vc.lemoyne.edu/relations/
This site contains an index to the complete English translation of the *Jesuit Relations*, with links to online versions of each volume, as they are added.

"Memoirs of Dell" (excerpt)
http://www.geocities.com/~hebridscots/religion.htm
An excerpt from an unpublished typescript by John Austin MacLeod on religion among the Hebridean Scots of Québec. Sections include Religion in the Home, Church Union or Dis-union (?), The Hampden Church, Gaelic Church Service and The Ordain.

Montréal (Diocese of) – History of the Diocese of Montréal
[French only]
- **History**: http://WWW.archeveche-mtl.qc.ca/histoire/diocese.html
- **Parishes and Missions**: http://www.archeveche-mtl.qc.ca/montreal/parmis/entree.html

This history of the diocese of Montréal contains many links to further information (text and images) of key people, places and events in the life of this ecclesiastical region.

Links to Your Canadian Past
Québec

Narration Annuelle de la Mission du Sault 1667-1685 [French only]
http://www.culture.fr/culture/nllefce/fr/sault/indexsa.htm
The text and drawings from this account, written for the most part by the Father Claude Chauchetière, a Jesuit missionary at the Saint-François-Xavier mission, at Sault-Saint-Louis. Part of the *Jesuit Relations*. Includes an extensive introduction to the text and period.

Québec (Diocese of) - History of the Diocese of Québec
[French only]
http://www.diocesequebec.qc.ca/Histoire/fr_texte.htm
This brief history of the diocese of Québec is divided into the following sections: In Search of a New World, The Birth of a Church, The Church Develops and The Church Fights for Survival.

Religious Heritage / Patrimoine Religieux – online exhibit
[English & French]
http://www.schoolnet.ca/collections/relig/
An online presentation of the religious heritage of Québec through a multimedia exhibit of text, music and images of the interior and exterior of many religious sites and the presentation of the religious art and artifacts of the province.

Saint-Jean-Longueuil (Diocese of) [French only]
http://planete.qc.ca/diocese/indxdioc.htm
Provides information on the history and geography of the diocese, with statistics on the population and priests of the diocese.

Links to Your Canadian Past
Québec

Tricentenaire de l'Arrivée des Ursulines à Trois-Rivières
[French only]
http://www.cgocable.ca/urstr/300e/ursul.htm
Dedicated to the Ursuline sisters who arrived at Trois-Rivières in 1697, this site presents their history through the following themes: Tercentenary Celebrations, Who Are the Ursulines?, The Arrival of the Ursulines in Canada, The Ursulines of Trois-Rivières, Works in the Region and Ursulines Throughout the World. You can also download a 300th anniversary game.

Geographical History and Information
Atlas du Québec et de Ses Régions [French only]
http://www.unites.uqam.ca/atlasquebec/
The "National" (Québec) atlas is viewable by Division of the Territory and Built, Cultural, Human, Institutional and Physical Environments. The Inter-Regional Atlas contains several maps, including 64 maps on demographic structure, 16 maps on settlement, 2 on migrations and 13 on culture. The Regional Atlases present the different areas of the province.

Bureau de la Statistique du Québec [English & French]
http://www.bsq.gouv.qc.ca/bsq/ang/bsq.htm
The BSQ is the official statistics office for the government of Québec. It provides data, graphs and other statistical publications and socio-economic studies on any matter of provincial jurisdiction. The BSQ offers publications for sale, including some from Statistics Canada.

Cartes des Origines Ethniques des Canadiens, 1901 [French only – maps]
http://www.uottawa.ca/~fgingras/doc/c1901index.html
A series of maps from the 1901 Atlas of Canada, presented in French, showing the ethnic origins of Canadians. Includes three maps for Québec (East, Center and West).

Links to Your Canadian Past
Québec

The Cartographic Creation of New England: Samuel de Champlain and New France
http://www.usm.maine.edu/~maps/exhibit2/sec2.htm
An exhibition by the University of Southern Maine chronicling the effects of European exploration and settlement in northeastern North America.

Eastern Townships Map
http://www.virtuel.qc.ca/simmons/MAP.HTM
A modern-day map showing the counties included in the Eastern Townships.

Dioceses of Québec
http://www.archeveche-mtl.qc.ca/histoire/quebec.html
This map depicts the present-day province of Québec divided into dioceses and archdioceses.

Géographie Québécoise [French only – list]
http://pages.infinit.net/histoire/geographie.html
Includes "Modern" maps: Québec in North America, Canada (all provinces) and the South of Québec (with principal towns) as well as the following "Historic" maps: New France in 1760, North America After the Conquest, Upper and Lower Canada after the Constitutional Act of 1791 and the Borders of Québec between 1867 and 1927.

Photocartothèque Québécoise [French only]
http://www.mrn.gouv.qc.ca/photocartotheque/index.htm
This department of the Québec government, part of the Ministry of Natural Resources, disseminates geographic and territorial information on the province of Québec, including maps, aerial photographs and survey information.

Links to Your Canadian Past
Québec

Places: Now and Then
http://www.geocities.com/Heartland/Bluffs/2005/endroits.htm
A list of place names from Québec and Acadia, with their modern or historic equivalent.

Ports of Québec
http://www.ist.uwaterloo.ca/~marj/genealogy/harbors.html
Reproductions of maps of Montréal and Québec City harbors, circa the 1870's. Also includes a link to a map of the harbor area of Liverpool, England.

Rare Map Collection: Colonial America (Hargrett Library, University of Georgia)
http://scarlett.libs.uga.edu/darchive/hargrett/maps/colamer.html
A list of rare maps (viewable online) from the colonial period in North America, including maps showing New France from the 17th and 18th centuries. A word of caution: The map names are in their original (often Latin) form, so don't pass them over just because they're not in French.

Siege of Québec
http://earlyamerica.com/earlyamerica/maps/quebecmap/index.html
An 1810 map by John Cary entitled "A Map of the Plan of the River St. Laurence with the Operations of the Siege of Québec, 1759." This site presents an image of the map and a textual description of the map and its importance.

Topos sur le Web: Noms et Lieux du Québec [French only]
http://www.toponymie.gouv.qc.ca/Accueil.asp
Search for geographic names (towns, rivers, topographical features, names of roads, etc.) for the entire province of Québec or a specific region, and the search engine returns a list of places that match your criteria, with links to maps. Find the hometown of your ancestors, or for fun, type in a last name and see what places are (potentially) named after your ancestor.

Links to Your Canadian Past
Québec

Les Trésors de la Cartothèque de l'Université de Laval [French only]
http://www.bibl.ulaval.ca/ress/carto2/welcome.html
This site has a twofold interest: it presents a virtual exhibition of some of the treasures of the cartography collection of the Université de Laval (Ste-Foy, Québec) and also provides access to the "Champlain" database, a catalogue of the nearly 4,500 printed maps and 12,000 microfilmed copies of maps of Québec and New France in the university's collection.

Virtual Museum of New France: Map Collection
http://www.vmnf.civilization.ca/reper/r-car-en.htm
This site presents the maps used in the online collections of the Virtual Museum, including a 1609 map by Lescarbot and 1688 maps by Franquelin of the Southern Part of America and Québec City. The "Overview of Cartography" contains several other maps of New France.

Local and Regional History and Photos

Cartes Postales du Québec d'Antan [French only]
- **Presentation**:
  http://www2.biblinat.gouv.qc.ca/antan/animation.html
- **Database**:
  http://www2.biblinat.gouv.qc.ca/carpos/bwcarpos.htm

Take a voyage through Québec's past, thanks to the postcard collection of the Québec National Library. Three circuits are offered: the Tourist circuit, Heritage circuit and Economic circuit, with each post card accompanied by historical text. The database is fully searchable.

The Early Modern City (1500-1800): French Colonial Towns
http://www.uoguelph.ca/history/urban/citybibV04.html
This site (actually part of a course at the University of Guelph) presents a bibliography of works pertaining to French colonial communities, including New France and Acadia.

Links to Your Canadian Past
Québec

Sites Internet des Municipalités, MRC et Organismes [French only]
http://www.mam.gouv.qc.ca/repmun/villes.htm
A list of the official Web sites of municipalities, Municipalités Régionales de Comté (County Regional Municipalities) and various official groups and organizations.

Ayer's Cliff – Old Tyme Photos
HTTP://www.interlinx.qc.ca/~tsharman/index.html
In addition to a great deal of photos of the town and surrounding region from the beginning of the 20th century, you'll also find a collection of old postcards depicting the city and information on the history of Ayer's Cliff.

Beauce – La Page d'Histoire Beauceronne [French only]
http://www.quebectel.com/histbeauce/
Sort of like "This Week in Beauce History," this site presents the history of the region by showing the important events that happened on each day in the current month.

Bécancour: Ville de Bécancour, A Place to Grow
http://www.ville.becancour.qc.ca/e-index2.html
The official Web site of this town presents brief information on the town's history, industry, location and an overview of town life, accompanied by photos.

Boucherville – History of Boucherville
http://www.geocities.com/Heartland/Hills/5727/Boucher/Boucherville.html
This page on the history of the town of Boucherville presents information on its founder, Pierre Boucher, the history of the colonial period and town history from 1854-present.

Links to Your Canadian Past
Québec

Buckingham: Ville Historique [French only]
http://ppp.atreide.net/infocomm/buck/buck2-f.htm
A very brief overview of the first settlers in the town of Buckingham.

Chambly – Ville de Chambly: Histoire et Patrimoine [French only]
http://www.ville.chambly.qc.ca/histoire/histoi.html
Sections include History of Chambly, Fort Chambly, the Chambly Canal, Heritage Tours and information on historic and heritage groups in the town.

Chicoutimi – Historique de Chicoutimi [French only]
http://ville.chicoutimi.qc.ca/historique.html
An illustrated timeline of the history of this urban center of the Saguenay-Lac-St-Jean region.

Coteau-du-Lac: Abrégé d'Histoire de Coteau-du-Lac [French only]
http://www.rocler.qc.ca/hbesner/
Scroll down past the information on the historical society and you'll find a brief history of Coteau-du-Lac and a list of society publications for learning more about this town.

Deux-Montagnes – Ville de Deux-Montagnes' History Chronicle
http://www.cloxt.com/ville-deux-montagnes/chapters.htm
This extensive history of the town of Deux-Montagnes is divided into eleven chapters covering the pre-colonial period, settlement and development of the town through various periods. For the final chapter (1966-present) click on "Back to the History Chronicle" at the bottom of the page.

Links to Your Canadian Past
Québec

Drummondville – Images Anciennes de Drummondville et Ses Cartes Postales [French only]
http://histoire-drummond.qc.ca/images2.htm
This collection of photos and postcards of old Drummondville is presented by the Société d'Histoire de Drummondville, which offers copies of the images for sale.

Eastern Townships Background
http://www.virtuel.qc.ca/simmons/TOWNSHIP.HTM
A brief look at what the designation "Eastern Townships" means, the colonization of this region of Québec and a list of cities found in the Eastern Townships, with their current counties.

Fort-Coulonge et la Région du Pontiac [French only]
http://www.qouest.net/~jljmt/coulonge/index.htm
A multi-part timeline of the history of this town and the Pontiac region of the Outaouais, broken down into pre-1600, 1600-1700, 1701-1759, 1760-1800, 1801-1900 and 1901-1998.

Gaspésie – Histoire [French only]
http://www.gaspesie.qc.ca/histoire.html
A brief look at the history of the Gaspé peninsula, including its geography, exploration by the Vikings and Jacques Cartier and development of the fishing industry and infrastructure.

Gatineau – Ville de Gatineau: History
http://www.ville.gatineau.qc.ca/c_lhistoire_e.htm
A brief look at the formation of the city of Gatineau from seven former municipalities.

Links to Your Canadian Past
Québec

Hull – History and Heritage [French only]
- **Hull en Bref**:
  http://www.schoolnet.ca/collections/patrimoi/hullbref.htm
- **Patrimoine Disparu**:
  http://www.schoolnet.ca/collections/patrimoi/disparu.htm
- **Patrimoine Existant**:
  http://www.schoolnet.ca/collections/patrimoi/existe.htm

Hull en Bref presents six pages on the history and development of the town, including a timeline, a page on the historic fires, old street names, tramways and more. Patrimoine Disparu includes several pages on heritage sites and building of Hull which have disappeared, while Patrimoine Existant features many heritage sites that can still be seen throughout the town.

Huntingdon County – Historical Highlights
http://www.rootsweb.com/~qchuntin/historic.htm
A timeline with brief descriptions of major events in the history of the county.

Jonquière: History
http://www.ville.jonquiere.qc.ca/anglais/histo.html
Brief information on the name, pioneer, first mayor and various industries in the town.

Kamouraska – Sur la Trace de Nos Ancêtres [French only]
http://www.kam.qc.ca/portrait/ancetres/ancetres.html
A great deal of information on the region, in the form or illustrated articles on the settlement, founding and history of the Kamouraska, the maritime life of the region and "Winter Among Our Ancestors." A very comprehensive and informative site.

Links to Your Canadian Past
Québec

Lachine – Historique [French only]
http://www.cum.qc.ca/LACHINE/fr/histoire.htm
The development of the town of Lachine from a simple fur trading post through the development of industry and Lachine's role as a major transportation hub.

La Prairie [French only]
- **Overview**: http://pages.infinit.net/shlm/arron.htm
- **Historic Photos**: http://pages.infinit.net/shlm/album000.htm
- **History "Capsules"**: http://pages.infinit.net/shlm/hist000.htm

Includes information on the Amerindian presence at La Prairie, ice cutting, water distribution, the railway, archaeology digs, and other articles on the people and traditions of La Prairie.

Laval – Les Pages d'Histoire de Marcel Paquette [French only]
http://www.total.net/~marpaque/
Several pages on the history of Laval and the former municipalities which now make up this municipality. Includes many photos and images from postcards of the town and region.

L'Islet [English & French]
http://www.appalaches.com/lislet/page200.html
The agricultural history, industrial development, forest and maritime industries of L'Islet and the surrounding area are presented on this site

L'Islet-sur-Mer – Légendes de l'Islet-sur-Mer [French only]
http://www.total.net/~clairc/index.html
This site presents several local legends about the people and places of L'Islet-sur-Mer, including the story of the Handsome Dancer, the legend of the black horse, "Devil's Eve" and stories concerning Captain Joseph Elzéar Bernier.

Links to Your Canadian Past
Québec

Longueuil – Dictionnaire Historique de Longueuil de Jacques-Cartier et de Montréal-Sud
[French only] http://pages.infinit.net/marigot/Dictionnaire.html
Just about everything you could want to know about the people, places and events that comprise the history of Longueuil and these two surrounding communities can be found in this encyclopedia-like historic dictionary.

Longueuil [French only]
- **Petite Histoire**: http://pages.infinit.net/marigot/petitehis.html
- **Maps**: http://pages.infinit.net/marigot/territoire.html

The history of Longueuil is well organized into chapters dealing with the pre-history of the town; Longueuil as seigneury, barony and parish (1657-1845); Longueuil as a municipality and village (1845-1919); and as a city in the periods 1920-1947, 1947-1969 and 1969-1997. The maps show the territorial evolution of Longueuil throughout the above periods.

Montréal – Adhémar Database [French only]
See Birth, Marriage, Death and Other Data Online/ Land Records.

Montréal – The History of Architecture in Montréal
http://www.cam.org/~fishon1/archit.html
This brief introduction to the architecture found in Montréal includes a section on the architectural influences of the city, plus some of the contributors to the city's built heritage.

Montréal (Diocese of) – History of the Diocese of Montréal
[French only]
See Religious History.

Links to Your Canadian Past
Québec

Montréal – Images of Montréal, Canadian Metropolis, 1872-1898 [English & French]
http://www.rescol.ca/collections/montreal/montreal.html
Sections of this collection of images include Current Events, Nature, Architecture, People, Social Life, Transportation, Winter, Industry, Technology, Monuments, Religion and Recreation, each section including several subsections or themes with illustrations depicting each subject.

Montréal – Important Dates
http://www.cityvu.com/ENGLISH/IMPDATES.HTM
A timeline of events from the city's history from 1535 to 1996.

Montréal – Municipalité et Métropole, 1920-1960 [French only]
http://www.schoolnet.ca/collections/mtl/
An online presentation of 301 photographs of the city of Montréal, divided into the categories Buildings, Places, Personalities and Municipal Services – each, in turn, divided into four to six subcategories, which provide access to the images. A search engine is also available.

Montréal – Vieux-Montréal (official site) [English & French]
http://vieux.montreal.qc.ca/
A wealth of information on the historic city center can be found on this site. Read about the history of Vieux-Montréal, from the founding of Ville-Marie and the creation of a fortified town to Montréal's metropolitan development or browse through "inventories" of historic buildings, people & events and bibliographic sources. You can also take a twenty-part guided (virtual) tour of the historic heart of Montréal through its six major historical periods.

Links to Your Canadian Past
Québec

Paspébiac [French only]
http://www.geocities.com/Heartland/3284/2.htm
A short timeline of events that contributed to the history of this Gaspé town.

Québec City [English & French]
http://www.quebecweb.com/tourisme/qucbec/villequebec/
While the focus of this site is on tourism, it nonetheless presents a brief history of the city and some photos of its historic locations. Follow the links in the text.

Québec City – The Historic District of Québec [English & French]
http://parkscanada.pch.gc.ca/unesco/QUEBEC/QUEBEC.HTM
A brief history of the founding and development of the city, with several photos of the buildings and sites that can be found in this UNESCO World Heritage Site.

Québec City – Photo-Historical Essay [English & French]
http://www.gel.ulaval.ca/~vision/quebec/quebec.html
A brief text accompanies several photos of the historic places and typical scenes of Québec City.

Québec City Places Gallery
http://www.harrypalmergallery.ab.ca/galquectyplaces/galquectyplaces.html
An online presentation from the Harry Palmer Gallery of photographs of monuments and buildings in and near the Old Town of Québec City.

Québec City – Québec, Québec, Canada: An Urban Analysis
http://mirror.syr.edu/analcity/Quebec/quebhome.html
A formal analysis of the urban characteristics and structure of

Links to Your Canadian Past
Québec

Québec City, divided into physical (cartographic) analysis and virtual (cultural) analysis. Includes a concise history of Québec City.

Québec City – Visite Virtuelle du Vieux-Québec [French only]
http://vieux-quebec.demarque.qc.ca/pagetitre.html
Choose between three themed walking tours of the Old Town: Winter Stillness, Summer Warmth or Autumnal Silence. Descriptive text accompanies photos of the historic buildings and locations that contribute to the charm of Québec City.

Québec: World Heritage City
http://www.ovpm.org/ovpm/sites/aquebe.html
This site, presented by the Organization of World Heritage Cities, showcases the reasons why Québec City is included on UNESCO's list of world heritage sites. Read about the city's history or view maps, photos and historical documents that make up the panorama of the past.

Québec (Diocese of) - History of the Diocese of Québec
See Religious History.

Rive-Sud – Chroniques de la Rive-Sud, 1947-1997 [French only]
http://pages.infinit.net/marigot/47-97.html
A yearly chronicle of events and observations for the Rive-Sud region, in and around the town of Longueuil. These accounts originally appeared in the newspaper *Courrier du Sud*.

Rivière-du-Loup – Historic of Rivière-du-Loup
- **English**: http://www.icrdl.net/mlagace/rdla.htm
- **French**: http://www.icrdl.net/mlagace/rdl.htm

This site presents a list of possible sources of the town's name, along with a timeline of important dates in the history of Rivière-du-Loup.

Links to Your Canadian Past
Québec

Saguenay-Lac-Saint-Jean – Historique [French only]
http://www.royaume.com/histoire/
Photos help illustrate the history of this region, which includes the contribution of the fur trade, the forest industry in the region, agricultural colonization, the railroad and industry.

Saint-Antoine-sur-Richelieu [French only – photos]
http://www.aei.ca/~barcelof/photos.html
Old photos of the church, former residence of the seigneurs of St-Antoine and the river.

Saint-Jean-Longueuil (Diocese of) [French only]
See Religious History.

Saint-Thomas-Didyme [French only]
http://www.erabliere-lac-beauport.qc.ca/didyme/didyme.html
The history of the founding, settlement, development and daily life of this parish, recounted through the narratives of several of its older residents.

Saint-Zénon [French only]
http://pandore.qc.ca/~matawinie/muni/zenon/html/histoire.html
A substantial look at the varied history of this town, including its geographic location, the history of the parish, milk and forest industries and other factors in the town's development.

Sunny Bank: Our Ancestral Home
http://surf.to/sunnybank
Information on the people and history of Sunny Bank, including sections on the Gaspé Fish Hatchery, Post Office, St. Andrew's Church, Schools, General Stores and more.

Témiscamingue – Histoire de la Navigation au Témiscamingue [French only]
See Professional Groups/Commercial History.

Links to Your Canadian Past
Québec

Prominent Figures

Historic Figures of New France
http://www.vmnf.civilization.ca/reper/glossair/r-glopen.htm
This site, part of the Virtual Museum of New France, presents links to biographical sketches of prominent people of New France. Each biography also includes several links to further information on each person or the places, events and groups of which they were a part.

Boucher, Pierre – Pierre Boucher: Interpreter and Explorer
http://www.vmnf.civilization.ca/boucher/index.html
This site, destined for senior elementary-level students, is an "Adventure in New France" in which the students are guided through the adventure by Pierre Boucher, founder of Boucherville.

Cartier, Jacques – Jacques Cartier: The Voyages of Jacques Cartier
http://www.mariner.org/age/cartier.html
A brief overview of the contribution of Jacques Cartier in the discovery and settlement of Canada. Presented by the Mariner's Museum in Newport News, Virginia.

Champlain, Samuel de – Living in Canada in the Time of Champlain
http://www.vmnf.civilization.ca/expos/champlain/indexeng.html
This presentation from the Virtual Museum of New France takes the visitor through important moments and places in the life of Champlain, from the first settlement in Québec through his first battle with the Iroquois and other steps in his attempts at colonization. Archaeological information presented on this site gives an idea of the daily life of Champlain and his men.

Links to Your Canadian Past
Québec

Champlain, Samuel de – La Mort de Champlain [French only]
http://www.crif.ca/textes/b_sulte_champlain.htm
This lengthy article, written by Benjamin Sulte, was originally presented to the *Société Royale du Canada* in May 1915. It seeks to examine what Chamaplain thought of the situation in New France and his attempts at colonization in the months preceding his death.

Champlain, Samuel de – Samuel de Champlain : Voyages (1604)
http://odur.let.rug.nl/~usa/D/1601-1650/champlain/voyag.htm
A passage taken from Champlain's own writings regarding the exploration of North America by France and her European ncighbors. "So many voyages and discoveries...have caused us French in late years to attempt a permanent settlement in those lands which we call New France."

Dion, Céline – Céline Dion : Arbre Généalogique [French only]
http://www.celine-dion.net/bio/arbre_f.htm
This site traces the lineage of the Canadian chanteuse back to Jean Guyon from Perche, France.

Hébert, Louis – Louis Hébert (1575-1627)
http://www.blupete.com/Hist/BiosNS/1600-00/Herbert.htm
This biographical sketch of Hébert focuses mainly on his expeditions and settlement of Acadia.

Hébert, Louis – Louis Hébert, Apothecary [English & French]
http://www.acpo.on.ca/claude/hebert-a.htm
A (very) brief introduction to Louis Hébert, with links to further information.

Links to Your Canadian Past
Québec

Hébert, Louis – Louis Hébert, Esclave et Seigneur [French only]
http://205.205.229.3/documents/nouvfrance/article6.html
An article from the series *Nouvelle-France: La Grande Aventure*, which originally appeared in the newspaper *Le Soleil*.

Hébert, Louis – Louis Hébert: A Legacy of Tenacity [English & French]
http://seeds.history.ca/~seeds/episodes/episode-0401/index.html
A description of this episode of the History Television series "A Scattering of Seeds: The Creation of Canada," which profiles Louis Hébert's contribution to the settlement of Acadia and New France. Also includes links to further information about the man and his legacy.

Hébert, Louis – Louis Hébert, Premier Colon au Canada [French only]
http://www.mlink.net/~ipm/gene/hebert.html
Excerpts from historical texts on Louis Hébert, "The first colonist in Canada."

Hébert, Louis – Medicinal Plants Cultivated by Louis Hébert [English & French]
http://www.acpo.on.ca/claude/plante-a.htm
A look at four plants whose medicinal properties Louis Hébert was taught by the Micmac Indians, and which he used in his practice as apothecary. Links to further information on each of the plants presented.

Jolliet, Louis – Short Biography of Louis Jolliet
http://www.navreshq.queb.dnd.ca/units/jolliet/story.htm
A brief sketch of the life of Jolliet – explorer, fur trade merchant and King's cartographer.

Links to Your Canadian Past
Québec

Lagimodière, Jean-Baptiste [French only]
http://uther.merlin.mb.ca/~dsfm/p-hist/baptiste.htm
An informative biography of this native of Saint-Anotine-sur-Richelieu who, with his wife Marie-Anne Gaboury, are credited as being the first French-Canadian couple in the West.

La Vérendrye [French only]
http://www.dlcwest.com/~acfc/Historique/Hommesmetis/verand/ptitre.htm
Biographical material on Pierre Gaultier de Varennes, Sieur de La Vérendrye, French-Canadian explorer who visited present-day Manitoba, Saskatchewan, Alberta and the northwest portion of the United States. Sections include New France in the Time of La Vérendrye, First Voyages of Discovery and La Vérendrye Reaches the Western Plains.

Madonna – Ascendance Maternelle de Madonna [French only]
http://www.acpo.on.ca/claude/arbres/madonna.htm
No, Madonna wasn't a *fille du roi*, but she is French-Canadian – on her mother's side. This site traces the lineage of Madonna's mother, Madonna Louise Fortin back to Julien Fortin and Marie Lavye, who were married in 1619 in France.

Marquette, Jacques [French only]
http://www.mlink.net/~lfournie/marquett.html
A brief biographical note on this 17th century Jesuit missionary and explorer who, with Louis Jolliet (*see above*), discovered the Mississippi River.

Martin, Abraham – Abraham Martin [French only]
http://205.205.229.3/documents/nouvfrance/article8.html
This article, which originally appeared in the newspaper *Le Soleil* as part of the series *Nouvelle-France: La Grande Aventure*, gives an overview of the life of the man who lent his name to the Plains of Abraham.

Links to Your Canadian Past
Québec

Martin, Abraham – Abraham Martin *dit* l'Écossais [French only]
http://www.mlink.net/~ipm/gene/martin.html
Excerpts of some biographical texts on one of the early founders of Québec.

Cultural Groups and Traditions in Québec

Cultural Associations and Groups
Alliance Québec – Montréal, QC
http://www.aq.qc.ca/
A volunteer-based community organization dedicated to preserving and enhancing the anglophone community in Québec. Includes sections on politics, important cultural and social issues, an Interactive Forum, tour of English-speaking communities and more.

Centre Mnémo – Drummondville, QC [French only]
http://www.mnemo.qc.ca/
A cultural group dedicated to the preservation and continuation of Québec's culture and traditions, particularly in the areas of dance and traditional music (francophone, anglophone and Amerindian). The group's database of collections is searchable online.

Centre de Valorisation du Patrimoine Vivant – Québec, QC [French only]
http://www.mcc.gouv.qc.ca/pamu/organis/cvpv/cvpv.htm
The center seeks to foster and preserve an interest and appreciation of living heritage – musical, oral, visual and physical expressions of culture and traditions – on a local, regional and national level. It produces various exhibitions and demonstrations of Québec culture and heritage.

Links to Your Canadian Past
Québec

Conseil de la Vie Française en Amérique – Québec, QC
[French only]
http://www.cvfa.ca/
An organization seeking to preserve and defend francophone culture in North America. The council awards a literary prize, Franco-American scholarship and the medal of honor *l'Ordre de la Fidelité Française*.

Corporation du Dévelopment Culturel de Trois-Rivières - Trois-Rivières, QC [French only]
http://sites.cgocable.ca/crc/CRC_pgs/P_Organs/sercultr.htm
The CDC de Trois-Rivières is the city agency that operates and maintains the city's cultural institutions, such as the La Maison de la Culture and the Salle J-Antonio-Thompson, where various exhibits and performances are held. It is also responsible for the city's cultural policy.

Fédération Acadienne du Québec – Montréal, QC [French only]
http://w3.franco.ca/faq/
The FAQ seeks to bring together Acadians living in Québec and those of Acadian descent for cultural, educational, social and other activities and to study and publish the history and genealogy of Acadians, particularly those now living in Québec.

Le Mouvement National des Québécoises et Québébois – Montréal, QC [French only]
http://www.cam.org/~mnq/index50.html
A group dedicated to defending and advancing the political, economic and cultural interests of the French-speaking population of Québec. The MNQ is a union of 16 regional societies.

Links to Your Canadian Past
Québec

Société Québécoise d'Ethnologie – Québec, QC [French only]
http://www.mcc.gouv.qc.ca/pamu/organis/sqe/sqe.htm
Dedicated to studying and presenting the traditions, culture and rites of the various ethnic groups in the province, with special attention to oral tradition and collective memory. Information on membership, publications and the society's mandate.

Société Saint-Jean-Baptiste de la Mauricie – Sherbrooke, QC [French only]
http://sites.cgocable.ca/crc/CRC_pgs/P_Organs/ssjbm.htm
This society seeks to promote and defend Québec nationalism and identity in the areas of politics, economics, education, culture and traditions.

United Irish Societies of Montréal, Inc.
http://www.ditton.net/uis/
This society preserves Irish culture and history in the Montréal area through an annual St. Patrick's Day parade, social and cultural events and charitable works.

Québécois French and Francophony
Le Français Québécois
http://www3.sympatico.ca/cousture/FRANC2.HTM
An introduction the history of the French language in Québec and its differences from other French-speaking countries or regions, with a list of Québécois expressions.

La Francophonie Canadienne: Statistiques [French only]
http://www.fl.ulaval.ca/CEFAN/DONN.HTM
Includes three tables of statistics on French-speaking Canada: percentage of francophone population from the 1991 census, evolution of statistics of native French speakers from the 1951, 1961, 1981 and 1991 censuses and indicators of French linguistic continuity.

Links to Your Canadian Past
Québec

La Francophonie Nord-Américain [French only]
http://www.fl.ulaval.ca/cefan/franco/
A comprehensive look at French-speaking North America. Includes a "Cartography" section with several maps of francophone distribution, a "Reading" section with various texts and excerpts of articles on regional francophony, a "Statistics" section with various charts and graphs and a "Contact" section with various online and real-world sources of francophone issues.

Glossaire Québécois [French only]
http://www.hostie.net/hostie/glossaire/glossaire.html
A glossary of 3,000 words and expressions from the everyday language of Québec.

La Parlure des Canadiens-Français [French only]
http://www.cyberbeach.net/~jrpellan/langue.html
A look at the various traits and nuances that make Canadian French distinctive from the language as spoken in France, and the influences on the language in Québec.

Phonétique du Français Québécois [French only]
http://www.ciral.ulaval.ca/phonetique/
This site presents research from the Université de Laval on the particularities of the French language as spoken in Québec. There are sections on the aspects of the Québécois accent, a list of theses and research documents on the subject and links to other sites on phonetics.

Links to Your Canadian Past
Québec

French-Canadian Traditions and Culture

9,000 Vieux Prénoms du Québec [French only]
http://cafe.rapidus.net/jhuriaux/index.html
A listing of 9,000 first names (male and female) from the late 19th and early 20th centuries in Québec, collected from visits to over 100 cemeteries and from published obituaries. This site also links to other sites with explanations of some names and lists of "saints' days."

Les Anciens Prénoms du Québec [French only]
http://planete.qc.ca/histoire/huriaux.asp
Each month, Jean-Claude Huriaux presents a series of old first names from Québec, grouped around a certain theme (having something to do with the current month). At the bottom of the page, you'll find a list of "archived" articles from past months.

Le Bon Vieux Temps (Chansons du Temps des Fêtes) [French only]
http://infoweb.magi.com/~yvondian/chanson/chanson1.html
This site is dedicated to traditional French songs from Québec, most of them from various holidays or celebrations. Here you'll find a list of songs, with lyrics. To hear audio files of some of these songs, check out *A French Thang*, below.

Christmas Traditions in France and in Canada [English & French]
http://www.chin.gc.ca/christmas/noel.htm
This Web site contains sections on Family Celebrations, Religious Ceremonies and Communal Festivities in the Middle Ages, 15th-18th Centuries and 19th and 20th Centuries, as well as the Origins of Christmas, a Bibliography and an Introduction to the entire site.

Links to Your Canadian Past
Québec

Les Costumes d'Antan [French only]
http://www.genealogie.org/manuel/costumes.htm
A look at "Clothing of Yesteryear" from Québec, including outfits specific to the bourgeoisie, peasants, military groups, religious communities and children, with accompanying diagrams.

Les Costumes de Nos Ancêtres en Nouvelle-France aux 17e et 18e Siècles [French only]
http://www.nouvellefrance.qc.ca/costumes.htm
An overview of the clothes our French-Canadian ancestors wore in the 17th and 18th centuries, with mention of the fabrics, colors and accessories that made up the outfits of the time. This site, part of the *Fêtes de la Nouvelle-France* Web site, also provides links to places where you can obtain the fabric or ready-to-wear costumes or rent outfits for the festival or personal use.

La Fête National du Québec [French only]
http://www.cam.org/~mnq/fn.html
The history, activities, customs, laws and organization behind the national holiday of Québec, June 24, Saint Jean-Baptiste Day.

Fêtes de la Nouvelle-France [French only]
http://www.nouvellefrance.qc.ca/Default.htm
For five days, costumed interpreters and celebrants convene on the Old Town of Québec City for festivities celebrating the history and heritage of New France (1608-1760).

French Language and Identity: A Vibrant Presence
http://www.infocan.gc.ca/facts/frenchid-e.html
Presented by Facts on Canada, this site is a look at various statistics and facts on the French-speaking presence in Québec and French-Canadian identity across Canada.

Links to Your Canadian Past
Québec

French Language and Identity: A Vibrant Presence
http://www.infocan.gc.ca/facts/frenchid-e.html
Presented by Facts on Canada, this site is a look at various statistics and facts on the French-speaking presence in Québec and French-Canadian identity across Canada.

A French Thang
http://www.geocities.com/Nashville/7886/index4.html
On this site you'll find links to RealAudio files of traditional French Christmas and holiday songs. (For lyrics, check out *Le Bon Vieux Temps*, above.)

Histoire du Temps des Sucres au Québec [French only]
http://www.erabliere-lac-beauport.qc.ca/histoire.htm
Texts and photos on the history of "maple sugaring" (making maple syrup and candy) in Québec. Includes looks at traditional methods of sugaring, the equipment used, a glossary of terms, tales and legends, "A Day in the Sugar Shack" and other aspects of this traditional activity.

L'Influence Amérindienne sur la Société du Régime Français [French only]
http://www.er.uqam.ca/nobel/m347370/index.html
This site presents the ongoing research of graduate history student Jean-François Mouhout into the influence of Amerindians on the society of New France under the French Regime. Sections include Anglo-Canadian Historiography on New France, Relations Between Europeans and Amerindians, Writings on New France and Amerindians According to Napoléon Bourassa.

Morton's Recipe Collection: Canadian
http://sunsite.auc.dk/recipes/english/cat70.html
This collection of Canadian recipes includes some Québec and French-Canadian dishes, such as French-Canadian Pea Soup, Jambon de la Cabane à Sucre, Maple Tourlouche, Pommes

Links to Your Canadian Past
Québec

Caramel, Québec Poached Salmon, Veau dans le Chaudron and three recipes for *tourtière*.

Petit Armorial de l'Amérique Française
http://tornade.ere.umontreal.ca/~baronial/heraldiq.html
A collection of (non-identified) coats-of-arms and crests from francophone North America.

Le Québec au Menu [French only]
http://saveurs.sympatico.ca/ency-voy/quebec/quemenu.htm
A collection of recipes from across the province, broken down into maple syrup-based recipes, bread and pastries, desserts, game dishes, hors d'oeuvres, vegetables, eggs, soups, seafood and shellfish, salads and cheese dishes, sauces, *tourtières*, meat & poultry dishes and condiments.

Recherche sur l'Américanité des Québécois [French only]
http://www.aieq.qc.ca/americanite.htm
Three articles from the newspaper *Le Devoir* on an inquiry into the "American-ness" of Quebecers: How much do citizens of Québec from all national and cultural groups consider themselves to be (North) American, do they share North-American values and to what extent to they act like typical North Americans?

Vexillologie Québécoise et de l'Amérique Française [French only]
http://tornade.ere.umontreal.ca/~baronial/vqaf.html
A look at the study and use of flags and banners to identify various groups within Québec throughout history and their use among French-Canadian groups in Canada and the U.S.

The Huguenots: History, Culture and Traditions
Experiences of the French Huguenots in America – The King's Refugees
http://pages.prodigy.com/VRHZ10A/ressegui.htm

Links to Your Canadian Past
Québec

The text of an article written circa 1908 by Col. James Tompkins Watson, including "Investigations into the Lives and Fortunes of Exiles who Fled to America during the Reign of Louis XIV when he Promulgated the Revocation of the Edict of Nantes in 1685, Persecutions of the Huguenots and Their Experiences in the New Western World and Exhaustive Historical Researches." While this article deals mainly with Huguenots in New York State, it still provides an insight into the reasons they left France and their lives in the New World.

Huguenot Database [English & French]
http://pages.infinit.net/barbeaum/fichier/index.htm
A multi-part table of information on documented French Protestants who either passed through or settled in Québec from the origins of the colony until 1763. The information presented includes first and last name, origin, spouse (with date and place of marriage), "proof," notes and a reference to the source of the information given.

Les Huguenots en Nouvelle-France [French only]
http://pages.infinit.net/barbeaum/hugue.htm
This informative article on the French Protestants is divided into three parts: Origins of the Huguenots, Role of the Huguenots in the Discovery and Colonization of North America and The Huguenots of New France.

The National Huguenot Society – Bloomington, MN (USA)
http://huguenot.netnation.com/index.htm
A comprehensive site with sections on Who Were the Huguenots, Important dates in Huguenot History, a Bibliography of Huguenot history, a Listing of Documented Huguenot Ancestors and Selected Publications for Huguenot Genealogical Research, in addition to membership info.

Links to Your Canadian Past
Québec

Our Huguenot Ancestors
http://pages.infinit.net/barbeaum/huga/index.htm
An online version of a lecture presented by Michel Barbeau on the history of the Huguenots in France and the discovery, settlement and development of New France. Includes images of slides, with accompanying text.

<u>*Other Cultural Traditions and Groups*</u>
Hebridean Scots of the Province of Québec
http://www.geocities.com/~hebridscots/
This comprehensive site includes the following sections: Genealogy, History, Geography, Culture, Arts, Music, Photos, Addresses and Links.

The **Huron Relation of 1635**
See Religious History.

Family Associations/Surnames

- An *address in italics* indicates an official family association.
- If you don't see a particular name, try adding one of the following prefixes: De, De la, Des, La or Le *or* try looking under a *dit* name.

Lanaudière, Un Air de Famille – St-Gabriel-de-Brandon, QC
[French only]
http://pages.citenet.net/users/ctmx2098/
Not a genealogy society or family association, but an event space dedicated to hosting family association gatherings and reunions. Located in the Lanaudière region of Québec.

Links to Your Canadian Past
Québec

The Dit Name and Other Name Problems

The Dit Names
http://members.aol.com/GFSJudi/dit_names.html
A three-part article by Denis Beauregard broken down into What Are Dit Names?, How to Deal With Them and Other Name Variations.

"Dit" Names: What Are They and How Were They Used in French Canada?
http://members.aol.com/GFSJudi/dit_names.html

A simple overview of the use of *dit* names in New France by AOL's genealogy coordinator.

Name Variations: Dit Names
http://ourworld.compuserve.com/homepages/lwjones/dit.htm
A nice introduction to the practice of using *dit* names in French-Canadian genealogy, with a long (but still partial) list of surnames with *dit* name equivalents and a section on first name problems.

Quirks With Names
http://www.virtuel.qc.ca/simmons/NAMES.HTM
A very useful introduction to common name problems and obstacles encountered by French-Canadian genealogists, particularly in the Eastern Townships and New England. Includes a useful list of French surnames and their anglophone or anglicized equivalents.

Province-wide and Regional Surnames

Associations de Familles [French only]
http://www.total.net/~benoitp/ass_fam.htm
A list of contact information for official family associations in Québec, many of which do not have their own Web sites.

Links to Your Canadian Past
Québec

Le Bas-du-Fleuve: Les Grandes Familles [English & French]
http://www.microtec.net/~lutrin/Families/index.html
This page from the Bas-du-Fleuve GenWeb site is a sort of genealogical dictionary in progress on "The Principal Families of the Lower Saint Lawrence."

Eastern Townships Century Family Certificate
http://www.interlinx.qc.ca/~e-dhealy/cfcie.htm
Any family that has lived in the Eastern Townships for one hundred years or more can apply for a "Century Family Certificate." Details are provided on this site.

Eastern Townships of Québec Genealogy
http://www.virtuel.qc.ca/simmons/acccuil.htm
Marlene Simmons, a professional researcher, owns many records and indexes of Eastern Townships (and Vermont) genealogical information. For a fee, she will look up queries in these records and/or provide extracts, if available.

Fédération des Familles Souches Québécoises, Inc. (Federation of Québec Founding Families)
See Genealogical, Historical and Cultural Societies / Professional Groups and Federations

French-Canadian GEDCOMs
http://www.visi.com/~pjlareau//gedcom3.html
A collection of downloadable genealogy files in GEDCOM format. Includes a brief description of the content and size of each file.

Gaspé Genealogy Register
http://geocities.com/Heartland/Fields/7220/
A sort of guestbook for people with roots in Gaspé to register their research interests for the region. Register your own interests or browse the registry.

Links to Your Canadian Past
Québec

GeneaNet des Francophones d'Amérique du Nord
- **French-speaking**:
  http://www.geocities.com/Heartland/Meadows/3699/
- **English-speaking**: http://www.autumnstar.com/GeneaNet/

A sort of repository or registry of information for French surnames of North America. Type in the name you are looking for, and the search engine returns a list of information on individuals in its database with that surname, with links to the person that contributed the information. Search others' information on your French-Canadian families, or contribute what you have to the pool.

Index des Patronymes (Surname Index) [French only]
http://www.smartnet.ca/users/roberochon/listedes.htm
A list of many of the founding families of New France, with links to articles on individual biographies of heads of families. Articles are taken from the book series *Nos Ancêtres*, translated into English as *Our French-Canadian Ancestors*.

Kamouraska's Founding Families
http://www.kam.qc.ca/portrait/genealogie/enframegen.html
Links to brief descriptions of the original families who settled in the Kamouraska region.

Northeast Surnames
http://members.mint.net/mdenis/surnames.html
A bulletin board for surname queries pertaining to the New England states of the United States, the Maritime Provinces of Canada and Québec.

Québec GenWeb Queries
See the regional/county site for the desired location on the main Québec GenWeb site (Genealogy and History Societies / Online Directories and Resources).

Links to Your Canadian Past
Québec

Québec Queries – Canadian Genealogy Made Easy
http://www.geocities.com/Heartland/4051/qq.htm

Individual Surnames and Family Associations
Alarie/Alary: [French only] *http://WWW.CAM.ORG/~jalarie/*

Allee/d'Ailly, etc. (mailing list)
- **all**: allee-roots-l-request@rootsweb.com;
- **digest**: allee-roots-d-request@rootsweb.com

Anctil: [French only] http://pages.infinit.net/anctil/

Angrignon: http://WWW.CAM.ORG/~guyyug/

Aubé/Auber/Aubert: http://pages.infinit.net/slowgo/

Aubin: http://www3.sympatico.ca/paubin/genealogie.htm

Auclair: http://pages.infinit.net/shlm/auclair.htm

Audet: http://www.microtec.net/~boblap/ancetre.htm

Babin: (GenForum) http://genforum.familytreemaker.com/babin/

Baillon: http://fp-www.wwnet.net/~dulongj/baillon/Baillon.htm

Barbe: http://www.mlink.net/~ipm/gene/barbe.html

Bard:
http://ourworld.compuserve.com/homepages/lwjones/bard.htm

Baril: [English & French] http://pooka.nunanet.com/~pbaril/
- (mailing list) http://happyones.com/genealogy/baril/mailing-lists.html

Links to Your Canadian Past
Québec

Barrette: *http://www.barrette.qc.ca/*

Bastarche/Bastrash/Basque:
- [English & French]
  http://www.geocities.com/Heartland/Woods/4407/accueil.htm

Bauché/Beauché/Baucher: *See Morency*

Bayer: *See Payer/Payeur.*

Beauchamp: (GenForum)
http://genforum.familytreemaker.com/beauchamp/

Beauchesne: [French only]
http://members.tripod.com/~beauchesne/

Beaudry: (GenForum)
http://genforum.familytreemaker.com/beaudry/

Beaulé/Bolley: [English & French]
http://www.cablevision.qc.ca/beaule/
- [English & French]
  http://www.mediom.qc.ca/~beaulep/wbolleyf.html

Beaulieu: *See Hudon.*

Beaumier: http://www.ida.net/users/beaum/BeWeb.html

Beauregard: [English & French]
http://www.cam.org/~beaur/gen/beaure-f.html

Links to Your Canadian Past
Québec

Beauvais:
http://ourworld.compuserve.com/homepages/J_Beauvais/descenda.htm (mailing list)
- **all**: beauvais-l-request@rootsweb.com;
- **digest**: beauvais-d-request@rootsweb.com

Bédard: [English & French]
http://www.angelfire.com/pa/archild/index.html
- (GenForum): http://genforum.familytreemaker.com/bedard/

Belley: [French only] *http://home.ican.net/~rbelley/indexbel.htm*

Belzile: *See Gagnon.*

Bergeron (GenForum):
http://genforum.familytreemaker.com/bergeron/
- **Mailing List**:
  http://www.onelist.com/viewarchive.cgi?listname=Bergerons

Bibeau/Bibaud: http://www.sorel-tracy.qc.ca/~jean/

Bilodeau: [French only]
http://www.genealogie.org/famille/bilodeau/bilodeau.htm
- [English & French]
  http://daisy.lino.com/~frabilod/geneal_e.htm

Blanchet(te): [English & French]
http://www.quebectel.com/blanchet/
- [same site] *http://www.globetrotter.qc.ca/blanchet/index.htm*
- http://www.internest.qc.ca/blanchette.html

Bois/Boies: [English & French]
http://www.virtuel.net/users/chabi/

184

Links to Your Canadian Past
Québec

Boissonneau/Bussineau: [English & French]
http://users.aol.com/bussineau/findex.html

Boisvert: [English & French]
http://pages.infinit.net/boisvert/index.htm
- See also De Nevers.

Bondu: [French only] http://www3.sympatico.ca/johanne.bondu/

Bordeleau: [French, some English – comprehensive.]
http://www.acpo.on.ca/claude/

Bouchard:
http://ourworld.compuserve.com/homepages/lwjones/bouchard.htm
- [French only]: http://www.famille.bouchard.com/genealogy/ind0000.html

Boudreau/Boudreault/Boudrot:
http://www.saglac.qc.ca/~boudroal/

Bouffard: http://www.thecore.com/~thomas/tree/treefr.htm

Boulanger: [English & French] *http://jeanbou.citeweb.net/*
- http://www2.zone.ca/~fpelleti/anbou/
- See also Lefebvre.

Bourdon: HTTP://pages.infinit.net/jacco/bourdon.html

Boulay/Boulé:
http://www.interlinx.qc.ca/~rboulay/boulay/boulay.htm

Bourgeois: [French only]
http://www.genealogie.org/famille/bourgeois/bourgeoi.htm

Links to Your Canadian Past
Québec

Boutin: [English & French]
http://www.geocities.com/Heartland/Flats/8678/boutin.html

Branchereau/Branchaud/Brancheau:
http://home.earthlink.net/~djmill/branchereau.html

Brasseur: http://www.mlink.net/~ipm/gene/brasseur.htm

Brochu: [French only] *http://www.abacom.com/brochu/*

Brulot(te): http://www.mlink.net/~ipm/gene/brulotte.html

Caisse: http://users.neca.com/ldragon/

Campagna: *http://www.multimania.com/campagna/*

Cantin/Quentin: [English & French]
http://www.qbc.clic.net/~rop_rom/

Carle: http://pages.infinit.net/muy/page2.htm

Caron: [French only]
http://www.genealogie.org/famille/caron/caron.htm
- http://www.genealogie.org/$spindb.query.requete.g-caron

Carrier/Carrière: http://www.geocities.com/Paris/Rue/9014/
- [English & French] http://www.andre-carriere.qc.ca/genealogie/

Casault/Cazeau: [English & French]
http://www.genealogie.org/famille/cazeau/cazeau.htm
- [French only]
http://www.er.uqam.ca/merlin/gh291590/casault.htm

Links to Your Canadian Past
Québec

Champeau/Champoux:
http://www.geocities.com/Heartland/Fields/8742/

Charbonneau: [English & French]
http://w3.laval.com/~charbono/

Charron/Ducharme: [French only]
http://pages.infinit.net/charronl/

Chartrand: [English & French]
http://www3.sympatico.ca/rocha/shartran2.html

Chassé: [English & French]
http://www3.sympatico.ca/mchassey/homes.htm

Chenard: http://members.mint.net/frenchcx/chenard.htm
- http://members.mint.net/frenchcx/chenard2.htm
- [English & French]: http://www.microtec.net/~gchenard/
- http://www.multimania.com/limbour/chenard.htm

Chevrette: http://www.microtec.net/~rhguay/famcheve.htm

Choquet(te): [English] http://jchoquette.org/english/
- [French] http://jchoquette.org/francais/

Cloutier: [French only]
http://www2.cadvision.com/cloutiem/famille.htm

Comeau: [French only] http://home.iSTAR.ca/~acomeau/aca/

Connolly:
http://www.geocities.com/Baja/Dunes/5175/CONNOLLY.htm

Conseiller: http://www.mediom.qc.ca/~navy/conseiller.html

Links to Your Canadian Past
Québec

Corbin: http://www.geocities.com/Heartland/Pointe/3343/
- http://www.hawk.igs.net/~letanu/biograph.htm

Côté: http://cafe.rapidus.net/renecote/genealogie.html
- http://web.ionsys.com/~microart/personal.html

Courtemanche: *http://www.total.net/~mcourt/*
- http://pages.infinit.net/clode/

Courville: http://www.geocities.com/Heartland/Hills/7517/

Couture: http://home.earthlink.net/~knotbad2/
- [English & French]: http://www3.sympatico.ca/cousture/COUST.HTM
- http://ourworld.compuserve.com/homepages/lwjones/couture.htm

Couturier: http://www.interlinx.qc.ca/~rboulay/couturi/coutur.htm

Creste/Crête: http://www.odyssee.net/~gilcrete/jehan.htm

Cyr: http://personal.nbnet.nb.ca/jimcyr/cyr/index.htm

Cyrenne/Syrenne: http://www3.sympatico.ca/gpfern/HOME.HTM

Croteau: [French only] http://205.151.63.184/

D'Amours: [French only] http://www.genealogie.org/famille/damours/damours.htm

D'Aoust: [English & French] http://members.xoom.com/daoust/

De Lessard: *See Lessard.*

Links to Your Canadian Past
Québec

Demers: [English & French]
http://www3.sympatico.ca/clegare/Demers.htm/
- See also Dumais/Dumay.

De Nevers: http://pages.infinit.net/boisvert/histden2.htm

Denoncourt: http://www.cedep.net/~denoncd/

Deschênes: *See Miville.*

Descoteaux/Decato/Descoteau/Decoteau:
http://www.mbay.net/~swdecato/swdecato.htm

Deslandes: http://www.cyber-surfer.com/CHAMP02/champ02.htm

Deslauriers: [French only] http://nlegault.citeweb.net/

Desportes: http://perso.wanadoo.fr/lettre.arthur/lettre.arthur/

Dion: *See Guyon.*

Doucet: http://www.bulli.com/~owenr/doucet/doucet.htm

Doyon: http://www.dsuper.net/~leroi/SITE.DOY.html

Dragon: http://www.oxclove.com/dragon/genealog.htm

Drapeau: [English & French]
http://www.interlinx.qc.ca/~drapeau/

Drouin: http://www.travel-net.com/~drouin/

Links to Your Canadian Past
Québec

Dubé:
http://www.geocities.com/Heartland/Pointe/4910/dpage2.html
- [English & French]:
http://www.globetrotter.net/gt/usagers/placombe/
- http://www3.sympatico.ca/any.cummings/Dube.html

Dubois: *http://members.aol.com/duboisdbfa/index.html*
- [French only] http://www.web-solut.com/dubois/

Ducharme: *See Charron.*

Dufour: [English & French] *http://saglac.qc.ca/~jpdufour/*

Duhamel: [English & French] http://www.dsuper.net/~jcduh/

Dulong: http://fp-www.wwnet.net/~dulongj/Dulong.htm

Dumais/Dumay: [English & French] *http://www.qbc.clic.net/~lrdumas/*
- http://PPP.ATREIDE.NET/adat/dumais/
- *See also Demers.*

Dumas: [English & French] http://www.qbc.clic.net/~lrdumas/english/eindex.html

Dumont: (mailing list) http://happyones.com/genealogy/dumont/mailing-lists.html
- *See also Guérêt.*

Dupré: [English & French] http://www.multi-medias.ca/Dgdupre/duprea.htm

Duquette: [English & French] http://www.DUQUETTE.org/

Links to Your Canadian Past
Québec

Durand: [French only] *http://www.clic.net/~durandm/*
- http://www.familytreemaker.com/users/d/u/r/Roger-E-Durand/index.html

Dussault: *See Toupin.*

Émond/Hemond/Aymond: [English & French] http://www.aidus-hemond.com/gedpage/hemond.html

Faneuf/Farnsworth: *See Phaneuf.*

Ferland: http://www.interlinx.qc.ca/~rboulay/ferland/ferland.htm

Filion/Fillion/Philion/Phillion: http://www3.sympatico.ca/mario.filion/index.htm

Fluet(te)/Fleuette: *http://www.kersur.net/~fleuette/*

Fortier: [English & French] http://www.dsuper.net/~efortier/

Fortin/Fortain/Forthin/Furtaw: [English & French] http://www.total.net/~yahwe/
- http://pages.Prodigy.net/rfurtaw/
- [French only] http://www.chez.com/fory/famille/

Fournier: [English & French]
http://www.geocities.com/Pentagon/Bunker/3790/AFAAccueil.html
- http://ourworld.compuserve.com/homepages/lwjones/fournier.htm
- (GenForum): http://genforum.familytreemaker.com/fournier/

Fréchette: [English & French]
http://www.angelfire.com/ca/frechette/

Links to Your Canadian Past
Québec

Gagné/Gagnier/Bellavance: *http://www.microtec.net/~jybell/*
[French, some English]
- http://home.eznet.net/~jgagnier
- http://cpcug.org/user/jlacombe/gagnier.html
- http://www.geocities.com/Heartland/Meadows/9951
- (GenForum): http://genforum.familytreemaker.com/gagne/

Gagnon/Belzile: http://www.microtec.net/~aphane/english.htm
- [French only] http://www.franco.ca/gagnon/
- http://ourworld.compuserve.com/homepages/lwjones/gagnon.htm
- (GenForum) http://genforum.familytreemaker.com/gagnon/

Galaise *dit* Léveillé: [English & French]
http://ww.total.net/~patgal/Geneo/bienvenue.htm

Gallant (GenForum):
http://genforum.familytreemaker.com/gallant/

Garceau dit Tranchemontagne: [French, some English]
http://www.microtec.net/~garceauj/

Gaudet (GenForum):
http://genforum.familytreemaker.com/gaudet/

Gauld: http://www.geocities.com/Heartland/Bluffs/1314/

Gauthier: http://home1.gte.net/momtonya/index.htm
- http://www.geocities.com/Athens/5844/english.html
- (GenForum): http://genforum.familytreemaker.com/gauthier/

Gautreau/Gaudreault/Gautrot/Godreau: [French only]
http://gautreau.freeservers.com/

Gauvin: [French only] *http://www.interlinx.qc.ca/~mggauvin/*

Links to Your Canadian Past
Québec

Gélinas: http://www.globalserve.net/~gelinas/

Gervais(e): http://pages.prodigy.net/rjgervais/yourpage.htm

Giguère: http://www.execpc.com/~gmgordon/gigre.html

Giroux: http://members.mint.net/frenchcx/giroux1.htm
- http://members.aol.com/tomgiroux/
- (GenForum): http://genforum.familytreemaker.com/giroux/

Godbout: http://people.ne.mediaone.net/godbout/index.html

Gosselin: http://www.umoncton.ca/etudeacadiennes/centre/white/gosselin.html
- http://www.cam.org/~le_prof/
- (GenForum): http://genforum.familytreemaker.com/gosselin/

Goudreau/Goodrow: (GenForum) http://genforum.familytreemaker.com/goodrow/

Goulet: http://home1.gte.net/goulet/family.htm

Goyette: [English & French] http://www.goyette.com/
- http://denisgoyette.fsn.net/trnadine.htm
- (GenForum): http://genforum.familytreemaker.com/goyette/

Guay: http://www.microtec.net/~rhguay/famguaye.htm

Guérêt: http://home.HiWAAY.net/~dumont/

Guyon/Dion: [French only] http://www.netrover.com/~monicdio/dion.html

Hazeur: http://www.aidus-hemond.com/gedpage/lazure.html

Links to Your Canadian Past
Québec

Héroux: [English & French] http://www.qbc.clic.net/~syheroux/
- http://pages.infinit.net/roluc/menu.html

Hétu/Etu/Estu: http://home.ican.net/~rhetu/

Houde/Houle: [English & French]
http://www.mediom.qc.ca/~famhoude/
- [French only]: http://www.cam.org/~stcroix/houde.html
- http://ourworld.compuserve.com/homepages/Ronald_Houde/

Hudon:
http://ourworld.compuserve.com/homepages/lwjones/hudon.htm
- http://www3.sympatico.ca/jorge.bolieux/

Hunault: http://www.familytreemaker.com/users/l/a/c/Frances-J-Lachance/index.html

Huot: http://www.qbc.clic.net/~jmhuot/

Janson: http://www3.sympatico.ca/fjanson/

Jomphe: http://www3.sympatico.ca/any.cummings/jomphe.html

Jubinville: [English & French] http://www.microtec.net/~promed/

Julien: http://www.total.net/~bjulien/

Kirouac/Keroack/Kérouac: [French only]
http://www.genealogie.org/famille/kirouac/kirouac.htm

Labelle: [English & French]
http://www.geocities.com/Athens/Atlantis/3712/
- http://www1.glen-net.ca/genealogy/labelle/index.html

Links to Your Canadian Past
Québec

Laberge: http://ourworld.compuserve.com/homepages/LaBarge_C/laberge.htm
- http://www.cs.usask.ca/homepages/undergrads/tnc131/470a/history.htm

Labre: HTTP://pages.infinit.net/jacco/ancetre.html

Labrecque: http://www.total.net/~gamase/g/genealog.htm

Labrosse: http://www3.sympatico.ca/rlabrosse/

Lacroix: http://www.geocities.com/Heartland/Ridge/5412/index.html
- *Also see Corbin.*

Lafontaine: *See Robert.*

Lafortune: *See Tellier.*

Lagacé/Lagassé: [English & French]
http://www.icrdl.net/mlagace/asslag.htm

Lalonde: [English & French] http://web.uvic.ca/~lalonde/history/
- http://www.mlink.net/~ipm/gene/lalonde.html

Lamarche: http://www3.sympatico.ca/guy.lamarche/

Lambert: [French only]
http://*www.genealogie.org/famille/lambert/lambert.htm*

Lamontagne: http://www.geocities.com/Heartland/Lane/5638/

Landry: *http://www3.nbnet.nb.ca/landryp/landry.htm*

Links to Your Canadian Past
Québec

Lapierre: http://www.familytreemaker.com/users/l/a/p/Brian-A-Lapierre-/GENE0001-0001.html

Lapointe:
http://www.geocities.com/Baja/Dunes/5175/ROBIN.htm
- *See also Audet.*

Laporte: [French & English]
http://www.genealogie.org/famille/laporte/
- [English & French]: http://members.xoom.com/efortier/
- http://www3.sympatico.ca/h.lederm/index.htm

Larivière: http://pages.infinit.net/papa/
- http://www.netrover.com/~jacql/INDEX.HTM

Larocque/LaRoque, etc.: [English & French]
http://www.easynet.on.ca/~larocque/laroc1f.htm

Lauzon: [English & French]
http://www.geocities.com/Heartland/7967/

Lavergne: http://www.geocities.com/Heartland/Bluffs/2368/

Laviolette: http://www.execpc.com/~gmgordon/lavlt.html

Lavoie: [French only]
http://www.genealogie.org/famille/lavoie/lavoie.htm
- http://www.geocities.com/Heartland/Meadows/2443/index.html
- http://www3.pei.sympatico.ca/galavoie/ARMOIRIES.HTM

Lazure: http://www.aidus-hemond.com/gedpage/lazure.html

Lebeau: http://www.geocities.com/Heartland/9221/Lebeau.html

Links to Your Canadian Past
Québec

Lebel: [French only] http://www.uquebec.ca/~uss1007/Lebel.html

Leblond: [English & French] http://www.genealogie.org/famille/leblond/choix.html

Leclerc: http://www3.sympatico.ca/ffrancoeur/

Lebrun: *See Carrier.*

Leduc: [English & French]
http://www.geocities.com/Heartland/5063/
- http://www.islandnet.com/~duke/genealog.htm

Lefebvre: [French only]
http://www.mtl.net/~rboulan/associat.htm
- http://www.genieaudio.com/lefebvre/
- *See also Denoncourt.*

Legault: *See Deslauriers.*

Legendre: http://www.multimania.com/rleg/index.htm

Legris [French]: http://www3.sympatico.ca/robert.legris/PRESGEN.HTM

Lemieux: [English & French] *http://WWW.CAM.ORG/~blex/*

LeNeuf: http://fp-www.wwnet.net/~dulongj/leneuf/Leneuf.htm

Le Normand: *See Normand*

Lereau: *See L'Heureux.*

LeRoux: [French only] http://www.angelfire.com/la/LeRoux/

Links to Your Canadian Past
Québec

Lessard: [French only] *http://www.total.net/~lessardc/afl_inc.htm*
- http://pages.prodigy.com/CUGF40A/
- http://www.gendex.com/users/dbltrbl/gen_et.htm

L'Étoile: [English & French]
http://www.genealogie.org/famille/letoile/letoile.htm

Levasseur: [English & French]
http://www.genealogie.org/famille/levasseur/levasseur.htm

Lévesque: [English & French]
http://www.genealogie.org/famille/levesque/levesque.htm
- http://www.geocities.com/Eureka/Plaza/4458/index2.html
- http://www3.nbnet.nb.ca/normap/levesque.htm

L'Heureux: [English & French]
http://happyones.com/genealogy/simon_lereau.html
- (mailing list):
  http://happyones.com/genealogy/lheureux/mailing-lists.html

Lucier: *See Lussier.*

Lussier: http://www.cnwl.igs.net/~nlussier/
- http://www.cnwl.igs.net/~nlussier/jacques.htm

Mailly: http://pages.infinit.net/timinou/famille.htm

Martel: [English & French]
http://www3.sympatico.ca/martel.andre/treemar.htm
- [French only]: http://pages.infinit.net/croixlys/Ghmfr.htm
- (GenForum): http://genforum.familytreemaker.com/martell/

Mathieu: http://www.genealogie.org/famille/mathieu/mathieu.htm

Links to Your Canadian Past
Québec

Mathon/Matthon/Matton/Maton:
http://www3.sympatico.ca/jacquest/matton.htm

Meilleur: [French only]
http://pages.infinit.net/meilleur/MEILLEUR.htm

Ménard: http://www.mlink.net/~jpmenard/
- http://www.mlink.net/~ipm/gene/menard.html

Messier: [French only]
http://www.geocities.com/Athens/Atlantis/3590/

Michaud: [English & French]
http://www.genealogie.org/famille/michaud/page1f.html
- [English & French]:
  http://www.geocities.com/Heartland/Valley/4098/
- http://members.tripod.com/~colinmichaud/

Mimée: [English & French]
http://pages.infinit.net/urba/mimee/index.html

Miville: http://www.iac.net/~rayjd/Homepage.html

Moisan:
http://www.geocities.com/Baja/Dunes/5175/MOISAN.htm

Montplaisir: [English & French]
http://www.online.ru/people/danmontp/

Moquin: http://www.wrra.org/moquin.htm

Morency: [French only]
http://www.qbc.clic.net/~remo/Morency.html
- [English & French]:
  http://www3.sympatico.ca/michel_morency/

Links to Your Canadian Past
Québec

Morissette: [English & French]
http://www.genealogie.org/famille/morissette/morissette.htm
- http://www.interlinx.qc.ca/~rboulay/morisset/moriss.htm

Nadeau: http://members.xoom.com/nadeau/

Nau(lt): [English & French] *http://www.nau.org/*

Néron: http://pages.infinit.net/badie/genealog/pmichfra.htm

Nicol:
http://www.geocities.com/Heartland/Flats/4694/racina00.html

Noël: [French only] http://pages.infinit.net/raymond/geneal.html

Normand: *http://www.enter-net.com/~anormand/*

Ouellet(te)/Willet(te), etc.:
http://www3.sympatico.ca/jeannine.ouellet/

Ouimet: [English & French]
http://www.geocities.com/~couimet/lehouymet.html

Pageot/Pageau/Pajot: http://www.novagate.com/~rpaggeot/

Paradis: *http://www.graphor.com/afpnet/index.html*

Paré: http://www.mlink.net/~ipm/gene/pare.html

Parent: [English & French] *http://pages.infinit.net/afpa/*

Payer/Payeur: [French only] *http://ww.total.net/~jlpayer/*

Pearson: http://www.er.uqam.ca/nobel/g17176/pearson/index.html

200

Links to Your Canadian Past
Québec

Pelland: [English & French]
http://www.cyberbeach.net/~jrpellan/pellan1.htm

Pelletier: http://association.pelletier.net/
- http://genealogy.org/~gapellet/
- http://www.execpc.com/~gmgordon/peltr.html
- http://www3.nbnet.nb.ca/normap/PELLETIE.TXT

Perreault: [French only]
http://www3.sympatico.ca/pperrot/index.html

Perron: [English & French]
http://www.oricom.ca/pperron/index.htm
- [same site] http://www2.intercime.qc.ca/afpa/perron.htm

Phaneuf/Farnsworth:
http://www.microtec.net/~aphane/english.htm
- http://www.sjc.com/farnsworths/

Piché/Pichet/Picher: [English & French] http://www.multi-medias.ca/Dgdupre/
- [same page] http://www.abacom.com/~dgdupre/webpage1.htm

Picot: http://Fox.nstn.ca:80/~nstn1528/index.html

Piet(te): http://www3.sympatico.ca/jacquest/jean.htm

Pilon: [English & French] http://www.magma.ca/~rmpilon/

Pinard: [English & French] http://www.enternet.com/~9sflauzi/pin.html

Pinette: [English & French]
http://www.dallas.net/~cpinette/genealogy/index.html

Links to Your Canadian Past
Québec

Plamondon: [French only]
http://www.qbc.clic.net/~mrplam/plamgenf.html

Plourde:
http://ourworld.compuserve.com/homepages/lwjones/plourde.htm

Poirier: [French only] http://famille.poirier.net/
- http://ourworld.compuserve.com/homepages/lwjones/poirierj.htm
- http://ourworld.compuserve.com/homepages/lwjones/poirierp.htm
- (GenForum): http://genforum.familytreemaker.com/poirier/

Poulin/Pooler: (GenForum)
http://genforum.familytreemaker.com/pooler/

Pratt: [French only] http://pages.infinit.net/marigot/Pratt1.html

Prévost: *See Provost.*

Provencher:
http://www.interlinx.qc.ca/~rboulay/provenc/provench.htm

Provost/Prévost: [English & French]
http://www3.sympatico.ca/cprovost/

Purcell: [English & French] *http://pages.infinit.net/purcell/*

Quay: *See Dragon.*

Quenneville: http://www.geocities.com/Paris/LeftBank/4595/

Quentin: *See Cantin.*

Links to Your Canadian Past
Québec

Raté: [French only]
http://www.genealogie.org/famille/rate/rate.htm

Raymond: [French only] http://www.cam.org/~gilray/cgi-bin/genealogie/raymond.dit.toulouse.pl/
- *See also Labrosse.*

Renaud: http://www.geocities.com/Heartland/Meadows/6257/

Richard: [French only]
http://www.genealogie.org/famille/richard/richard.htm

Riou(x): [French only]
http://www.genealogie.org/famille/rioux/rioux.htm

Robert: http://home1.gte.net/robertdp/r_72.htm

Robichaud: http://www.genweb.net/~robichaud/

Robillard: http://www.execpc.com/~gmgordon/rblrd.html

Robin: *See Lapointe.*

Rodrigue: [English & French]
http://www.genealogie.org/famille/rodrigue/rodrigue.html
- [French only]:
  http://www.interlinx.qc.ca/~doum/francois/an_rodr.html

Ross: [French only]
http://www.genealogie.org/famille/clanross/clanross.htm

Rouleau: [French only]
http://www.microtec.net/~multimac/Rouleau.html
- [English & French]:
  http://members.aol.com/MARouleau/AFRA.html

Links to Your Canadian Past
Québec

Roussel(le)/Russell/Rouxel: [English & French]
http://WWW.CAM.ORG/~mauricel/

Roy: [French only] *http://www.genealogie.org/famille/roy/roy.htm*
- [French only]: *http://members.xoom.com/associat95/index.htm*
- [French only]: http://www3.sympatico.ca/jean-guy/Roy.html
- [French only]: http://www.qbc.clic.net/~aroy/

Royer: [English & French]
http://www.intplsrv.net/jroyer/gen/genhome_fr.htm
- http://www.cet.com/~royerr/

Rozon [English & French]
http://www3.sympatico.ca/rocha/rozon1.html

Saint-Georges: *See Laporte.*

Saint-Laurent: [English & French]
http://www3.sympatico.ca/stl.jacinthe.remi/

Saint-Pierre-Dessaint: [French, some English]
http://www.total.net:8080/~jfortier/index.htm

Saumur/Saumure/Semeur:
http://www.magi.com/~saumure/saumure.html

Savard: [English & French]
http://www.geocities.com/Paris/Parc/9993/

Savoie: *http://personal.nbnet.nb.ca/savoimar/*

Sénécal/Sénéchal: [English & French]
http://www.gel.ulaval.ca/~senecal/genealog.htm

Sicard: http://www.geocities.com/Heartland/9221/Sicard.html

Links to Your Canadian Past
Québec

Simoneau: http://www.geocities.com/Heartland/Plains/8083/
- http://www.fortunecity.com/millenium/donald/302/index.html

Soucy/Soucisse/Sucese: [English & French] http://www.aidus-hemond.com/gedpage/soucy.html

Sutton: http://www.sutton.org/

Sylvestre: http://magi.com/~aemau/

Syrenne: *See Cyrenne.*

Taillon: http://pages.infinit.net/xelf/taillon.htm

Talbot: [English & French]
http://www.geocities.com/CapitolHill/1213/talbot.html

Tanguay: [French only]
http://www.genealogie.org/famille/tanguay/tanguay.htm

Tardif: [English & French]
http://www.quebectel.com/tardif/index.htm
- [English & French – same page]:
  http://www.globetrotter.qc.ca/gt/usagers/jtardif/Assogn.htm

Tellier: [English & French] http://www3.sympatico.ca/mlafortu/

Terriault/Theriault/Theriot:
http://www.geocities.com/SunsetStrip/Balcony/1123/terriaultged.html

Therrien: [English & French]
http://www.genealogie.org/famille/therrien/therrien.htm
- http://www.globaldialog.com/banners/chart.html

Links to Your Canadian Past
Québec

Thibodeau/Thibodeaux/Thibaudeau:
http://www.qouest.net/~jljmt/index.htm

Tifault: [English & French]
http://www.genealogie.org/famille/tifault/tifault.htm

Toulouse: *See Raymond.*

Toupin: http://pages.infinit.net/gildus/index.html

Tourtellotte: (GenForum)
http://genforum.familytreemaker.com/tourtellotte/

Trahan: (GenForum)
http://genforum.familytreemaker.com/trahan/

Tremblay: [French only]
http://www.genealogie.org/famille/tremblay/tremblay.htm
- http://www.saglac.qc.ca/~sttremb/welcome.html
- (GenForum): http://genforum.familytreemaker.com/tremblay/

Trempe: http://www3.sympatico.ca/jacquest/

Trottier: http://www.geocities.com/Heartland/Prairie/5304/

Trudel(le): [French only] *http://www.microtec.net/~rtrudel/*
- [French only]: http://membres.tripod.fr/claude/

Vaillancourt:
http://ourworld.compuserve.com/homepages/lwjones/vaillanc.htm

Veilleux: [French only] *http://www.clic.net/~afvi/*
- [same site] *http://www.qbc.clic.net/~afvi/*

Links to Your Canadian Past
Québec

Whittom: [English & French]
http://www.geocities.com/Heartland/3284/whittom.htm

Chat Rooms and Mailing Lists
(See Notes section for mailing list instructions)

Association Internationale des Études Québécoises (AIEQ) Discussion List
http://www.aieq.qc.ca/discuss.htm
From this site, you can register for this discussion list or view recent postings.

Bonaventure County Mailing List:
majordomo@listserv.northwest.com
`subscribe bonaventure-pq`

Eastern Townships Mailing List (QC-ETANGLO-L)
http://www.geocities.com/Heartland/Acres/3500/etanglo.html
Pertaining to the genealogy and history of the Anglo-Protestant settlers of Brome, Compton, Missisquoi, Shefford, Stanstead, Sherbrooke, Richmond, Megantic, Drummond, Arthabaska and Wolfe counties, Québec.

Forum de Généalogie – Centre de Généalogie Francophone d'Amérique [French only]
http://www.genealogie.org/forum.htm
A moderated discussion list on varying themes related to North American francophone genealogy. The discussion list is in French, and you must obtain a free access code.

French-Canadian Culture Chat Room (The Mining Company)
http://frenchcaculture.tqn.com/mpchat.htm
Open to topics of "what makes French-Canadian culture unique," including genealogy, history, customs and traditions. The site provides instructions and help.

Links to Your Canadian Past
Québec

GÉchanges Mailing List – Québec
http://www.egroups.com/list/gechanges_quebec/

"Généalogie Canadienne-Française" Mailing List (Stéphane Luce) [French only]
http://pages.infinit.net/mercure/liste.htm

Francophone Genealogy Mailing List (GEN-FR) Includes Francophone Canada
- **all**: gen-fr-l-request@rootsweb.com • **digest**: gen-fr-d-request@rootsweb.com
- **index**: gen-fr-i-request@rootsweb.com

Francophone Genealogy Mailing List (GEN-FF) Includes Francophone Canada
- **all**: gen-ff-l-request@rootsweb.com • **digest**: gen-ff-d-request@rootsweb.com
- **index**: gen-ff-i-request@rootsweb.com

Native Trail Chat Room For First Nations history, culture and concerns.
http://www.nativetrail.com/cgi-bin/en/chat/chat.cgi

Québec Mailing List (Genealogy, History, General Interest): majordomo@listserv.northwest.com
- **all**: subscribe quebec • **digest**: subscribe quebec-digest

La Société des Musées Québécois Discussion List
http://www.unites.uqam.ca/musees/fr/discu.html

Upper Ottawa Valley Genealogy Mailing List (UOVGEN)
http://www.valleynet.on.ca/~aa127/uovgen/uovgen.html
Includes not only Renfrew County, Ontario, but also Pontiac County, Québec.

Links to Your Canadian Past
Québec

Other Canadian Provinces

French-Canadian Genealogical, Historical and Cultural Societies

Directory
Histoire et Généalogie (Francophones) [French only – list]
http://www.cvfa.ca/Accueil/Publications/R_pertoire/Division_Th_matique/Patrimoine___Famille/histoire___g_n_alogie.html [*note: long spaces above are 3 spaces (underscores) long.*]
A list of francophone-oriented history and genealogy societies throughout Canada and the United States.

Alberta
La Société Généalogique du Nord-Ouest
http://www.genweb.net/~pbg/sgno.htm
The society seeks to assist all persons interested in the genealogy and family history of French Canadian descendants and develop a suitable center for genealogical research.

Société Historique et Généalogique du Smoky River [English & French]
http://www.telusplanet.net/public/genealfa/
The largest francophone genealogical and historical center west of Winnipeg. The site details the society's mission, extensive resources and services, with contact information.

Links to Your Canadian Past
Québec

Manitoba
Société Historique de Saint-Boniface – Winnipeg, MB [English & French]
http://home.ican.net/~shsb/
A wealth of information on the French presence in Manitoba. Includes chronological histories of French Manitoba and the diocese of Saint-Boniface, histories and genealogies of local families, a list and description of items in their archives, and a genealogical research request form.

Nova Scotia
Louisbourg Heritage Society – Louisbourg, NS
http://fortress.uccb.ns.ca/historic/heritage.html
Dedicated to studying, preserving and presenting the history of Louisbourg and Cape Breton in geeral. The site details the history of the town and society, its activities and publications.

Ontario
Société Franco-Ontarienne d'Historie et Généalogie – Cornwall, ON [English & French]
http://www.glen-net.ca/sfohg/
Focuses on the francophone presence in Ontario, with a large research collection and activities.

Saskatchewan
La **Société Historique de la Saskatchewan** [English & French]
http://www.dlcwest.com/~acfc/Associations/socihist/intro.html
Dedicated to studying and promoting the francophone history, heritage and genealogy of the French-speaking population of Saskatchewan.

Links to Your Canadian Past
Québec

Archives, Libraries and Research Centers

Ontario
Institut Franco-Ontarien: Laurentian University – Sudbury, ON
http://www.laurentian.ca/www/admn/grad_study/research/ifoe.html
Responsible for maintaining the J.N. Desmarais Library, hosting conferences and producing publications, including the journal *Revue du Nouvel-Ontario*.

Birth, Marriage, Death, Census and Other Data Online

Newfoundland
Plaisance Area Census Data [French only]
- **1701**: http://www.infonet.st-johns.nf.ca/project21/1701/1701_census.htm
- **1706**: http://www.infonet.st-johns.nf.ca/project21/1706/1706.htm

These censuses of the French-speaking area of Newfoundland are transcribed entirely in French. 1701 shows the *habitants*, fishermen who wintered with them, names of the fishermen who will return to France, and any consideration paid by the King. 1706 shows *habitants* and wives, boys and girls over/under 12 years and fishermen. Translation of some terms given for both censuses.

Links to Your Canadian Past
Québec

Nova Scotia
From Montbéliard to a New World
http://www.uwindsor.ca/library/leddy/people/art/resource.html
A brief introduction to the immigration from the former French province of Montbéliard to Nova Scotia, with a list of subjects from the *seigneurie* of Héricourt (Montbéliard) who left for Nova Scotia and a list of emigrants from Montbéliard in 1793.

Ontario
Migration of Voyageurs from Drummond Island to Penetanguishene in 1828
http://users.aol.com/bussineau/tree/drummond.html
A short article on the voyageurs that accompanied the British garrison, with a list of names.

Saskatchewan
Société Historique de la Saskatchewan: Banque de Données
http://www.dlcwest.com/~acfc/Associations/socihist/Banques/donnees.html
Indexes to *Histoire des Franco-Canadiens de la Saskatchewan* by Richard Lapointe and Lucille Tessier and *Les Français dans l'Ouest Canadien* by Donatien Frémont, with others to be added.

Museums and Historic Sites and Groups

Directory
Musées (Francophones)
http://www.cvfa.ca/Accueil/Publications/R_pertoire/Division_Th_matique/Communication_et_Culture/mus_es.html
A list of contact information and addresses for francophone museums across Canada.

Links to Your Canadian Past
Québec

Alberta
Bonnyville and District Museum – Bonnyville, AB
http://www.town.bonnyville.ab.ca/museum.html
Displays honoring the Native, French and Ukrainian contributions to the history of the area, including re-created log church, fur trader's shack, schoolhouse and other early buildings.

Rocky Mountain House National Historic Site – Rocky Mountain House, AB [English & French]
http://www.worldweb.com/ParksCanada-Rocky/index.html
This site of rival posts of the North West Company and Hudson's Bay Company commemorates the fur trade in the region. Many history articles available online.

Manitoba
Compagnie de Sieur de la Vérendrye [French only]
http://www.franco-manitobain.org/cielaverendrye/index.html
This historical reenactment group takes on the lifestyle and history of the *Compagnie Franche de la Marine* that accompanied the *Sieur de la Vérendrye* in his explorations to the west of the Great Lakes in present-day Manitoba, Saskatchewan and the American midwest.

Fort Dauphin Museum, Inc. – Dauphin, MB
http://susan.chin.gc.ca:8016/BASIS/guide/user/search/DDW?M=1&U=1&W=GUIDE_KEY=1318
Pioneer buildings and artifacts from the fur trade and settlement eras, surrounded by the palisade of an 18th century fur trading post. Also an archaeological resource center and archive.

Links to Your Canadian Past
Québec

Fort La Reine Museum and Pioneer Village – Portage la Prairie, MB
http://susan.chin.gc.ca:8016/BASIS/guide/user/search/DDW?M=1&U=1&W=GUIDE_KEY=1328
Includes a replica of La Vérendrye's Fort La Reine, an 1879 log cabin, pioneer church and school, blacksmith shop, trading post, trapper's cabin and other recreated buildings and displays.

Newfoundland
Castle Hill National Historic Site – Jerseyside, NF [English & French]
http://parkscanada.pch.gc.ca/parks/newfoundland/castle_hill/castle_hille.htm
The remains of French and British fortifications from the 17th and 18th centuries, with exhibits on the daily life of French fishermen and soldiers at Placentia. The history, services, exhibits and operating information of this site are described, along with photos of the site.

Nova Scotia
Fortress of Louisbourg National Historic Site – Louisbourg, NS
http://parkscanada.pch.gc.ca/parks/nova_scotia/fortress_louisbourg/fortress_louisbourge.htm
The official site from Parks Canada for this reconstructed 18th century French fortified town.

Fortress of Louisbourg – Louisbourg, NS
http://fortress.uccb.ns.ca/parks/fort_e.html
Information on the history and activities of the Fortress of Louisbourg on Cape Breton Island. Reconstructed buildings and costumed staff re-enact life in the fort community from the summer of 1744. Experience the daily life of the soldiers and townspeople and eat in a period restaurant serving traditional 18th century food.

Links to Your Canadian Past
Québec

Fortress of Louisbourg – Louisbourg, NS
http://www.schoolnet.ca:80/collections/louisbourg/index.html
A comprehensive site about the fortress, with a clickable map and sections on the History of the Fortress, Peoples of Louisbourg, Archaeology, Legends and Folklore, Subject Directory, Parish Genealogy Records and Geography.

Montbéliard Memorial – Lunenburg, NS
http://www.geocities.com/Heartland/6625/memorial.html
A tribute to the settlers from the former principality in France, with cairns for each ship and a list of passengers.

Port Morien French Mine Site – Port Morien, NS
http://www.ednet.ns.ca/educ/museum/arch/sites/morien/morien.htm
The history of this site, the first commercial coal mine in North America, started by the French in 1720. Includes a brief history of the coal industry on Cape Breton Island.

Port-Royal National Historic Site – near Annapolis Royal, NS
http://parkscanada.pch.gc.ca/parks/nova_scotia/port_royal/port_royale.htm
A reconstruction of the 17th century French village, with costumed interpreters.

Ontario
Lake of the Woods Museum – Kenora, ON
http://netra.voyageur.ca/~lwmchin/museum.html
Dedicated to the history of Kenora (formerly Rat Portage), Keewatin and Lake of the Woods, in the areas of exploration, settlement, population, education, arts, trade, transportation, etc.

Links to Your Canadian Past
Québec

Musée Sturgeon River House Museum – Nipissing, ON
http://www.city.north-bay.on.ca/west_nip/msrhm.htm
This former fur trading post now depicts the history of the fur trade in the area.

Saint-Louis Mission National Historic Site – Honey Harbour, ON [English & French]
http://parkscanada.pch.gc.ca/parks/ontario/st-louis_mission/st-louis_missione.htm
The site of a former Huron village and Jesuit mission that was attacked by the Iroquois in 1649.

Prince Edward Island

Port-la-Joyce / Fort Amherst National Historic Site – Charlottetown, PEI [English & French]
http://parkscanada.pch.gc.ca/parks/pei/fort_amherst_plj/fort_amherst_plje.htm
Remains of French and British forts at the site of the first permanent settlement in the province.

Saskatchewan

Willow Bunch Museum – Willow Bunch, SK [English & French]
http://www.quantumlynx.com/fts/musee/
Celebrating the history of the community and its prominent citizens, including many francophone families. Extensive information online, with a virtual gallery tour.

Regional, Provincial and Local History

National
Un Brin d'Histoire [French only]
http://francalta.ab.ca/Histoire.htm

Links to Your Canadian Past
Québec

If this page had a title, it might be "This month in French-Canadian History." You'll find entertainment, political and historical highlights for each day of the current month.

The Canadian West
Les Canadiens Français de l'Ouest: Espoirs, Tragédies, Incertitude [French only]
http://www.fl.ulaval.ca/cefan/franco/my_html/LALONDE.html
An excellent and lengthy look at the presence of French-Canadians in the Western Provinces of Canada. Sections include Colonization, Vitality of the Culture and The Ravages of Assimilation. This study is complemented with notes and two superb maps: The French-Canadian Presence in the West and Two Centuries of Francophone Colonization of the West.

British Columbia
The French Presence in Canada and in British Columbia
http://www.corp.direct.ca/news/french/french1.shtml
An overview of the achievements and contributions of the francophone population, with emphasis on its origins and development in British Columbia.

L'Histoire des Francophones de la Colombie-Brittanique [French only]
http://www.ffcb.bc.ca/federation/exposition.html
This site presents the written accompaniment to an exhibition from the offices of the Fédération des Francophones de la Colombie-Brittanique. The text showcases the francophone people, places and events that contributed to the history of the province, including a look at *voyageurs*, explorers and trappers; religious leaders, missionaries and institutions and other notables.

Links to Your Canadian Past
Québec

Manitoba
Fisher Branch History
http://www.evergreen.freenet.mb.ca/fisherbranch/history.html
A detailed and informative three-page history of the settlement of the town by French and Ukrainian pioneers and its subsequent development, accompanied by photographs.

Portage la Prairie History
http://www.cpnet.net/portage/city/history.html
A brief overview of the city's history, with a list of historic facts.

Winnipeg: Our Colourful Past
http://WWW.Tourism.Winnipeg.MB.CA/Intr_TT.htm
Includes an overview of fur trade and settlement, Jean-Baptiste Lagimodière, the Riel Rebellion, "Chicago of the North" and Winnipeg Today.

New Brunswick
Barachois – L'Église St-Henri de Barachois et les Débuts de l'Établissement de Barachois
http://www.rbmulti.nb.ca/shmr/eglbara.htm [French only]
A history of the church building, parish and town of Barachois.

Cap Pelé – Historique [French only]
http://www.rbmulti.nb.ca/cap-pele/histoire.htm
The French-language history of this community, including its first settlers, the use of *aboiteaux* to dry the marshes, the presence of buccaneers and the town's settlement and incorporation.

La Mer Rouge [French only]
http://www.rbmulti.nb.ca/shmr/merrouge.htm
An article from *Sur l'Empremier*, the journal of the Société Historique de la Mer Rouge on the origin and historical and

cultural significance of the name "Red Sea" for the water between New Brunswick and Prince Edward Island.

Néguac – Village of Néguac
http://www.rpa.ca/neguac/otho.htm
A description of some of the historical buildings and sites in the village, including the Otho-Robichaud House, the Saint-Bernard Church, Rendez-Vous Festival and the town's name.

Nova Scotia
Colchester County – A Brief History of Colchester
http://www.shelburne.nscc.ns.ca/nsgna/col/history.htm
From early native presence to French land grants and English and Scottish settlement.

Ontario
Darling – The French Settlement in Darling Township
http://www.globalgenealogy.com/LCGS/A-FR.HTM
A brief but interesting article on the francophone history of this town by a descendant.

Sault Ste. Marie: A Community's History Through the Prism of Its Heritage Sites
http://www.schoolnet.ca/collections/ssm/pages/english/home.html
An excellent visual and textual presentation of the town's rich history.

Le Toronto Francophone [French only]
http://www.miquelon.net/toronto/
A guide to the French-language resources and attractions of this city. Sections include News and Media, Arts & Cuture, Education, Business, Institutions, Recreation & Tourism and Health.

Links to Your Canadian Past
Québec

Vanier – Municipalité de Vanier: Histoire [French only]
http://www.intergov.gc.ca/mun/on/vanier/histoirf.html
A (very) brief history of this town, formerly known as Cummings Island, Janeville and Eastview.

Prince Edward Island
Prince Edward Island Place Names Past and Present
http://www.isn.net/~dhunter/peiplace.html
A list of the French and Mi'Kmaq names and their present-day names or location. Also includes a link to a map of the island before 1758.

Saskatchewan
Un Bout d'Histoire / La Parlure Fransaskois [French only]
http://www.dlcwest.com/~lgareau/lgareau/archives/Archives.html
Archived articles on the history of francophone communities and traditions, together with articles describing the particularities of Franco-Saskatchewan speech.

Francophone Communities of Saskatchewan
- **English** :
  http://www.schoolnet.ca/collections/fransaskois/Communaute/commun.html
- **French** :
  http://www.schoolnet.ca/collections/fransaskois/Communaute/communaute.html

Brief notes on the various French-speaking communities throughout the province.

Historique de la Communauté Fransaskoise [French only]
http://www.schoolnet.ca/collections/fransaskois/Historique/historique.html
Articles on Franco-Saskatchewan pioneer women and men, Métis leaders, and a brief chronology of the history and contribution of the French-speaking population in the province.

Links to Your Canadian Past
Québec

Regina – Le Réginois [French only]
http://www.gpfn.sk.ca/culture/acfc/odonymie.html
A description of the Franco-Saskatchewan flag and the francophone origins of street names and place names for the city of Regina.

Yukon Territory
La Francophonie Yukonnaise: Une Mine d'Or à Découvrir! [French only]
http://www.fl.ulaval.ca/cefan/franco/my_html/YUKON.html
Excerpts from a thesis by Marie Tremblay, examining the various reasons for the immigration of French-Canadians to the Yukon and how the French-speaking community of the territory developed and what elements comprise it.

Histoire et Chroniques [French only]
http://w3.franco.ca/afy/histoires/histoire.htm
Articles on some of the prominent francophone people and places in the Yukon Territory, as well as everyday people, traditions and forgotten locations that are part of French Yukon.

French-Canadian Culture and Cultural Groups

Directories/Canada-wide
Atlas du Développement Des Communautés Francophones Hors Québec [French only]
http://aix1.uottawa.ca/~andrelan/index.html
Various maps, charts and statistics showing the distribution and development of French-speaking communities in Canada outside the province of Québec. This project plans to include photos of francophone communities and other data and images to complement this analysis.

Links to Your Canadian Past
Québec

Centres Culturelles (Francophones) [French only – list]
http://www.cvfa.ca/Accueil/Publications/R_pertoire/Division_Th_matique/Communication_et_Culture/centres_culturels.html
A list, by province or state, of French-Canadian cultural centers and groups across Canada and in New England and Louisiana in the United States.

CiCaFra (La Culture et la Civilisation Canadiennes-Françaises [French only]
http://www.usask.ca/frenchciv/cicafra/
This site is an ambitious undertaking to be an online multimedia resource not only on historic, but also contemporary French-Canadian culture. It seeks to create a database of articles, stories, personal narratives, photos and other expressions of the "French-Canadian experience" and present them together as a sort of collective encyclopedia, created by anyone who wishes to contribute.

Fédération Culturelle Canadienne-Française – Ottawa, ON
http://francoculture.ca/fccf/
An umbrella organization bringing together many provincial and national francophone cultural groups into five sectors of activity: literary arts, broadcast media, visual arts, community cultural development, song/music and theater. The FCCF assures communication and advocacy for member groups in a minority francophone setting. The site offers a francophone discussion forum.

Francophonie Canadienne [French only]
http://www.franco.ca/
An online guide to francophone resources across Canada. Includes a searchable listing of events (Agenda), pen pal service (Correspondance), a directory of sites grouped by theme (Documentation), online news (Journal) and provincial francophone sites (Francovoyageur).

Links to Your Canadian Past
Québec

Répertoire FrancoSources [French only]
http://www.uottawa.ca/academic/crccf/francophonie/repertfs.html
This site serves as a directory of information on Web sites of minority francophone communities across Canada. It is divided into thematic sections (Culture & Heritage, Government, Language, Associations, etc.), with pages divided into Acadia, Ontario, the West and Territories.

Alberta

Alliance Française d'Edmonton – Edmonton, AB [English & French]
http://www.planet.eon.net/~infotel/afe.html
In addition to French language education and resources, the Alliance Française presents a variety of cultural activities, arranges French-language entertainment and other activities.

Association Canadienne-Française de l'Alberta – Edmonton, AB [French only]
http://francalta.ab.ca/acfa/provincial/
Working towards the community, cultural, social, educational and political development of the francophone community in the province of Alberta.

Sociétié Acadien d'Alberta [English & French]
http://www.connect.ab.ca/~acadie/index.htm
Basic information on the society, its activities and Acadian history.

British Columbia

Association Francophone de Campbell River – Campbell River, BC [French only]
http://oberon.ark.com/~franco/
Dedicated to the social, cultural, economic and community development of the francophone community in British Columbia, particularly in the area of Campbell River.

Links to Your Canadian Past
Québec

Fédération des Francophones de la Colombie-Britannique – Vancouver, BC [French only]
http://www.ffcb.bc.ca/
An association of 33 local societies whose aim is to offer support and development in the areas of communication, education, economy, community action, culture and lobbying government. The site also includes the text of an historic display located at the federation's center.

Manitoba

Centre Culturel Franco-Manitobain – Saint-Boniface, MB [French only]
http://francoculture.ca/ccfm/index.html
Dedicated to promoting francophone culture in the province of Manitoba as well as increasing awareness of Franco-Manitoban culture outside the province. Activities include participation in music, literary and art festivals, exhibitions and special activities.

La Société Franco-Manitobain – Winnipeg, MB [French only]
- http://www.franco-manitobain.org/sfm/
- **Site Franco-Manitobain**: http://www.franco-manitobain.org/

The official representative of the francophone community in Manitoba, working for the recognition, respect and celebration of the French-speaking community and its rights. The Franco-Manitoban site lists other resources and information on the francophone community.

New Brunswick

Conseil Provincial des Sociétés Culturelles – Moncton, NB [French only]
http://francoculture.ca/cpsc/index.html
An umbrella organization for various francophone/Acadian cultural societies, serving to provide communications, training, news, research, coordination and lobbying for its member groups.

Links to Your Canadian Past
Québec

Société des Acadiens et Acadiennes du Nouveau-Brunswick
[French only]
http://www.saanb.org/index2.asp
A group dedicated to the cultural identity and needs of the francophone population of New Brunswick, including linguistic, educational, legal and legislative concerns.

Newfoundland
Fédération des Francophones de Terre-Neuve et du Labrador – St. John's, NF [French only]
http://www.franco.ca/fftnl/index.htm
Dedicated to promoting and developing the francophone culture in Newfoundland and Labrador, particularly in the areas of Education, Communications and Media, Economy, Government Services, Culture and Tourism.

Northwest Territories/Nunavut
Association Francophone d'Iqaluit – Iqaluit, NWT
http://www.nunanet.com/~afi/
An association for the preservation of the French language and culture in the new territory of Nunavut, formerly the eastern part of the Northwest Territories. Also has links to *Le Toit du Monde*, the virtual magazine of Nunavut, and *l'Aquilon*, an online magazine of the NT.

Fédération Franco-Ténoise – Yellowknife, NWT [French only]
http://www.francoculture.ca/fft/
Dedicated to promoting and defending the cultural, political, economic, social and community life of the French-Canadian population of the territory.

Links to Your Canadian Past
Québec

Franco-Nord – online resource
http://www.franco-nord.com/
An online listing of the francophone cultural resources for the Northwest Territories. Sections include Organizations, Services, Education and Others

Ontario
Alliance Culturelle de l'Ontario – Vanier, ON
http://francoculture.ca/aco/
This group acts as the cultural and artistic forum for the francophone population of Ontario. It serves as a communications network and lobbying group for its members.

Association Canadienne-Française de l'Ontario – Toronto, ON
http://test.franco.ca/acfo/
The ACFO represents the francophone population of Ontario in the areas of culture, education, economy, politics and quality of life.

Prince Edward Island
Fédération Culturelle de l'Île-du-Prince-Edward [French only]
http://www.francoculture.ca/fcipe/
An organization encouraging the development and promotion of francophone culture and artistic expression in Prince Edward Island through artistic support, representation and lobbying.

Saskatchewan
Associations
http://www.dlcwest.com/~acfc/Associations/associations.html
A list of local and provincial francophone associations throughout Saskatchewan.

L'Association Canadienne-Française de Regina – Regina, SK
http://www.dlcwest.com/~acfc/Associations/acfr/acfr1.html
The ACFR seeks to develop and promote the French language and culture in Regina.

Links to Your Canadian Past
Québec

L'Association Culturelle (Catholique) Franco-Canadienne de la Saskatchewan [French only]
http://www.schoolnet.ca/collections/fransaskois/Associations/ACFC/acfc1.htm
Dedicated to promoting the interests and protecting and defending the rights of the French-speaking population of Saskatchewan.

Commission Culturelle Fransaskoise – Regina, SK [French only]
http://francoculture.ca/ccf/index.html
This organization seeks to assure and maintain the cultural development of the francophone community in Saskatchewan.

The Francophone Community of Saskatchewan [English & French]
http://www.schoolnet.ca/collections/fransaskois/english.html
Information on the Education, Culture, Economy, Associations, Activities and other aspects of the French-speaking population of Saskatchewan.

Pratiques Culturelles de la Saskatchewan Française [French only]
http://www.fl.ulaval.ca/CEFAN/cecff.html#pratiques
A research project from the Centre d'Études sur le Canada Français et la Francophonie on the French presence in Saskatchewan. The project seeks to draw up a portrait of the French-speaking popluation of the province and give it a better understanding of its cultural heritage.

Links to Your Canadian Past
Québec

Yukon Territory

L'Association Franco-Yukonnaise – Whitehorse, YK [French only]
- http://w3.franco.ca/afy/
- http://www.francoculture.ca/afy/

A group dedicated to promoting francophone interests in the territory in the areas of language, school, politics, social activities and history.

Surnames and Family Associations

Alberta

Bordeleau Families in Alberta
- **English**: http://www.acpo.on.ca/claude/albrta-a.htm
- **Français**:http://www.acpo.on.ca/claude/albrta-a.htm

Calihoo: Musée Héritage Museum Register Report
http://www.compusmart.ab.ca/museum/RR_IDX/SUR.htm
An in-house genealogy developed for the Calihoo family, with over 15,000 names for researchers of Métis, Aboriginal or francophone roots in Alberta.

Hiron/l'Hirondelle:
http://www.familytreemaker.com/users/h/i/r/Don-W-Hiron/COL1-0015.html

Pouchée, Pushee, Pushea, Pushie:
http://www.calgary.shaw.wave.ca/~dpushie/

Manitoba
Desautels: http://members.aol.com/marcjoli/Desautels.html

Gagné: http://www.geocities.com/Heartland/Acres/3364/

Links to Your Canadian Past
Québec

The Story of Hilaire Gagné and Adéline Hibour [French only]
http://home.ican.net/~shsb/bulletin/famillegagne.htm
The story of a branch of the family that immigrated to Manitoba in 1870. An insight into French immigration to Manitoba and early life in the new province.

Gervais: http://members.aol.com/marcjoli/Gervais.html

Jolicoeur: http://members.aol.com/marcjoli/Jolicoeur.html

Ouimet: http://members.aol.com/marcjoli/Ouimet.html

Proteau: http://members.aol.com/marcjoli/Proteau.html

Rajotte: http://members.aol.com/marcjoli/Rajotte.html

St. Jean: http://members.aol.com/marcjoli/StJean.html

Syrenne/Cyrenne: [English & French]
http://www3.sympatico.ca/gpfern/EHOME.HTM

New Brunswick
Dumaresq:
http://www.geocities.com/Heartland/Ranch/9002/dumaresq.htm

Lévesque:
http://www.geocities.com/Heartland/Pointe/6106/geneology1.html

Savoy/Savoie:
http://www.geocities.com/Athens/Styx/1600/savoy.jpg

Newfoundland
Gillette: http://www.gillette.net/

Links to Your Canadian Past
Québec

Roach/Roache/Roche: http://www.echelon.ca/jfroache/

Sceviour:
http://www.geocities.com/SiliconValley/1641/sceviour/index.htm

Nova Scotia
L'Ardoise – Early Families of L'Ardoise
http://www.execulink.com/~sonny1/photo.htm
A table of links to varying information on French, Scotch, German, Irish and other families.

Montbéliard – Nova Scotia's Montbéliard Names
http://www.uwindsor.ca/library/leddy/people/art/names.html
An introduction to the immigration from this former French province, with a description of the origin of the family and name, and where the families settled in Nova Scotia.

Montbéliard Settlers Genealogy
http://www.montbeliard.org/
An overview of the Montbéliard immigration and genealogies of individual families.

Bezanson:
http://www.geocities.com/Heartland/Plains/7525/Bezanson/bezanson.htm
- Mailing List: http://www.onelist.com/subscribe.cgi/bezanson

Boutilier: http://www.geocities.com/Heartland/6625/boutilier.html
- Baptism & marriage records from St. James Church, Port Dufferin:
http://www.geocities.com/Heartland/Prairie/6261/portduff.htm

Dauphinee: http://www.colba.net/~dauphinm/gen.htm

Links to Your Canadian Past
Québec

D'Entremont / La Tour:
http://fox.nstn.ca/~deonted/michlato.html

Deveau: http://www.cnwl.igs.net/~deveaupj/tree.htm

Jonah/Jeaunné: http://personal.nbnet.nb.ca/garlandb/jonah.html

Langille:
http://www.geocities.com/Heartland/Plains/7525/langille.htm

LeBlanc: http://personal.nbnet.nb.ca/leblanc2/gen.html

Ontario

Marlatt, Malott, Mellott:
http://members.aol.com/BMarlatt/homepage.html

Ouimet: http://www.geocities.com/~couimet/lehouymet.html
[English & French]

Renaud: http://www.geocities.com/Heartland/Meadows/6257/

Rodrigue:
http://www.genealogie.org/famille/rodrigue/rodrigue.html

Truax/du Trieux: http://home.ica.net/~runesmith/gene/truax.html

Valleau: http://www.geocities.com/Heartland/Prairie/1181/

Prince Edward Island

Prince Edward Island: Fortune River Settlement [English & French]
http://www.isn.net/~dhunter/anglo.html
A list of both francophone and anglophone surnames in this former Acadian settlement, in an effort to trace descendants of these families for a reunion and cemetery rededication.

Links to Your Canadian Past
Québec

Souris: Ancestry
http://www.peisland.com/souris/ancest.htm
A great page on the various ethnic groups that made up many of the early settlers of Souris and eastern Kings County: French/Acadian, Scots, Irish, English & Welsh and "Others," all with a list of early surnames. Also includes current surnames found in the area.

Poirier/Perry: http://members.xoom.com/peifam/perry.html

Saskatchewan

Campagne:
http://www.quantumlynx.com/fts/musee/promme72.htm

Chatelain:
http://www3.sk.sympatico.ca/robibn/chatelai.htm#CHATELAIN

Légaré: http://www.quantumlynx.com/fts/musee/promme15.htm

Chat Rooms and Mailing Lists
(See Notes section for mailing list instructions)

Nova Scotia
Montbéliard Settlers Chat Room
http://www.montbeliard.org/chat.htm

United States

Genealogical, Historical and Cultural Societies

Acadian Cultural Society – Fitchburg, MA
http://www.angelfire.com/ma/1755/index.html

Links to Your Canadian Past
Québec

Dedicated to helping Americans of Acadian descent trace their genealogy and learn more about Acadian history and heritage.

American-French Genealogical Society – Woonsocket, RI
http://users.ids.net/~afgs/afgshome.html
This society is dedicated to researching and publishing the genealogy of Americans of French-Canadian descent and works towards the preservation of French-Canadian culture in the United States. This site features membership benefits and application, an overview of library holdings, activities, publications, society news, member e-mail directory and queries policy.

American-Canadian Genealogical Society – Manchester, NH
http://www.acgs.org/
Information about this society, including membership, research services, *The American-Canadian Genealogist* quarterly publication and an abstract of the holdings of "the largest resource facility for French-Canadian research in the United States."

Association for Great Lakes Maritime History – Bowling Green, OH
http://www.aglmh.org/
A group of museums, historical societies, libraries, archives and individuals dedicated to preserving Great Lakes maritime history. Meetings, newsletter, special projects.

Franco-American Genealogical Society of York County – Biddeford, ME
http://www.state.me.us/sos/arc/mhrab/repos/rpage043.htm
Contact, location and other basic information on this society. Taken from the Maine Historical Records Repository Guide.

Franco-American Heritage Center – Lewiston, ME
http://www.state.me.us/sos/arc/mhrab/repos/rpage042.htm

Links to Your Canadian Past
Québec

Contact information and an overview of the holdings and schedule of this center, taken from the Maine Historical Records Repository Guide.

Franco-American Women's Institute – ME
http://members.aol.com/FAWI2000/index.html
A non-profit group dedicated to collecting, recording, celebrating and promoting the history, experience and contributions of women who are descendants of French-Canadians, Acadians, Métis and mixed blood ancestors.

French-Canadian Genealogical Society of Connecticut, Inc. – Tolland, CT
http://home.att.net/~rich.carpenter/fcgsc/
Information on this society includes the library schedule and list of holdings, upcoming events, services offered by the society and a membership e-mail directory.

French-Canadian Heritage Society of Michigan
http://fp-www.wwnet.net/~dulongj/fchsm/Fchsm.htm
Membership and activity information can be found on this site, as well as information on how to research your French-Canadian ancestors in Michigan. The society has three chapters throughout the state.

Great Lakes Shipwreck Historical Society – Sault Ste. Marie, MI
http://www.lssu.edu/shipwreck/
Includes information on the society's dive team, vessels and policies, historic wrecks of lake superior's coast, Whitefish Point Lightstation and Great Lakes Shipwreck Museum.

Links to Your Canadian Past
Québec

Northwest Territory, Canadian and French Heritage Center – Golden Valley, MN
http://www.mtn.org/mgs/branches/nw.html
A branch of the Minnesota Genealogical Society, the Center is one of the largest societies interested in French and Canadian genealogy and history research. Its main area of focus is the former Northwest Territories (American and Canadian West) and all of Canada.

Salt Lake City Genealogical Society
http://www.lds.hpl.com/Genealogy

Southern California Genealogical Society French-Canadian Interest Group – Burbank, CA
http://home.earthlink.net/~djmill/
This site details the meetings, activities, and holdings of this interest group affiliated with the Southern California Genealogical Society, which boasts "the largest collection in the Western United States except for the Family History Library at Salt Lake City."

US GenWeb Project: http://www.usgenweb.org/
Each state may have several counties or other divisions. See the main site for more info.
- **Connecticut:** http://www.99main.com/~jrothgeb/ctgenweb.htm
- **Louisiana:** http://www.rootsweb.com/~lagenweb/
- **Maine:** http://www.rootsweb.com/~megenweb/
- **Michigan:** http://www.rootsweb.com/~migenweb/
- **Minnesota:** http://www.rootsweb.com/~mngenweb/
- **Missouri:** http://www.rootsweb.com/~mogenweb/mo.htm
- **Montana:** http://www.imt.net/~corkykn/montana.html
- **New Hampshire:** http://www.geocities.com/Heartland/5275/nh.htm
- **New York:** http://www.rootsweb.com/~nygenweb/
- **North Dakota:** http://www.rootsweb.com/~ndgenweb/

Links to Your Canadian Past
Québec

- **Oregon**: http://www.rootsweb.com/~orgenweb/
- **Vermont**: http://www.rootsweb.com/~vtgenweb/vtgenweb.htm
- **Washington**: http://www.rootsweb.com/~wagenweb/
- **Wisconsin**: http://www.rootsweb.com/~wigenweb/
- **Wyoming**: http://www.rootsweb.com/~wygenweb/

Vermont French-Canadian Genealogical Society
http://members.aol.com/vtfcgs/genealogy/index.html
Located in Burlington, VT. Information on membership, activities, workshops and conferences, an abstract of their publication *Links* and a form for research queries.

Wisconsin's French Connections – online resource
http://gbms01.uwgb.edu/~wisfrench/index.htm
A collection of (virtually) all things French-Canadian in, of and about Wisconsin. This site is divided into "rooms" – library, kitchen, study, etc. Lots of information and contacts for history, genealogy and culture both on and off this site. Individual sections indexed below.

Archives, Libraries and Research Centers

American Council for Québec Studies
http://acqs.plattsburgh.edu:81/
Not much information here beyond a list of the executive board, indexes to (not very recent) issues of the *Québec Studies Journal* and links to government, political and cultural sites. You can fill out a membership form, but they don't tell you what they do.

Association for Canadian Studies in the United States
(Washington, DC)
See National / Archives, Libraries and Research Centers / Canadian Studies Centers and Programs.

Links to Your Canadian Past
Québec

Center for Maine History: Genealogy Room – Portland, ME
http://www.mainehistory.com/genealogy.html
This site features a list of genealogy resources available at the Center, an online genealogy forum, information on fee-based research and information on contacting or visiting the Center.

Connecticut State Archives – Hartford, CT
http://www.cslib.org/archives.htm
Information on the state archives, which since 1909 has officially been housed at the Connecticut State Library (*See below*).

Connecticut State Library – Hartford, CT
- **Main Page**: http://www.cslib.org/
- **History and Genealogy**: http://www.cslib.org/handg.htm
- **(French-)Canadian Finding Aid**:
  http://www.cslib.org/canada.htm

Includes separate pages on vital records, church records, family bible records, cemetery inscriptions, newspaper notices, census, land, probate, military and land records found at the library, as well as several informative guides, finding aids, a records search request and online catalogue to all state library materials.

Folger Library, University of Maine (Orono, ME) – Maine Old Cemetery Assn. Materials
http://www.rootsweb.com/~memoca/fogler.html
A listing of the materials produced by the Maine Old Cemetery Association housed at the Folger Library at the University of Maine. Includes printed and microfilmed materials.

Maine State Archives – Augusta, ME
- **General**:
  http://www.state.me.us/sos/arc/general/admin/mawww001.htm
- **Genealogy**:
  http://www.state.me.us/sos/arc/archives/genealog/genie.htm

Links to Your Canadian Past
Québec

Contact and visitor's information on the archives, plus further information on the state archives' collections, services (useful section!) and exhibits. The Genealogy section contains descriptions of the vital, military, legal and judicial material available at the archives.

Maine State Library: Genealogical Resources – Augusta, ME
http://msl1.ursus.maine.edu/refgenealogy.htm
A description of the materials available for genealogical research at the Maine State Library, with links to further information about the library's location, services and collections.

Massachusetts State Archives – Boston, MA
- **Main**: http://www.magnet.state.ma.us/sec/arc/arcidx.htm
- **Family History Resources**:
  http://www.magnet.state.ma.us/sec/arc/arcfam/famidx.htm

Includes a general introduction to the state archives and overviews of the vital records, passenger lists, census schedules, military, colonial, judicial and other records held by the state.

Massachusetts State Library – Boston, MA
http://www.magnet.state.ma.us/lib/Homepage.htm
An overview of the services and collections of the state library, including an online interface to the library's catalogue.

Michigan: State Archives of Michigan – Lansing, MI
http://www.sos.state.mi.us/history/archive/archive.html
Information on all aspects of the archives, including requests, "circulars" pertaining to various types of records, the county clerks' genealogy directory and visitor information.

Michigan: (State) Library of Michigan – Lansing, MI
- **Main Page**: http://www.libofmich.lib.mi.us/
- **Genealogy & Local History**:
  http://www.libofmich.lib.mi.us/genealogy/genealogy.html

Includes information on the genealogical and historical sources found at the library, guides to doing research, selected bibliographies and a link to the library's online catalogue.

National Archives and Records Administration –Washington, D.C.
- **Main Page**: http://www.nara.gov/
- **Genealogical Research**: http://www.nara.gov/genealogy/

The Genealogical Research page includes sections on policy issues affecting genealogists, genealogical publications and information leaflets, regional centers, workshops and courses and further information for conducting research at the National Archives.

New Hampshire Division of Records Management and Archives – Concord, NH
http://www.state.nh.us/state/archives.htm

This Web site presents an overview of the governmental, judicial, municipal, military and land records available at the archives and provides an online guide to the archives, as well as indexes to some archival collections. (Note: Vital records are housed a the Bureau of Vital Records.)

New Hampshire State Library – Concord, NH
- **Main**: http://www.state.nh.us/nhsl/
- **Genealogy Section**:
  http://www.state.nh.us/nhsl/history/index.html

These pages present an overview of the library and its services, as well as the specific records and materials available for genealogists, including family histories and town records.

New York State Archives and Records Administration (SARA) – Albany, NY
- **Main Page**: http://unix6.nysed.gov/

Links to Your Canadian Past
Québec

- **Genealogical Sources**:
  http://www.sara.nysed.gov/holding/fact/genea-fa.htm
General information on this state office, plus descriptions of services and publications, a workshop catalog, online exhibit and an index to all of the records series preserved in the State Archives, searchable by keyword, creating agency or government, and subject.

New York State Library – Albany, NY
- **Main Page**: http://unix2.nysed.gov/
- **Genealogy**: http://www.nysl.nysed.gov/gengen.htm

Provides information on the scope of the genealogical material in the state library, guides to finding information and using specific records and access to the library's online catalogue.

Rhode Island State Archives – Providence, RI
gopher://archives.state.ri.us/
Note: This is a "gopher" site, which will display in your browser like a folder directory.
Presents information on the holdings of the state archives, which date from 1638 to the present and include vital records (births, marriages, deaths), military records (revolutionary war through the Vietnam War), census records (1865 to 1935), legislative records, maps, photographs and other related historical materials.

University of Washington Center for the Study of the Pacific Northwest
http://www.washington.edu/uwired/outreach/cspn/
Makes available some of the university's resources in this field, including curriculum materials, news and events, articles from the *Pacific Northwest Quarterly*, a discussion list, etc.

Vermont Public Records (General Services Department) – Montpelier, VT
http://www.state.vt.us/gsd/pubrec.htm
The Public Records division of the Department of General Services provides records management for "inactive" archival material, a microfilm service for the state and municipal governments and a research area for publicly available vital and municipal records.

Vermont State Archives – Montpelier, VT
http://vermont-archives.org/
Sections of this site include Reference Services, Publications List, Vermont Historical Records Advisory Board, Public Records, Guide to Records at the Archives and a Searchable Catalog.

Wisconsin: State Historical Society of Wisconsin – Madison, WI
- **Main**: http://www.shsw.wisc.edu/index.html
- **Archives**: http://www.shsw.wisc.edu/archives/index.html
- **Library**: http://www.shsw.wisc.edu/library/index.html

The SHSW, both a state agency and private member society, serves as both the state archives and library of Wisconsin, preserving the historical materials of the state in published, manuscript, photographic and other forms. Searchable catalogues of the library and archives are available online, as are research guides, finding aids and information on holdings and services.

Birth, Marriage, Death, Census and Other Data Online

Vital Statistics and Parish Records - General

Social Security Death Index
http://www.ancestry.com/ssdi/advanced.htm

Links to Your Canadian Past
Québec

Search over 60 million names in the SSDI. Enter first name, last name, Social Security Number and state or any combination of the above and the search returns a list of possible matches. Advanced searching capabilities are also available.

US Sites With Genealogical Source Material
http://freespace.virgin.net/alan.tupman/sites/us.htm
A listing, by state, of sites that have online genealogical data. Includes links to cemetery pages, censuses, vital statistics information and more. Browseable by state.

U.S. Vital Statistics Offices
http://www.gov.ns.ca/bacs/vstat/usoffices.htm
Contact information for the vital statistics offices of all 50 states and U.S. territories.

Vital Records Information – United States
http://vitalrec.com/
A very comprehensive site on obtaining vital records for U.S. states and territories. This site not only provides contact information for state vital records sources, but will link to the official state office Web site (where available) and also provide useful information on county- and town-level vital records sources and related genealogical/historical groups. There's also a Guidelines section to help you through the entire process.

Vital Statistics and Parish Records – By State
Maine – Biographies of Some Pre-1915 Franco-Americans of the State of Maine
http://members.mint.net/frenchcx/meframer.htm
Extracted information from the book *Franco-Americans of the State of Maine*. Not really biographies, but birth, marriage and death information for selected individuals.

Links to Your Canadian Past
Québec

Maine – Catholic Churches in Maine
http://members.mint.net/frenchcx/mecath1.htm
A table of contact information for the state's Catholic churches. Listed by town, the table includes the name of parish, year established, rectory address, zip code and county.

Maine – Maine State Archives Records Search Forms
- **Marriage**:
  http://thor.ddp.state.me.us/archives/plsql/archdev.Marriage_Archive.search_form
- **Death**:
  http://thor.ddp.state.me.us/archives/plsql/archdev.death_archive.search_form

Search for marriages between 01 January 1892 and 31 December 1996 by groom's name or bride's name. You can also request a copy of a marriage certificate by e-mail. Death records available for search span the period 01 January 1960 to 31 December 1966.

Maine (Old Town) – St. Joseph's Catholic Church, Old Town, Maine: Supplement
http://members.mint.net/frenchcx/otownbk.htm
Additions and corrections to the marriage catalogue of St. Joseph's Church published in 1993.

Maine (Waterville) – Marriages of the Children of Waterville's French-Canadian Families of 1840
http://members.mint.net/frenchcx/1840cens.htm
Information, listed by family, on the marriages of the children of French-Canadian families found in the 1840 Waterville census (*See Census Information and Similar Records*).

Maine – Pre-1892 French-Canadian Records in Selected Maine Town Registers
http://members.mint.net/frenchcx/metown.htm

Links to Your Canadian Past
Québec

Extracted information for the towns of Frenchville, Fort Fairfield, Houlton, Presque Isle, Wallagrass, Winn and Winthrop, Maine.

Massachusetts Registry of Vital Records and Statistics – Boston, MA
http://www.magnet.state.ma.us/dph/vitrecs.htm
Information from the Bureau of Health Statistics, Research and Evaluation on availability of records, who may obtain records and how to do so.

Michigan – Genealogical Death Indexing System
http://www.mdch.state.mi.us/PHA/OSR/gendis/search.htm
A searchable database of recorded death information in the state of Michigan for the years 1867-1882. The search returns a list of possible matches with decedant's name, date of death, father's name and county. Full records include this information, plus record location info, place and cause of death, race, marital status, occupation, age, birth date and place and parent's names and residence.

Michigan Division for Vital Records – Lansing, MI
http://www.mdmh.state.mi.us/PHA/OSR/vitframe.htm
Information from the state Department of Community Health, which preserves records of births, marriages, and deaths filed with the state since 1867 and Michigan divorce records since 1897.

Montana – Métis Marriages
http://www.televar.com/~gmorin/marriages.htm
Marriage records compiled by Gail Morin for the Métis of Fergus, Sheridan and Valley Counties, Montana.

New York State Department of Health: Vital Records – Albany, NY
http://www.health.state.ny.us/nysdoh/consumer/vr.htm

Links to Your Canadian Past
Québec

Includes information on where and how to obtain records for genealogy, a records request form and information on adoption and related records.

Wisconsin Vital Records – Madison, WI
- **Main Page**:
  http://www.dhfs.state.wi.us/VitalRecords/index.htm
- **Genealogy Information**:
  http://www.dhfs.state.wi.us/VitalRecords/genereq.htm

Information from the Department of Health and Family Services on how to obtain vital records for genealogical purposes, with an overview of how to make a request, earliest dates (by county) for births, marriages and deaths and a list of time periods covered by indexes.

Cemetery Information

Maine (Waterville) - French-Canadians/Franco-Americans Buried in Pine Grove Cemetery
http://members.mint.net/frenchcx/pinegrov.htm
Contains burial/headstone information on the French-Canadians buried in this cemetery, which opened in 1851 and those whose graves were moved from the older cemetery (Monument Park).

Maine (Waterville) – Halde Cemetery/Father Doyon Memorial Cemetery
http://members.mint.net/frenchcx/haldecm1.htm
An extensive Web site on this cemetery. After the Introduction, History and Restoration information, you'll find links to headstone information, further genealogical information, church and funeral home records, an index and excellent cemetery map and a 1993 newspaper article.

Links to Your Canadian Past
Québec

Michigan Cemetery Page
http://www.rootsweb.com/~migenweb/mi-cemetery.html
A list of cemeteries throughout the state, with location and telephone contact numbers.

Census Information and Similar Records
Clues in Census Records 1850-1920
http://www.nara.gov/genealogy/cenclues.html
Information from the National Archives on how to get more information out of census records.

Maine - French-Canadians in the 1840 Waterville Census
http://members.mint.net/frenchcx/1840wtvl.htm
Extracted information from this census, with expanded genealogical listings for the families contained in it. Also links to a second page which expands on the marriage of the children of the families found in these listings (*See Vital Records/Parish Data*).

Maine – Old Canada Road
http://members.mint.net/frenchcx/canroad.htm
A list, by town in Québec (mostly from the Beauce region) of French-Canadians who followed the "Old Canada Road" or Chaudière-Kennebec Trail from Québec to the middle Kennebec valley, Maine before the American Civil War. Based on 1830-1870 census records and other vital statistics.

Montana – 1917 Rocky Boy Census (Métis)
http://www.televar.com/~gmorin/rockyboy.htm
Extracted information on the Métis found in the Tentative Roll of Rocky Boy Indians taken 30 May 1917 at Rocky Boy, Montana, copied by Verne Dusenberry, 15 Apr 1953.

North Dakota – Métis Census Information
- **1850: Pembina County (formerly MN):**
  http://www.televar.com/~gmorin/1850mncen.htm

Links to Your Canadian Past
Québec

North Dakota – Métis Census Information
- **1850: Pembina County (formerly MN)**:
  http://www.televar.com/~gmorin/1850mncen.htm
- **1892 Turtle Mountain Chippewa**:
  http://www.televar.com/~gmorin/1892cen.htm

Information compiled by Gail Morin from these two censuses. The 1892 Turtle Mountain Chippewa census was conducted in Belcourt, North Dakota.

Wisconsin – 1990 Census Information: French Ancestry
http://gbms01.uwgb.edu/~wisfrench/family/stats/90census.htm
A listing, by county, of the number of people who reported French or French-Canadian as their first ancestry. No surnames included – just a total of individuals by county.

Immigration/Border Crossings/Naturalization

California – Registered Voters in California from Prince Edward Island, 1872
http://www.isn.net/~dhunter/calislander.html
A list of registered voters in California in 1872 who voluntarily stated their place of birth as Prince Edward Island, Canada.

Fanny Passenger List – 1849
http://www.isn.net/~dhunter/fanny.html
Passenger list of this ship, which was chartered to bring men from Prince Edward Island to the Gold Rush in California.

Immigration Records at the National Archives
http://www.nara.gov/genealogy/immigration/immigrat.html
Sections include what the NARA has and doesn't have for given periods, sample immigration records, where to find immigration records and information for further research.

Links to Your Canadian Past
Québec

Indiana – Madison County Naturalzation Records Search
http://www.acsc.net/~apl/natu.htm
You can search the records of all individuals who applied for naturalization in Madison County between 1890 and 1958. Search by individual's name, country or date of record. The search returns a list of names, country of origin and date of record.

Immigration and Passenger Arrivals on Microfilm (National Archives)
http://www.nara.gov/publications/microfilm/immigrant/immpass.html
Includes US Customs Service Records for Great Lakes Ports, INS records for New Bedford and Gloucester, MA; Portland, ME; Providence, RI and St. Albans, VT.

Location of Naturalization Records By State
http://www.rootsweb.com/~fianna/citizen/naturloc.html#ct
An incomplete list of where to find records for naturalizations that occurred in certain states.

Massachusetts – Prince Edward Islanders in Massachusetts Censuses
- **1870 Boston Census**:
  http://www.isn.net/~dhunter/boston1870.html
- **1920 Massachusetts Census**:
  http://www.isn.net/~dhunter/mass1920.html

Extracted information relating to individuals from Prince Edward Island in these censuses.

Naturalization Records at the National Archives
http://www.nara.gov/genealogy/natural.html
An introduction to the naturalization process, what records are involved and where to find them.

Links to Your Canadian Past
Québec

Naturalization Resources
http://www.rootsweb.com/~fianna/citizen/naturl.html
An overview of the history of the US naturalization process, the location of certain naturalization records, and how to interpret and gain information from naturalization papers.

Newfoundlanders to the United States
http://members.tripod.com/CyndiJ/NFtoUS/Newfoundlanders_to_the_US
Attempts to compile data on Newfoundlanders who went to the US to work prior to the 1950's.

Legal and Other Data

Canadians Who Served in Maine Militias in the Civil War
See Museums and Historic Sites and Groups / New England and New York.

Franco-Americans of Waterville Who Served in the American Civil War
See Museums and Historic Sites and Groups / New England and New York.

Museums and Historic Sites and Groups

Directories

French Colonies in America
http://www.southalabama.edu/archaeology/old_mobile/fr_america.htm
A directory of the archaeological sites of former French forts, outposts and colonies in America, presented by the Center for Archaeological Studies of the University of Alabama. Individual sites are catalogued below in the appropriate region.

Links to Your Canadian Past
Québec

Tribes and Bands of the United States and Canada
http://www.hanksville.org/sand/contacts/tribal/US.html
A geographical interface to lists of contact information and (where available) links to Web sites of tribal and native groups throughout the United States and Canada.

New England and New York
Canadians Who Served in Maine Militias in the Civil War
- http://www.bitheads.ca/nbgenweb/me_militia.htm
- [same info w/ search]
  http://www.isn.net/~dhunter/mainem.html

A lengthy table of data on men from Canada who served in Maine state militias during the American Civil War. Data includes name, age, rank, company & regiment, place of residence, married or single, date of muster, date attained rank and miscellaneous remarks.

Fort at No. 4 – Charlestown, NH
http://www.chesulwind.com/fort-at-no4/
Once the northernmost British settlement in North America, this 1740's fort is now a living history museum depicting life during the French and Indian Wars and the late 18th century.

Fort Carillon – NY
http://www.digitalhistory.org/fort_carillon.html
A brief overview of the building of this fort, begun by De Lotbinière in 1755 and completed in 1758. After falling to the British, the fort was renamed Ticonderoga (see below).

Fort Carillon/Ticonderoga – NY
View a photomontage of the fort's monuments, take a virtual tour of the recreated fort or see what is left of the original fortifications.

Links to Your Canadian Past
Québec

Fort Ticonderoga – NY
http://cahpwww.nbc.upenn.edu/~thomsen/forts/fort_ti.html
A short timeline of the history of this fort, which began as the French Fort Carillon (see above).

Franco-Americans of Waterville Who Served in the American Civil War
http://members.mint.net/frenchcx/civwar.htm
A list of sixty Franco-American soldiers from this town who fought in the American Civil War. Data includes name, birth date, unit, parent or spouse and miscellaneous additional information.

Old Fort Niagara History – Youngstown, NY
http://www.oldfortniagara.org/history.htm
The extensive history of this former strategic fort, the "Guardian of the Great Lakes" for 300 years. The fort was originally French, being successively named Fort Conti and Fort Denonville, before falling to the British and seeing action in the War of 1812, 1837 Rebellion and the American Civil War.

Central and Western United States
Cahokia Courthouse – Cahokia, IL
http://www.southalabama.edu/archaeology/old_mobile/cahokia_courthouse.htm
This house, probably built circa 1737, later served as a courthouse for the town of Cahokia, itself founded in 1699 by seminary priests from Québec. This site presents a brief overview of the house's history, accompanied by historic photos.

The Cahokia Courthouse – Cahokia, IL
http://www.state.il.us/hpa/CCRTHOUS.htm
The history and significance of this former residence, "a unique remnant of the French in Illinois." The site also presents photos of the structure and a history of the town of Cahokia.

Links to Your Canadian Past
Québec

Compagnie Franche de la Marine du Detroit – Detroit, MI
http://www.richnet.net/~kamoore/
This site presents the history of the original *Compagnie Franche de la Marine* and the present-day company of historical re-enactors who continue their memory and traditions.

Compagnie Franche de la Marine du Saint Joseph – Niles, MI
http://members.aol.com/Ngiwani/index.html
A re-enactment group with members from lower Michigan, northern Illinois and northeast Indiana, dedicated to portraying the French colonial presence in the area and to helping restore the former Fort Saint Joseph. Includes links to a timeline of events around the world during the time of Fort Saint Joseph and a collection of photos of artifacts from the Saint Joseph era.

Les Coureurs du Bois de Fort de Chartres – Prairie du Rocher, IL
http://www.wincowindow.com/employee/phil/homepage.htm
A club that celebrates and re-creates the French experience in mid 18th century Illinois with black powder rifle shoots, rendezvous, woods walks, dancing, etc. This site provides information on the group's activities and a brief history of the fort.

Fort de Chartres – Prairie du Rocher, IL
http://www.state.il.us/hpa/FORTC.HTM
Photos of the restored and reconstructed areas of the third French fort built on this site complement the textual history of the fort and Illinois Country presented here.

Fort de Chartres III – Prairie du Rocher, IL
http://www.southalabama.edu/archaeology/old_mobile/fort_de_chartres_iii.htm
A brief historical introduction and photos of this French fort, first built in 1718 and now the site of a reconstruction, museum and historical re-enactments.

Links to Your Canadian Past
Québec

Fort Ligonier – Ligonier, PA
http://www.ligonier.com/fortligonier.html
Re-live the history of the French and Indian War and the struggle for the conquest of the continent at this full-scale, on-site reconstruction of the 1758-1766 original fort.

Fort Michilimackinac – Mackinaw City, MI
http://fishweb.com/maps/cheboygan/mackinawcity/fort/index.html
Click on any of the numbered buildings or areas in this map of the recreated fort and view a photo of the given attraction.

Fort Michilimackinac – Mackinaw City, MI
http://www.southalabama.edu/archaeology/old_mobile/fort_michilimackinac.htm
A brief introduction to this reconstructed fur trading fortification, which is the most intensely excavated French historic site in the United States. The reconstruction presents aspects of the fort from both the French and British periods of occupation. Photos available.

Fort Michilimackinac – Mackinaw City, MI
http://www.sos.state.mi.us/history/preserve/phissite/fortmich.html
Photos of the reconstructed fort help illustrate the history of the French presence in this stronghold from 1715 to 1761.

Fort Necessity National Battlefield – Farmington, PA
http://www.nps.gov/fone/
Visit this site, where a 22-year-old George Washington lost the opening battle of the French and Indian War. The 900-acre site includes the reconstructed fort and Mount Washington Tavern.

Links to Your Canadian Past
Québec

Fort Ouiatenon – near Lafayette, IN
http://www.tcha.mus.in.us/fort.htm
This site presents a lengthy history of this French fort, trading post and mission, which was built in 1717 – the first fortified European settlement in the present-day state of Indiana.

Fort Ouiatenon Collections Management Report
http://www.gbl.indiana.edu/abstracts/93/jodi_93.html
This site, whose full title is "Fort Ouiatenon: A French and Indian Occupation Along the Wabash River in Tippecanoe County, Indiana – A Collections Management Report," presents a brief history of the fort and a lengthy description of the archeological digs at the site and a description of the articles recovered, with links to images and photographs.

Fort Saint Charles – Lake of the Woods, MN
http://www.entreeltd.com/fortStCharles.htm
A very extensive and informative site on the history of Fort Saint Charles, its founding by La Vérendrye, daily life, and use in explorations, the fur trade and mission work, its rediscovery and restoration – all accompanied by photos, maps and sources of further information.

Fort Saint Joseph – Niles, MI
http://www.sbtinfo.com/011198/local_ar/28960.htm
An online article from the South Bend *Tribune* on the possible discovery of the former Fort St. Joseph in Niles, Michigan, "the only site in Michigan to be ruled by four different countries."

History and Archaeology: New Evidence of the 1730 Mesquakie Fort – IL
http://www.parkland.cc.il.us/sshs/len/idotfx.htm
A lengthy examination of the history and new archeological evidence concerning the location of the Mesquakie Indian fort

besieged in 1730 by the French and their Indian allies. Includes a look at a newly discovered narrative of the siege and details of structures uncovered in the dig.

Holy Family Militia/Milice de Sainte-Famille – IL
http://www.angelfire.com/il/milicedestefamille/
This group is both an historical re-enactment club for the historic sites in the French Colonial District of southern Illinois and a support group for the state-owned sites in the region. This site presents the group's activities and events.

Pierre Ménard Home at Fort Kaskaskia – Kaskaskia, IL
http://www.state.il.us/hpa/PIERRE.htm
This site presents the history of the home of Pierre Ménard, along with a biography of the man who was a fur trader, entrepreneur and the first lieutenant governor of Illinois. The site also presents the history of Kaskaskia and information on related and nearby historic sites.

St. Clair Flats Historical Encampment – Algonac, MI
http://www.i-is.com/st.clairflats/
Get information and photos of this event, an historic re-enactment of the daily life, tasks and skills of the native and European peoples who inhabited the Great Lakes region during the mid 1700's, including a group of French "marine" re-enactors, *coureurs du bois* and natives.

Tippecanoe Ancient Fife and Drum Corps – Lafayette, IN
http://virtual-indiana.com/TAFDC/index.html
This re-enactment company portrays 18th century French music and the French marine presence in colonial North America. This Web site also provides a history of the *Compagnies Franches de la Marine* and the overall French presence in North America in the colonial period.

Links to Your Canadian Past
Québec

The South

Fort Gaines Historic Site – Dauphin Island, AL
http://dauphine.net/fortgaines/
This site, first dubbed "Massacre Island" by d'Iberville, was once the center of French colonization along the Gulf Coast of North America. It became capital of the Louisiana Territory, and successively passed from French control to British and Spanish rule. This Web site presents the fort's history, current events and visitor information.

Fort Saint Jean-Baptiste – Natchitoches, LA
http://www.southalabama.edu/archaeology/old_mobile/fort_jean_baptiste_natchitoches.htm
A brief introduction to and photos of this off-site reconstruction of a French fort, built by Juchereau de St-Denis in 1716 on the border with New Spain.

Fort Saint Jean-Baptiste State Commemorative Area – Natchitoches, LA
http://www.crt.state.la.us/crt/parks/ftstjean.htm
An overview of the history and modern re-creation of Fort St. Jean Baptiste, the first permanent European settlement in what later became the Louisiana Purchase.

Fort Toulouse – Wetumpka, AL
http://www.southalabama.edu/archaeology/old_mobile/fort_toulouse_wetumpka_alabama.htm
A brief history of this fort, built by the French among the Alabama tribe. The site contains photos of the recreated fort complex.

Fort Toulouse/Jackson Park – Wetumpka, AL
http://www.wetumpka.al.us/fort.html
This Web site presents the history and current events and activities at the site of the former Fort Toulouse, built by the French in 1717 on the eastern border of the Louisiana Territory.

Links to Your Canadian Past
Québec

La Pointe-Krebs House – Pascagoula, MS
http://www.southalabama.edu/archaeology/old_mobile/krebs_house_pascagoula.htm
Built between 1772 and 1780, this is the oldest standing structure in the state of Mississippi. It displays the use of French colombage construction as well as *bousillage* to fill the walls.

La Salle's French Fort – near Victoria, TX
http://www.thc.state.tx.us/belle/FortSL.html
Details the discovery and recovery of eight iron cannons near Victoria, Texas, confirming the location of Fort Saint-Louis, established by La Salle in 1685.

Old Mobile – Axis, AL
http://www.southalabama.edu/archaeology/old_mobile/old_mobile.htm
This site presents the ongoing archeological dig being conducted by the University of Alabama on the site of former colonial buildings in Mobile, once the capital of French Louisiana.

Old Mobile Archaeology Home Page – Mobile, AL
http://www.southalabama.edu/archaeology/old_mobile/index.htm
This site presents the Center for Archaeological Studies of the University of Alabama and their work in uncovering and studying (among other things) remnants of French colonial presence in the Gulf Coast region of the United States. Sections of the site include French Colonies in America (*See Directories, above*), Artifacts of Colonial Mobile and links to ongoing digs.

Links to Your Canadian Past
Québec

Regional and Local History and Historic Photos

New England and New York

The Aroostook War: Maine vs. New Brunswick
http://www.stanford.edu/~jenkg/family/aroostook.html
The history of this bloodless border "war" of 1839 and its resolution.

Historical Perspective on Waterville's 19th century Franco-Americans
http://members.mint.net/frenchcx/frcanwtv.htm
This lengthy essay takes a look at the various reasons for and patterns of French-Canadian migration to New England, with a focus on Maine and the city of Waterville. Includes a list of many of the families who emigrated, and facts on the French-Canadian population of Maine.

Un Milieu de Vie Difficile [French only]
http://www.fl.ulaval.ca/cefan/franco/my_html/Francam.html
A look at some statistics on the 573,000 French-Canadian immigrants in New England in 1900. Brief introductory notes and two tables of data help situate these immigrants in society.

WPA Life Histories From Maine
http://memory.loc.gov/ammem/wpaintro/mecat.html
A collection of 29 (mostly) first-person accounts of life in Maine, collected by the Works Progress Administration during the Great Depression. Subjects include Folklore, Religion, Industries and Occupations and French-Canadians, and a look at a list of the titles reveals that the majority of interviewees are of French-Canadian origin.

Links to Your Canadian Past
Québec

WPA Life Histories From New Hampshire
http://memory.loc.gov/ammem/wpaintro/nhcat.html
Part of the WPA Writer's Project, this series of narrative accounts of life in New Hampshire includes the subjects French Canadians (social activities, fraternal organizations, French language newspapers, songs, acculturation and relations with Irish Americans) and two documents entitled "Franco-American Grandmother" and "French-Canadian Textile Worker."

WPA Life Histories From Rhode Island
http://memory.loc.gov/ammem/wpaintro/ricat.html
A collection of six (mostly) first-person accounts of life in Rhode Island, collected by the Works Progress Administration during the Great Depression. Subjects include of the textile industry, unemployment and French Canadian textile workers.

WPA Life Histories From Vermont
http://memory.loc.gov/ammem/wpaintro/vtcat.html
Titles of some of the 129 documents in this Works Progress Administration series of narrative accounts of life in Vermont include Alcide Savoie, Boarding House Keeper – French, French Stonecutters – Father and Son and many other articles on stonecutting and life in Vermont.

Central and Western United States
At Home on the French Frontier: 1700-1800
http://www.museum.state.il.us/exhibits/athome/1700/welcome.htm
This online exhibit of the Illinois State Museum covers many aspects of the French colonial period in the central and Midwestern U.S. in the 18th century. It includes an historical timeline, maps, activities, presentation of artifacts, resource documents and more.

Links to Your Canadian Past
Québec

Les Communautés Canadiennes-Françaises du Midwest Américain au 19e Siècle [French only]
http://www.fl.ulaval.ca/cefan/franco/my_html/QUILLAN.html
This lengthy and informative essay examines the French-Canadian settlements along the agricultural, forestry and mining frontiers in the American Midwest in the 19th century, as well as in the major cities. It looks at the survival of French-Canadian identity among immigrants and suggests areas of further research. Several maps and diagrams complement the text.

Iowa – The Historic Period
http://www.uiowa.edu/~osa/cultural/historic.htm
A look at the founding and settlement of the state of Iowa, which examines the explorations of Jolliet and Marquette and the influence of French-Canadian city founder Julien Dubuque.

Peoria, Illinois – History
http://www.bradley.edu/convention/history.html
A brief history of this city, which was first explored and settled by French-Canadians.

Waterville Township, WI – The French-Canadian Settlement of Waterville Township
http://gbms01.uwgb.edu/~wisfrench/family/pepin/intro.htm
The table of contents and extended introduction to this book, dealing with the early French-Canadian founders of Waterville Township, Pepin County, Wisconsin. The table of contents includes a list of families, many of which have links to genealogical data.

Wisconsin's French Connections Library
http://gbms01.uwgb.edu/~wisfrench/library/index.htm
A large collection of links to articles and historical information both on- and off-site. Categories include History of French-speaking People in Wisconsin, On-line Articles, Maps, Wisconsin

Links to Your Canadian Past
Québec

Information and Related Historical Information. The subjects covered range from the contributions of French-Canadian explorers and residents, local francophone communities, religious history and traditions to family histories and interaction with native and other societies.

Wisconsin's French Connections Study
http://gbms01.uwgb.edu/~wisfrench/study/index.htm
Research papers and projects by students from Wisconsin (from middle school through college) on French-Canadian history, heritage and ancestors. Subjects include French Place Names in Wisconsin, explorers, French-Canadian culture and traditions and local history.

Military History
1755: The French and Indian War Page
http://web.syr.edu/~laroux/
Includes soldier lists, reference books, places to visit and a "document of the month."

The Aroostook War: Maine vs. New Brunswick
See New England and New York.

Battle of Lake Champlain
http://odur.let.rug.nl/~usa/E/champlain/champxx.htm
A look at this battle during the American Revolution when Benedict Arnold invaded Québec.

Documents on the American War of 1812
http://www.hillsdale.edu/dept/History/Documents/War/FR1812.htm
A series of primary source documents on this North American conflict, divided into the sections Political Issues, Naval Actions, the Northwest Campaigns, Eastern Campaigns, Southern Campaigns and Support Issues.

Links to Your Canadian Past
Québec

History and The Last of the Mohicans: Seeing Through the Distant Haze
http://www.mohicanpress.com/mo08000.html
This site takes a look at the French and Indian War through the James Fennimore Cooper book *The Last of the Mohicans*. History pages includes topics such as Le Marquis de Montcalm: Adieu à France et Candiac, Fort William Henry: The Siege and Massacre and The Delicate Art of Scalping.

Re-living History: The War of 1812
http://library.advanced.org/22916/exmain.html
This comprehensive site includes an "Explore History" section with the causes, timeline, battles, people and aftermath of the war, an "Expand Your Knowledge" section with an atlas of maps and three quizzes and an "Exchange Information" section with a discussion forum.

Surnames and Family Associations

Anglicized French Surnames
http://members.mint.net/frenchcx/angname.htm
A long list of anglicized French surnames, whether they are misspellings or phonetic transcriptions of the actual French name or an outright translation.

Regional Surnames

Illinois – Petit Canada Project [English & French]
http://members.aol.com/DJKboysrus/index.html
The Petit Canada Project is gathering information on a number of French-Canadian families who settled in this Illinois community 2 ½ miles northwest of Bourbonnais Grove, Kankakee County Illinois between 1832 and 1865. Links to genealogical information on several families.

Links to Your Canadian Past
Québec

Michigan – French Names found in Alpena, Alcona, Montmorency and Presque Isle Counties
http://members.aol.com/alpenaco/migenweb/frnames.htm
A compiled list of French-Canadian surnames from these Michigan counties and their anglicized or translated counterparts that are often found in local records.

Northeast Surnames
http://members.mint.net/mdenis/surnames.html
A query bulletin board for surnames of families located in Québec and the Maritime Provinces, as well as Maine, Massachusetts, New Hampshire and Vermont.

Wisconsin's French Connections: Histories of Wisconsin Families of French Origin
http://gbms01.uwgb.edu/~wisfrench/family/history/index.htm
An index to several family histories and stories (some with photos) of French-speaking families who immigrated to Wisconsin from Canada.

Wisconsin French Family Names
- **Southeast Wisconsin**:
  http://gbms01.uwgb.edu/~wisfrench/family/stats/senames.htm
- **Madison**:
  http://gbms01.uwgb.edu/~wisfrench/family/stats/madnames.htm

Two lists of family names of French origin compiled from phone book listings and other sources.

Wisconsin – Waterville Township: The French-Canadian Settlement of Waterville Township
See History and Photos.

Links to Your Canadian Past
Québec

Individual Surnames

Branchaud/Brancheau/Branchereau:
http://home.earthlink.net/~djmill/branchereau.html

Bordeleau: [English & French]
http://www.acpo.on.ca/claude/bor-us-a.htm

Lévesque:
http://www.geocities.com/Heartland/Pointe/6106/geneology1.html

Michaud:
http://www.members.tripod.com/~Scott_Michaud/index-3.html

Pageot/Pageau/Pajot: http://www.novagate.net/~rpaggeot/

Thibaudeau/Thibodeau/Thibodaux:
http://www.qouest.net/~jljmt/a_menu.htm

Chat Rooms and Mailing Lists

Franco-American Women's Listserv (FAFEMM-L):
LISTSERV@MAINE.MAINE.EDU
SUBSCRIBE FAFEMM-L Your Name